D0903127

DE HAVILLAND

Philip J.Birtles

JANE'S

Copyright © Philip J. Birtles 1984

First published in the United Kingdom in 1984 by
Jane's Publishing Company Limited
238 City Road, London EC1V 2PU

ISBN 0 7106 0303 7

All rights reserved. No part of this publication
may be reproduced, stored in a retrieval system,
transmitted in any form by any means electrical,
mechanical or photocopied, recorded or
otherwise without prior permission of the
publisher.

Designed by Geoffrey Wadsley

Typesetting by
D. P. Media Limited, Hitchin, Hertfordshire

Printed in the United Kingdom by
Biddles Ltd, Guildford, Surrey

Contents

Author's Note

de Havillands were among the most prolific of aircraft manufacturers, in addition to their production of aero engines, propellers, missiles and other equipment. Their World Enterprise supported the many products of the companies in the important overseas markets, building up goodwill not only for the company, but for British products and their support.

It has been interesting, but difficult to write this book within the strict confinement of the allocated space. Therefore, in the introductory chapters, I have attempted to map out the history of the organisation, dealing with the major personalities, and also covering in some detail the activities of the Engine and Propeller Companies.

Having worked at Hatfield for over twenty years, I would like to thank all my colleagues who encouraged me to write this book.

P.J.B. Hatfield

The founder Directors: Francis St. Barbe, Charles Walker, Sir Geoffrey de Havilland, Wilfred Nixon and Frank Hearle (*de Havilland*)

4

Pioneering

1.

Had it not been for the encouragement and generous financial support of Jason Saunders, the de Havilland aerial activities may have never occurred. Jason Saunders, the maternal grandfather of Geoffrey de Havilland, was a hard working farmer who had, in the 1860s, built up his own business of transport, removal and warehousing in Oxford, in addition to his own self-sufficient farm at Medley.

Geoffrey de Havilland, who had a great enthusiasm for mechanical and electrical apparatus, as well as an interest in natural history, was expected to follow in his father's footsteps by entering the church, but instead became a draughtsman with the Motor Omnibus Construction Company of Walthamstow, London. Born on 27 July 1882, he was by this time 27 years old, and his interest in Sir Hiram Maxim's flying machine experiments was further aroused by news of the successful flying attempts by the Wright Brothers and other pioneers.

de Havilland was confident that he could design a suitable engine to power a flying machine and he asked a new-found friend, Frank Hearle (later his brother-in-law), if he would join him in building an aircraft. Hearle, who was working as a mechanic with the Vanguard Omnibus Company, agreed to leave his job and join forces with him. Their immediate problem was finances: de Havilland's father, a poorly paid rector, was unable to help, but de Havilland's grandfather Saunders was willing to invest £1,000, a sum which he intended to leave to Geoffrey de Havilland in his will.

de Havilland acquired an office in Bedford Square, where over a period of four months he designed a flat-four water-cooled engine estimated to develop 34 kW (45 hp) at 1,500 rpm. He then approached Mr Knowles, a director of the Iris Motor Company, who agreed to build the prototype engine for £250, allowing time for work to commence on the design and construction of the airframe.

A modest workshop was rented in Bothwell Street, Fulham, for one pound per week, and all the necessary tools were purchased for less than £20. At that time, the novice aircraft constructors had not even seen an aeroplane fly. With de Havilland's good mechanical background and experience, the engine did not present too much of a challenge. However, he intended to design, build, and fly an aircraft from scratch, possessing none of the skills with which so many other pioneers had worked, giving varying degrees of success.

The first de Havilland
aeroplane in the Fulham
workshop (*de Havilland*)

The chosen layout was a biplane wing with the engine mounted in the fuselage driving the two propellers through bevel gears. The tailplane was fixed with the elevator out at the front. Very little of the aircraft was drawn, with quite a bit of designing done during construction. The majority of the materials were bought commercially, the main special items being turn-buckles for the wire bracing and the fabric covering. The engine was completed, and apart from minor modifications, ran well.

The search for a suitable flying ground commenced, the well known fields at Brooklands, Hendon, and Eastchurch being too expensive and public. A suitably isolated site was located at Seven Barrows, near Beacon Hill, on Lord Carnarvon's estate close to Newbury. A pair of sheds had been erected by J. T. C. Moore-Brabazon, later Lord Brabazon, for an aircraft, but he decided to use Eastchurch, and was therefore persuaded to sell these sheds for £150. In November 1909, the airframe and engine were moved out of the Fulham workshop, which was too small to allow assembly. Soon after at Seven Barrows, the assembled aircraft was pushed out for the first time for engine runs. The first run was a great success, although during the second, one of the bevel gears

The first de Havilland
aeroplane was wrecked on
its first take off
(*de Havilland*)

driving the propellers collapsed as the first of a number of annoying, but expected snags. With the mechanical problems largely solved, the next challenge was to fly, but the machine obstinately refused to leave the ground, often due to unsuitable flying conditions. What was needed was a gentle steady breeze blowing up the slight incline of the field.

On an unrecorded date in December the conditions were just right, and de Havilland, with a determination borne of long frustration, taxied to the top of the slope, turned, and started off down the hill. The speed built up, and for the first time in all the taxiing trials, the aircraft gave an indication that it was capable of flying. Due to overcontrol, it lurched into the air, and before de Havilland could correct by pushing the nose down, there was a crack as the main spar broke, and the aircraft ended up in a pile of pieces with a slightly bruised novice pilot.

It had suffered structural failure due to the inexpert handling of the pilot, and the structure itself was almost certainly marginal in strength. About all that was left to salvage was the undamaged engine and one propeller with its gearing. Everything was loaded onto a lorry and returned to Fulham, to build an aeroplane that would fly.

With the finances running low, it was decided that speed and simplicity of construction and materials was essential. The twin propeller layout was therefore abandoned and replaced by a direct drive wooden pusher propeller, which allowed the heavy flywheel to be discarded. The undercarriage was improved with main wheels and tail-skid and the general layout of the aircraft was simplified. It had spruce and ash framework and wing construction which made it more robust.

By the summer of 1910, Aircraft Number Two was ready for transport back to Seven Barrows, where it was soon assembled and after two or three weeks of taxiing trials, all appeared ready for a flying attempt.

It was a beautiful evening on 10 September with the breeze light enough and in the right direction. On some of the fast taxiing runs the aircraft appeared to be ready to fly, and de Havilland asked Hearle to lay down on the ground close to the flight path to see if there was daylight under the wheels as it went by.

de Havilland went to the top of the slope, turned, and opened up the engine. The fragile aircraft rolled forward gathering speed until he eased back on the stick and the vibration from the ground ceased. de Havilland eased back on the throttle, coming to a halt at the bottom of the field, chased by an excited Hearle, who was able to confirm that the aircraft had flown several inches off the ground for a distance of about 18 metres (20 yds). Having proved that the aircraft could fly, they packed up for the day and planned carefully the next stages, since due to lack of finance, there was no possibility of a further rebuild if there was an accident.

Gradually, the height and duration of the hops were increased, not only to prove the aircraft, but for de Havilland to teach himself how to fly. Then one day when airborne, he decided to climb above the point which would allow a landing straight ahead. He rose up to some 15 metres (50 ft) and gently turned to the left in a half circle, trying out the controls on the downwind leg. He then turned to the left again, lining up

Geoffrey de Havilland at
the controls of his second
aircraft (de Havilland)

for the inevitable landing, with the ground at a frightening distance below. There were no flaps, so by reducing power and putting the nose gently down, the aircraft was aimed at the take-off point. de Havilland had to estimate the speed to be just above the stall, and when he thought he was about three metres (10 ft) off the ground, cut the throttle and levelled out, to stall into landing. The aircraft struck the ground sharply once, bounced, and settled on its wheels and skid, rolling to a rest.

Controlled flight had been achieved and as confidence grew, a passenger seat was fitted for Hearle to have a well earned ride, followed by de Havilland's wife Louie and their eight week old son, Geoffrey Jnr, probably making him the youngest aircraft passenger in the world at that time.

By November 1910 the money was all but spent, and the two pioneers needed to find a buyer for the aircraft, and employment for themselves. Fortunately, a chance meeting with Fred Green at Olympia was their salvation. Green and de Havilland had been colleagues at Daimlers in Coventry, but Green was now working at the Government Balloon Factory at Farnborough. Here, they had only been dealing with lighter than air craft, but Mervyn O'Gorman, the Superintendent, was keen to have aeroplanes as well. After a meeting, it was agreed that providing the aircraft passed some basic tests, it would be purchased for £400, and the two aviators hired. And so Aircraft Number Two became the first aeroplane to be purchased by the British Government, de Havilland was taken on to supervise its development and design new aircraft, and Hearle was the mechanic to look after the engineering.

The main work at Farnborough was on the development of man-carrying observation kites and balloons and semi-rigid and non-rigid airships. These departments suffered from a great deal of jealousy, making a rather unhappy atmosphere which was not improved by the advent of experiments with aeroplanes. The efforts to produce airships

at Farnborough were rather unsuccessful and only three locally designed ones were built before all efforts were abandoned.

The second de Havilland aeroplane was sold to the British Government (*de Havilland*)

There were also other difficulties for the aircraft designer. The independent aircraft manufacturers had formed their own trade organisation and by lobbying politically and through the trade journals, they managed to prevent the design and construction of new aircraft at Farnborough.

Under O'Gorman, this ruling was circumscribed by repairing or reconstructing damaged aircraft, making use of odd pieces or the engines of crashed machines. The reconstruction could then involve adding new ideas; the result was an entirely new aircraft. However, the same group that had achieved the limitation on Farnborough also managed to force the resignation of O'Gorman. This had the disastrous effect of the immediate cessation of important research work, slowing down the vital early aeronautical development so soon before the First World War.

On arrival at Farnborough, the de Havilland aeroplane had to be proven by flying for an hour to gain its Royal Aero Club certificate. This important test was carried out in the bitterly cold weather of January 1911, requiring a couple of intermediate landings to thaw out the exposed pilot and refuel the short endurance tank. Having achieved its certificate, it was designated the F.E.1, which stood for Farman Experimental Number One, part of an illogical system devised by the Civil Service based on French aircraft. (All pusher propeller types were known as Farman Experimental, all tractor types as Blériot Experimental or B.E., and any tail-first or canard layouts were Santos Dumont Experimental or S.E. Later, S.E. stood for Scout Experimental adding further confusion.)

de Havilland included in his duties the task of being the sole initial test pilot at Farnborough, and soon also commenced designing using the

The tail-first S.E.1 was the first aircraft to be designed by de Havilland at Farnborough (*Crown Copyright*)

vastly superior facilities and experience in stressing, aerodynamics and structural testing of other members of the staff. The first effort was an improvement of his F.E.1 powered by a 37 kW (50 hp) Gnome rotary engine and with some protection from the elements for the pilot. Known as the F.E.2, it first flew on 18 August 1911, and it was in this aircraft that de Havilland achieved the Royal Aero Club Special Certificate No. 4. Another development was the replacement of wheels by a float. A successful flight was made from Fleet Pond, but with the extra drag the engine was not powerful enough and a 52 kW (70 hp) Gnome was fitted allowing water take-offs with pilot and passenger. Later in 1912, a Maxim machine gun was installed in the nose, and the following year a 52 kW (70 hp) Renault V-8 engine was fitted. Other improvements included new outer wing panels increasing the span to 12.8 m (42 ft), a raised tailplane and a smaller rudder. It now resembled the larger F.E. types which were soon built in quantity. The F.E.2 was destroyed when it spiralled into the ground at West Wittering on 23 February 1914 killing the passenger, but the pilot survived.

The next aircraft was the unorthodox S.E.1 canard biplane powered by a pusher 45 kW (60 hp) E.N.V. engine salvaged from a crashed Army Blériot monoplane. The two-bay biplane wings were mounted at the rear of a long slim fuselage with the elevator in the extreme nose. First flight was made on 8 June 1911, but it was not a successful aircraft, being difficult to turn, and was initially unstable in pitch. On 18 August, much against de Havilland's advice, Lt T. J. Ridge, the Assistant Superintendent, who had only recently learnt to fly and was therefore limited in experience, decided to pilot the S.E.1. Once airborne, he stalled it off a gliding turn over Farnborough, went into a spin, crashed and was killed.

de Havilland followed up the S.E.1 with the rather more successful B.E.1. This was a 'reconstruction' of a Voisin biplane, but the 45 kW (60 hp) Wolseley engine was the only connection. The B.E.1 was a two bay biplane of orthodox layout with a tractor engine, capable of carrying two people. Lateral control was by wing warping and there was no fixed fin. de Havilland made the maiden flight on 27 December 1911 and the first passenger was Hearle, on 3 January 1912. Despite being a reasonably successful aircraft after the rigging was corrected, the engine installation was cumbersome and caused too much drag. This was replaced by an air-cooled 45 kW (60 hp) Renault which made it relatively quiet. The B.E.1 led to the mass-produced B.E.2, the first de Havilland production design used widely during the First World War. The prototype had a useful career; first testing early radio equipment, and then with No. 2 Squadron RFC with the identity 201 for service trials, finally crashing at Farnborough in January 1915.

In one of the early B.E.2s, de Havilland gained the international height record of 3,218 m (10,560 ft) during the Military Aircraft Trials on Salisbury Plain on 12 August 1912. He carried Major Sykes, Commandant of the Royal Flying Corps as a passenger and the record stood for about three years. The B.E.2 was later converted by Edward Busk into the very stable B.E.2C which could be flown hands and feet off the controls. Unfortunately, Busk lost his life when the engine of a B.E.2C he was flying caught fire and the machine crashed in a ball of flame. It

B.E.2 was de Havilland's most successful Farnborough design

B.S.1 was de Havilland's last design before joining Airco (*MoD/RAE*)

was in a B.E.2 that de Havilland first tried simple aerobatics by looping, despite the limitation of low power and unknown structural and mechanical safety when inverted. This manoeuvre was carried out using no safety straps or parachute.

The last aircraft designed by the team led by de Havilland at Farnborough was the rather more advanced B.S.1 (Blériot Scout No. 1). One of the team at this time was H. P. Folland, a junior draughtsman, who designed the famous S.E.5 fighter and later formed Folland Aircraft Ltd, the makers of the Gnat lightweight jet fighter and advanced trainer. The B.S.1 was a single-seat single-bay biplane scout powered by a tractor 75 kW (100 hp) Gnome engine. It was the first aircraft in the world to be designed as a fast scout, and the slim wooden fuselage was a circular section monocoque structure well ahead of its time. Lateral control was by wing warping and no fin was fitted. It was first flown early in 1913, and in March 1913 it achieved 147 km/h (91.4 mph) over a measured course. However, directional control was poor resulting in a crash in a flat spin which injured its designer/pilot, Geoffrey de Havilland.

During the extensive repairs, a 60 kW (80 hp) Gnome engine was fitted and control was very much improved by fitting small fins above and below the fuselage and a divided elevator to accommodate a larger rudder. The aircraft was redesignated B.S.2, later changed to S.E.2, and the sole example was issued to No. 5 Squadron RFC in January 1914. It then served with No. 3 Squadron at Netheravon before going to France in October 1914, and was flown on offensive patrols until March 1915 armed with two rifles mounted on the fuselage firing outside the arc of the propeller.

Before the outbreak of war in 1914, de Havilland's employment at Farnborough came to an end, to his regret. This was due to the design and manufacture of aircraft being allocated to private companies. His experience, however, stood him in good stead and he was offered the job of Inspector of Aircraft in the Aeronautical Inspection Directorate. Geoffrey de Havilland reluctantly accepted the position, disappointed at being away from the design of aircraft.

He made a break to return to his design career after having an opportunity to talk to George Holt Thomas, who had formed the Aircraft Manufacturing Company, known as Airco. During a visit by Holt Thomas to Farnborough, de Havilland suggested that he had his own design department to produce aircraft, instead of licence-building Farman biplanes. This suggestion was accepted and he resigned from the A.I.D. to become designer and pilot with Airco.

Airco and the First World War

2

On 2 July 1914, Geoffrey de Havilland joined Airco to design, supervise the construction, and test-fly any aircraft required by the company. For this he was to be paid £600 per year with a commission of £50 per aeroplane on the first 20 sold in one year, and £25 per aeroplane on any further sales. With the high volume production resulting from military orders, this unanticipated benefit proved a significant extra source of income.

A month later war was declared. While at Farnborough, de Havilland had joined the Royal Flying Corps Reserve and as a result, within a month of starting his new job, he was recalled to Farnborough for military service. He had not fully recovered from his crash with the B.S.1, so although found fit for flying, he was limited to home duties. In the same month he was posted to Montrose, on the east coast of Scotland, where Sgt Carr and himself were allocated the task of protecting British shipping from German U-boats between Aberdeen and the Firth of Forth. For this important task they were supplied with two unarmed 37 kW (50 hp) Blériot monoplanes with a speed of up to 80 km/h (50 mph) and a very short range. Sgt Carr patrolled the northern section from Aberdeen to Montrose, while de Havilland watched over the section down to the Firth of Forth. Fortunately, they did not spot anything, as they would have been hard pushed to identify friend or foe, and without radio they would have been unable to call assistance.

Before the end of August, the folly of having a talented aircraft designer risking his life daily in an unreliable, obsolete foreign aircraft on fruitless missions was realised. Captain de Havilland returned to

D.H.1 prototype, de Havilland's first Airco design (*Flight*)

Farnborough by the end of the month, but it was a further three months before he was released to re-commence work at Hendon in the design office. As an officer, he was expected to wear uniform and be ready for instant call-up since his design work was treated as a secondment.

Work was started on a tractor biplane, but before construction could begin the War Office requested the less efficient pusher layout to give the gunner a clear field of fire forward. A successful interrupter gear to fire a gun between the rotating propeller blades had yet to be developed. This aircraft, which became the D.H.1, was a two-seat reconnaissance biplane fitted with a Renault inline engine. However, as it was underpowered, and only a small number were built until the Beardmore engine was available; the improved aircraft was produced by Savages Ltd as the D.H.1A.

This left Airco free to concentrate on the urgent design and production of a single-seat high-performance fighter to combat the latest German aircraft, which in the event proved to be the formidable Fokker monoplanes. By working day and night, the new D.H.2 aircraft was flying by July 1915. Like the D.H.1 it was a pusher, powered by a Gnome Monosoupape rotary engine and armed with a single nose-mounted Lewis gun. Some 400 were built, requiring a dramatic expansion at Hendon, but the resulting aircraft did useful service at the front.

de Havilland's first twin-engined design was the pusher Beardmore-powered D.H.3, a bomber capable of reaching German industrial areas and Berlin. A modified version powered by two more powerful Beardmore engines became the D.H.3A. Production had commenced with an order of 50 aircraft, but it was abruptly cancelled in the belief that the strategic bombing of Germany would be unnecessary. The prototypes were dumped at Hendon and eventually burned, but with the German bombing of London in 1917 the idea was rapidly revived in the form of the later D.H.10.

de Havilland's first really successful design was the D.H.4 high performance two-seat day bomber. The Germans had developed a gun interrupter device and soon after the similar Constantinesco gear became available to the Allies. It was therefore practical to return to the tractor layout and take full advantage of the new more powerful engines. The pilot, who was also the bomb-aimer, was armed with a fixed forward firing machine gun and the observer, separated from the pilot by the fuel tank, had a defensive Lewis gun. Not only was the

Twin-engined D.H.3 had folding wings to save hangar space

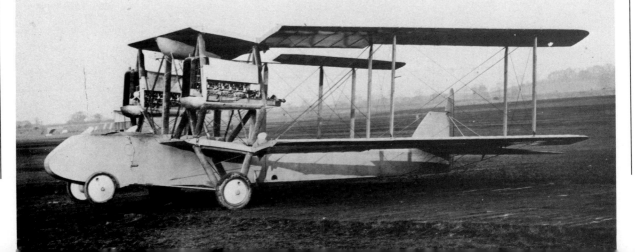

D.H.4s ready for
operations on the Western
Front during the First
World War
(*Hawker Siddeley*)

Modified D.H.4B for the
carriage of the U.S. Mail
(*de Havilland*)

D.H.4 faster than any contemporary bomber, but it could hold its own against most of the fighters. Two 103 kg (230 lb) bombs could be carried on under-fuselage racks and four 50.8 kg (112 lb) bombs under the wings. The prototype was powered by a BHP engine, but after a number of alternatives were tried, the Rolls-Royce Eagle became fairly standard. When adopted by the USA, a 12-cylinder Liberty engine was used. The success of the D.H.4 was due to its simplicity, optimum size, attention to detail and a reliable engine. The simplicity helped production, maintenance, reliability, weight saving and cost. The attention to detail reduced drag, improving performance, and the optimum size gave versatility. Many thousand D.H.4s were built around Britain and, more significantly, in the USA by such well known companies as Boeing.

The introduction of the Constantinesco interrupter gear of course benefited many more aircraft than just the D.H.4. One of these was de Havilland's own answer to the outdated and outperformed D.H.2, the D.H.5 tractor biplane. The unusual feature of this le Rhône-powered

15

D.H.5 prototype with a flat sided fuselage

D.H.6 K-100 was the first registered British civil aircraft (*Hawker Siddeley*)

single-seater was the backward stagger of the biplane wings in an effort to give the pilot the good view of the pusher-engined aircraft by seating him ahead of the top wing. The armament was a single Vickers machine gun conveniently close to the pilot on the fuselage top to clear any stoppages.

de Havilland was later to become famous for training aircraft, and his first was the angular and very simple D.H.6. It was a primary trainer conceived to an urgent requirement in 1916, and was therefore designed for ease and speed of manufacture, as well as cheapness and simplicity of repair. All major assemblies were straight-sided, and rumour had it that the wings were built by the mile and cut off by the yard! A number of D.H.6s were also used for coastal patrols.

The D.H.7 and D.H.8 were both fighter designs which were abandoned due to non-availability of suitable engines.

In the meantime, the D.H.4 had proved so successful that the best replacement was an improvement, designated D.H.9. The same wings and tail surfaces were used, and an improved fuselage was designed putting the two crew in adjacent cockpits for better communications. With so many similar parts, it was relatively easy to change some of the existing D.H.4 contracts to D.H.9, but the major downfall of this new aircraft was the choice of the Puma engine. This had originally been rated at 224 kW (300 hp), but due to serious teething troubles it had to be derated to 172 kW (230 hp), giving the new aircraft a lower performance than the one it was designed to replace. This poorer performance was made worse by the unreliability of the engine which resulted in serious losses in combat. The situation did not improve until the American Liberty engine was installed, the aircraft then becoming the successful and long-serving D.H.9A. This was developed and pro-

No. 601 Squadron D.H.9A connected to a Hucks starter (*Hawker Siddeley*)

duced by Westland, to allow the parent company to concentrate on the new twin-engined D.H.10.

The D.H.10 Amiens was a direct development of the abandoned D.H.3, and the first de Havilland design to be given a name. The new aircraft was somewhat larger, and in its production version was powered by a pair of tractor Rolls-Royce Eagle or American Liberty engines. Only eight had been delivered to the RAF by the Armistice, too late for operational use, although the Amiens remained in service for at least another five years.

With the ending of hostilities, aircraft orders were drastically cut back and the expected enthusiasm for commerical aircraft did not materialise. Airco meanwhile were continuing to work on improved bomber designs, but the three types built did not progress beyond the prototype phase. They then entered the small airliner field with the D.H.16 and D.H.18, but because the British Government would not subsidise commercial aviation unlike other nations, many of the emerging airlines and manufacturers were forced into liquidation.

By the end of the First World War, Airco were producing over 300 aircraft per month in a factory covering several acres and employing over 2,000 workers. During this wartime period great advances had been made in aircraft, their engines and armament. de Havilland had also built up a team of experienced people who were to help him form the de Havilland Company less than two years afterwards.

Among these people was Charles Walker, with a thorough training in civil and mechanical engineering, who took on the contrasting tasks of stressing and aerodynamics. Wilfred Nixon came from Farnborough to look after the finances of Airco and was an obvious choice to take charge of the financial side of the new company, later becoming Secretary, Financial Director and eventually Chairman. Francis St. Barbe was in charge of sales at Airco before de Havilland arrived, and retained this responsibility and for de Havillands until his retirement in 1961. He built up the comprehensive world-wide sales organisation on which the enterprise was based.

Frank Hearle had already left Farnborough in November 1912 before de Havilland joined Airco, to become Works-Foreman at the Deperdussin Aircraft Company at Highgate. When that company failed a year later, Hearle joined Vickers, and one of his responsibilities was to start up the factory at Weybridge. He joined Airco in 1917 to take charge of the Experimental Shop, later becoming one of the founders of the de Havilland Company.

With the high volume of aircraft being produced at Hendon de Havilland was unable to carry out all the test flying as had been planned, and so B. C. Hucks was hired as Chief Pilot after being invalided home from France, and was joined by a staff of another two pilots, Birchenough and Gresswell. Hucks also invented the 'Hucks Starter' for the swinging start of propellers by mechanical means. This relief from test flying also gave de Havilland time to fly to France to obtain first-hand information on any technical problems from the front-line squadrons. These visits also helped formulate the requirements of future designs.

However, the great pressure of work during the war took its toll and Geoffrey de Havilland suffered a nervous breakdown in the later part of 1918. The recovery was slow, but sure, although much less was then known about nervous exhaustion.

Without the anticipated civil aircraft expansion Airco was soon in financial difficulties, and was taken over in 1920 by the Birmingham Small Arms Company, who were not interested in aviation but simply wanted the buildings and plant. The sudden and sad ending forced the staff to make plans for their future, and with some of the work in hand at Hendon released by BSA, the foundations for the de Havilland Aircraft Company were laid.

Not only were Airco in difficulties but their subsidiary, Aircraft Transport and Travel, a company formed by Holt Thomas, also found it could not compete with the European government-subsidised SNETA (later SABENA), KLM and French airlines. AT & T made its last commercial flight on 15 December 1920 and was forced to close down.

The de Havilland Aircraft Company

Early Airliners and Experimental Military Aircraft

3

Geoffrey de Havilland secured the release from his contract which BSA had bought amongst the assets of Airco, and also obtained, for a modest price, the aviation assets including the D.H.18, completion of the two D.H.14s and D.H.9A repair work. His next problem was how to create the new company. He put up £3,000 for a start, and then canvassed for additional funds from friends and acquaintances. It was Holt Thomas, however, who came to the rescue by promising £10,000 over a period of time, on the condition that A. E. Turner, finance director of Airco, should be the chairman of the new company.

One of around 150 D.H.9As overhauled by de Havillands for the RAF
(*P. T. Capon*)

The de Havilland Aircraft Company was incorporated on 25 September 1920, and ten days later moved into the small airfield at Stag Lane, just off the Edgware Road, formerly used as a flying school by the London & Provincial Aviation Company. The two partially completed D.H.18s were moved in by road, together with materials and a selection of tools. Wilfred Nixon became secretary and looked after the tenuous finances, Charles Walker was the stressman (later Chief Engineer) and Frank Hearle became works manager. St. Barbe continued his duties on the business side to generate sales. In charge of the design office, under de Havilland as Chief Designer, was Arthur Hagg, who had been with Airco and was later to achieve a classic design style which reached its peak in such aircraft as the Albatross and Ambassador. The total initial employees of the company were about 60, all from the Airco factory,

de Havilland Aeroplane Hire Service operated a number of converted D.H.9s (*Flight*)

de Havilland School of Flying used D.H.9s for advanced training (*de Havilland*)

D.H.9AJ Stag powered by a Jupiter engine was the ultimate D.H.9 version (*de Havilland*)

and as the new organisation became established, more of the ex-Airco employees joined de Havillands in the following year or two.

The total accommodation at Stag Lane consisted of two sheds for aircraft manufacture and assembly, and two huts. One of the huts was used for the design office, and the other for administration. These huts were unheated, and when it was really cold, de Havilland would call everyone out for a ten minute game of football as a warm-up. Often, the relative importance of design and manufacturing had to be decided, as the generator was shared, and if a heavy cut was being taken on a main spar, the lights went dim in the drawing office. The administration hut was eventually moved to Hatfield, and is now the home of the de

Havilland Museum housing many of the records and artifacts of the company, including the spare propeller made for Biplane No. 2 but never used.

Prospects however slowly began to show signs of improvement within a year or two, with de Havillands on the Air Ministry contractors tender list, and the abortive Airco sales missions were expected to be of benefit to the new company. A number of war surplus aircraft were sold to overseas governments, including D.H.4s and D.H.9s. Although this inhibited demand for new aircraft, it did give a chance to provide spares and support, creating valuable goodwill for future sales. Some 150 D.H.9As were overhauled for the Air Ministry and other customers using spares from a number of low priced sources, including serviceable engines from the Aircraft Disposal Company for as little as 25 shillings (£1.25 at today's rate).

Not only did the new company work on aircraft, but also became involved in the operation of a variety of tasks including early crop dusting with a D.H.6, and charter flying for press and newsreels. One of these pioneer pilots was Alan Cobham, the inventor of in-flight refuelling and founder of the Flight Refuelling Company. The first private pleasure charter from Stag Lane was a tour of Europe with a wealthy American. Sir Sefton Brancker, the Director of Civil Aviation, also chartered aircraft for many official trips. The de Havilland Aeroplane Hire Service, as the charter company became known, was supplemented by the Reserve Flying School which started operations on 1 April 1923 and continued for 30 years. This varied operation gave the engineers a broad experience in the maintenance of aircraft, allowing them to build greater reliability into later designs, and to more fully understand the needs of private flying.

Early in 1921, the Air Ministry ordered two prototypes of each of two new designs, the D.H.27 Derby day bomber biplane and the D.H.29 Doncaster high monoplane wing research/long-range transport aircraft. In both cases, the design had been initiated at Airco and these contracts were very encouraging for the company, as even modest orders were not plentiful. It was the Government's intention to keep the industry ticking over thereby advancing technology on a low budget. The morale of the company increased greatly with the work on the first new aircraft since Airco days, and it was quite a challenge for such a small organisation where costs were watched very carefully.

D.H.14A long-range civil mail carrier version
(*de Havilland*)

D.H.29 Doncaster military prototype (*P. T. Capon*)

Of the two aircraft, the more advanced and efficient Doncaster monoplane was the first to fly piloted by de Havilland on 5 July 1921, but problems were experienced with fore and aft control. Despite a great deal of effort on the D.H.29 Doncaster, it was reluctantly decided to abandon it in favour of the D.H.34 biplane airliner in which Daimler Air Lines were interested, followed by Instone. Delivery dates were critical for a cross-Channel service to be started in the spring of 1922, and design work went through quickly during the autumn and winter of 1921 to meet these requirements.

A more domestic problem was the lease of the Stag Lane factory and airfield, the owners demanding evacuation or purchase of the freehold. The asking price was £20,000. Further difficulties then came from the landlords, and the directors took the bold decision to purchase the Stag Lane site at the requested price without knowing where the money would come from. Profits for the first year had been over £2,300, but for the £7,500 deposit an overdraft had to be raised.

Soon after this, a request came from a Mr Alan S. Butler to have a touring aircraft designed and built to his requirements. de Havilland felt that an order for such a special aircraft would come to nothing, and in order to put off Butler, decided to ask for £3,000. When St. Barbe submitted this figure to Butler, he did not object. Alan Butler visited Stag Lane to talk about his prospective two to three seater with adequate range and room for luggage, and upon his departure unexpectedly asked de Havilland if he could invest in the company, stating that he was interested in the aviation business. This offer came in the nick of time because the money was required urgently to buy the premises. After his investment, Butler was invited to join the board, and the purchase of Stag Lane went through smoothly. He was elected chairman on 13 February 1924.

The D.H.34 airliner was first flown on 26 March 1922 by Alan Cobham, and it proved to be a great success for Daimler Hire and Instone Air Line. Butler's special D.H.37 flew in June 1922, and was used by its owner touring widely around Europe. A second was later delivered to Australia.

Business began to grow with orders coming in from a number of overseas countries as far afield as Japan and Canada. The factory was expanding and the Aeroplane Hire Service continued to gain experience and publicity. The first overseas licence agreement was made to

SABCA of Belgium in 1922 for D.H.9s starting the great World Enterprise.

The RAF were continuing to fly reconditioned wartime-vintage aircraft and there appeared to be no urgency to re-equip with more modern types. Many projects were investigated and then abandoned, but the D.H.42 fighter-reconnaissance biplane was built, although only as three differing prototypes. For the hard pressed company to survive, they had to take opportunities in the commercial market, and with the experience gained from the Aeroplane Hire Service, a four-passenger cabin version of the D.H.9 was designed. Known as the D.H.50, it was ideal for light charter work and first flew in August 1923. Within a few days, the aircraft was flown by Alan Cobham to the Göteborg Exhibition in Sweden and won the £1,000 first prize for its reliability and economy. Seventeen D.H.50s were built at Stag Lane, the majority going to Australia, where eleven more were built locally. Further licence production was in Belgium and Czechoslovakia. The most outstanding achievements with the D.H.50 were the long-distance flights by Cobham between 1924 and 1926 to Rangoon, Cape Town and Melbourne, for which he gained a knighthood.

The company were still keen on touring aircraft, but there was concern that the only reasonably powered and priced engines available

D.H.42A Dingo I army co-operation biplane (*Aerofilms*)

Sir Alan Cobham about to land the D.H.50J on the Thames on return from Australia (*de Havilland*)

23

were the outdated and inefficient war surplus examples. They were inexpensive to purchase, but did not provide the answer for the private owner. There was simply not an engine available for a light aircraft that could be used widely to get any but the most wealthy in the air. de Havilland discussed this one afternoon with Frank Halford, a gifted engine designer who had been a friend since the Farnborough days. At that time the rather large D.H.51 three-seat tourer powered by a 67 kW (90 hp) RAF (Royal Aircraft Factory) 1 engine was under construction. This engine was a copy of a First World War Renault inline, and only three of the aircraft were built.

One of the few company failures was the D.H.52 glider. It was the only de Havilland glider and two were built rapidly for the trials at Itford in Sussex in 1922. However, the lateral control was poor and the structural integrity of the aircraft was insufficient as one of the wings failed during the trials, fortunately without serious injury to the pilot.

At the lower end of the power scale, the companies had been encouraged to participate in the light aeroplane competitions, and de Havilland had built and entered the D.H.53 Humming Bird. Although it was not a prize winner, it was the only aircraft to be put into production and actually received an RAF order. The low power however was its limitation, demonstrated on one occasion when Alan Cobham was flying against a strong cold headwind over the snowy fields of Flanders. When he was overtaken by a train, Cobham gave up and arranged to ship the aircraft home.

With these aircraft, de Havilland realised that the ideal popular tourer formula had not been reached, but he was forming in his mind the ideal specification which was to result eventually in the Moth. de Havilland definitely decided not to enter for the 1924 light aeroplane competition which called for a two-seater powered by a 1,150 cc engine.

Meanwhile, with the airline success of the D.H.34, a larger replacement was required to Air Ministry Specification 40/22. This aircraft was the single-engined D.H.54 Highclere with two crew in an open cockpit ahead of the wing and 12 passengers enclosed in a cabin. Full span automatic camber changing flaps were fitted to reduce the high landing speed, and the undercarriage could be jettisoned if ditching were imminent. A toilet and luggage accommodation were provided, as well as heating for the cabin. Flight trials were successful, but Imperial Airways announced abruptly that all their passenger aircraft would be multi-engined types for greater safety, so the Highclere was relegated to development work. It was destroyed at Croydon on 1 February 1927 when a hangar roof collapsed under the weight of snow.

The final experimental military aircraft at this time was the D.H.56 Hyena, a two-seat army co-operation development of the D.H.42. Two prototypes were built for evaluation at Martlesham Heath and Farnborough before the second aircraft participated in assessment trials at Manston with the Armstrong Whitworth Atlas, Bristol Boarhound and Vickers Vespa. Service evaluations continued at Old Sarum, Odiham and Farnborough, the contract being awarded to the Atlas.

The Moths

4

What was needed was a suitable engine, 45 kW (60 hp) at a weight of 159 kg (350 lb) would be practical, and de Havilland asked Frank Halford to produce one early in 1924. de Havilland's idea was to take a V-8 Airdisco engine, a developed Renault, and cut it in half to give two four-cylinder inline engines retaining as many parts as possible to keep down the cost. Finally, he persuaded an initially reluctant Halford to design the new engine for manufacture by the Aircraft Disposal Company, allowing Geoffrey de Havilland to start designing a light aircraft as the first private venture for the company.

This simple, but revolutionary, new aircraft should be a two-seater with provision for dual control and room for light luggage and a tool kit. It would need endurance of about three hours and a cruising speed of 128 km/h (80 mph). It must be easy to fly and operate out of modest fields. The first cost and running expenses had to be reasonable and maintenance simple, while wing folding would make hangarage cheaper and easier. A whole new range of less expensive materials had to be demonstrated as sound to the airworthiness authorities, and as

The Stag Lane factory in the heyday of the Moth (*Hawker Siddeley*)

25

Geoffrey de Havilland at his desk in later years (*de Havilland*)

The three sons of the founder, Peter, John and Geoffrey Jnr (*Fox Photos*)

Folding wings on the Moth allowed it to be towed on the road (*de Havilland*)

production increased some of the less acceptable equipment in use could be replaced by specially developed items.

de Havilland's life-long interest in entomology inspired the name Moth for his new creation, and Cirrus was the name chosen for the engine. He made the maiden flight of the prototype D.H.60 Moth G-EBKT on the Sunday afternoon of 22 February 1925, and this confirmed that the formula was right.

The Moth was a dramatic success despite its specification being completely different to the officially accepted ideas. The company fortunes made a sharp upturn as the Government was prepared to financially assist the light aeroplane clubs, now that a practical and cost-effective aircraft was available. Ninety Moths were ordered for the five state-aided clubs, in some cases as introductory equipment.

In the first year the prototype was flown on its initial long-distance flight by Sir Alan Cobham from Croydon to Zürich, covering the 800 km (500 miles) non-stop. He returned in the afternoon; a total flying time of 13 hours 51 minutes at an average speed of 114 km/h (71 mph). A service organisation was established and lock-up garages to house Moths were provided on the Stag Lane aerodrome. Excellent publicity was received for the Moth when Hubert Broad won the King's Cup Air Race in 1926, and Wally Hope won in 1927, both averaging 149 km/h (92.5 mph) on 45 kW (60 hp).

Not only was the Moth to revolutionise light aviation, but it was to have an important effect on the company. Business was building up rapidly, but there were worries about the continued availability of the Cirrus engines at the right price. Eventually the stocks of surplus parts would be exhausted and if the price increased too much, the price of the Moth could become too expensive for the growing popular market.

Frank Halford was therefore approached again to assist; at the time he was an independent designer. de Havilland considered that with their strong business position they could build their own engine to safeguard interests and also to satisfy a market for other manufacturers, both at home and overseas.

Halford and his team started design of the new engine on 29 October 1926. Keeping to the traditional layout of four in-line cylinders, it was a

King's Cup winner in 1926 was Hubert Broad in a Moth (*Flight*)

27

greatly refined design over the Cirrus, aiming at the desirable 75 kW (100 hp) at low weight. Halford had an excellent background of engine work having been part of the Beardmore-Halford-Pullinger team (BHP) during the First World War, and became a freelance designer in 1923. He later designed engines for both de Havilland and Napier, the H-type aero-engine leading to the powerful Sabre, also his creation.

To test and publicise this new engine it was decided to produce a monoplane racer designed around it. Additionally, it was hoped that by showing the efficiency and high performance of a cleanly-designed monoplane some of the more elusive military business might be attracted. To obtain the optimum size for this single-seat racer, the D.H.71 Tiger Moth, the test pilot Broad, who was not a big person, was sat on the floor by a wall, and chalk lines were drawn around him to determine the maximum size of the cockpit.

The new engine, with a capacity of 5.23 litres, was developing 101 kW (135 hp) at 2,650 rpm on the bench at Stag Lane, where the engine production was established in about four months. By downrating to 75 kW (100 hp), the reliability and life of the new engine, named Gipsy by de Havilland, was improved. The new combination of engine and airframe was to be called the Gipsy Moth. The first production engine was delivered on 20 June 1928, and immediately installed in a Moth.

The Gipsy engine had been tested under high loads in the D.H.71, but there was also a need to prove its reliability. A standard Gipsy engine, selected at random, was therefore installed in a Moth and flown for 600 hours with only routine external attention. Many pilots helped put the hours on during the nine months of flying, commencing 27 December 1928, and the drop in power at the end was only 2 kW (2½ hp). The total cost of replacement parts at the completion of this test was a mere £7.15. Another ordeal, more for the pilot than the engine, was to stay airborne for 24 hours on the 16–17 August 1928. Hubert Broad flew about 2,300 km (1,440 miles) averaging about 12.5 litres (2.75 Imp gallons) of petrol per hour. Hope flew the Gipsy Moth to winning place in the 1928 King's Cup Air Race at a speed of 170 km/h (105.5 mph).

Military business continued to be slow, so the profits had to be gained in the civil field. While Moth production was being established, de Havilland produced the D.H.65 Hound to a military high-performance general purpose biplane requirement. It was capable of 260 km/h (162 mph), as fast as the fighters then in service, and appeared to fulfil the requirements exactly. It also had a better performance than any of the competing designs, but the Westland Wapiti was chosen as it had more room for equipment at the expense of speed.

The next two military designs were started by de Havilland, but due to the volume of civil work were transferred to the Gloster Aircraft Company. The first was the D.H.67 metal-structured, twin-engined aerial survey aircraft. de Havilland completed the initial layout and design work, leaving Glosters the task of detailed design and construction. The resulting aircraft was known as the A.S.31 and only superficially resembled the original design. The second project handed over to Glosters, no

D.H.65J Hound was the military version of the D.H.65A to an Australian requirement
(*The Aeroplane*)

doubt with some relief by de Havillands, was the large D.H.72 three-engined night bomber. Manufacture was protracted due to Air Ministry inspired design changes and de Havilland's unfamiliarity with the new all-metal construction techniques using light alloy in the wings. The aircraft took such a long time being built that the planned Bristol Jupiter engines improved at a faster pace, allowing progressively later marks to be used. Eventually, the dismantled airframe was moved by road to Brockworth where it was completed and flown in 1931. The D.H.72 can be classed as one of de Havilland's least successful aircraft.

One other military prototype was produced before the Second World War, the D.H.77 all-metal interceptor, to further prove the efficiency and good performance of the monoplane. It was designed on similar lines to the Tiger Moth racer, but as the Air Ministry were reluctant to recognise a new engine supplier, Halford designed the new H-layout for Napier under an agreement that all engines over 6,621.86 cc (404.09 cu in) cylinder capacity were to be built by D. Napier and Son Ltd. The engine, which became known as the Rapier, developed 246 kW (330 hp) and was a supercharged air-cooled design with four banks of four cylinders driving two geared-together crankshafts. This layout gave extra power for a low frontal area. The aircraft was a private venture by de Havilland to Air Ministry Specification F.20/27, and only one was built. The clean monoplane efficiency was now twice proven, but no production orders resulted.

The company's business with aircraft until the Second World War was split between light touring and training aircraft of the Moth family and light to medium-sized transports. During the early 1920s, single-engined airliners were acceptable. Multi-engined aircraft could not continue to fly then if one engine failed due to lack of power. Therefore, the risk of engine failure and complexity was only increased. When engines became more powerful, it was desirable to have more than one to give the added safety, while at the same time increasing their reliability. These larger aircraft requirements suited the European environment, but in the developing areas of Australia, Asia, Africa and South America the smaller single-engined aircraft remained in demand.

In the spring of 1927, an inquiry came from Australia for a simple

**D.H.60 Cirrus Moth
G-EBLV is still airworthy at
Hatfield** (*P. J. Birtles*)

single-engined transport along the lines of a scaled-up D.H.50. Early
delivery was essential. The drawings of the resulting D.H.61 Giant
Moth were completed in ten weeks allowing the six- to eight-passenger
prototype to fly by December 1927. One of them was bought by Sir
Alan Cobham, who was by then in business on his own with his flying
circuses bringing aviation to the masses and campaigning for municipal
aerodromes.

Another important order was from Imperial Airways for the multi-
engined D.H.66 Hercules 12-passenger airliner powered by three
Bristol Jupiter radial engines. Total numbers of all airliners built tended
to be small, usually not more than about a dozen to suit the limited
British airline requirements for Europe, while the continental companies tended to use their own manufacturers. The initial order for the
Hercules was for five aircraft to a very rigid specification defining the
engines, passenger load, and overall span to fit existing hangars. First
flight was in September 1926, and three were delivered by the following
December. The aircraft had been conceived and entered service all within
the one year. Its introduction to service was excellent, giving complete
satisfaction and 100 per cent reliability for months at a time. A total of
eleven Hercules were built, four of which were sold in Australia.

There appeared to be better business opportunities in the light aircraft market, so de Havilland started looking at Moth improvements
and developments. In the five years from September 1924, the Moth
business had transformed de Havillands from a private company employing 300 people and with 48,843 £1 shares to a public company with
a 1,500 work force, subsidiaries in Australia and Canada, a branch
in India, agents worldwide and £400,000 paid-up capital. The de
Havilland World Enterprise was fully established and still expanding.
The Moth was the eventual answer to the worldwide interest in flying
aroused during the First World War. The Stag Lane factory was producing 20 Gipsy engines per week by the end of 1928 and 16 light aircraft a
week by 1929. By 1928, Moths were flying with flying clubs and private
owners in practically every country of the world.

The first overseas company was formed by Hereward de Havilland,
younger brother of the founder, in Australia on 7 March 1927. The
Canadian company was formed a year later by Bob Loader, to be the

foundation of the de Havilland Aircraft of Canada, still producing outstanding aircraft today. The basis for these companies was the Moth, which commenced to attain many records for aircraft in its class as well as the King's Cup successes.

Moths were adopted by the Royal Australian Air Force as their standard trainers in 1928, and the type was put into licence production in the USA the same year. The royal seal of approval was given in 1929 when the air-minded Prince of Wales purchased a Moth, which was eventually to lead to today's Queen's Flight. A staggering 85 per cent of all private aircraft on the British register were Moths and company profits rose dramatically. Moth had become a household word, and symbolised all light aircraft the world over. Even more publicity was generated by a number of epic long-distance flights, including the one by Francis Chichester to Australia.

Then in 1930 came the slump which hit light aviation hard and reduced the profit from nearly £49,000 in 1928–29 to £36,500 the following year. This worldwide depression came at a time when the company was expanding further, particularly as it had just purchased some open fields at Hatfield, so that the RAF Reserve Flying School could move away from the congestion at Stag Lane. They started flying at the new premises in June 1930. The Australian company had moved to larger premises, but showed a loss, and the American operation died, never to be revived. South Africa still showed promise, and in 1930 a subsidiary was formed there by St. Barbe.

In 1931 the depression worsened, and the restrictive legislation which had grown up around light aviation only made things worse for de Havillands and easier for the emerging competition. Despite the difficulties, the company was able to survive by opening up new over-seas markets, and morale was much improved in 1930 when Amy Johnson made the first solo flight to Australia by a woman, taking nineteen and a half days by Gipsy Moth. During that year many other long-distance flights were made in Moths in ever decreasing times.

Basic development of the D.H.60 Moth continued over the years, much of the progress being made with the power plant. The arrival of the Gipsy engine was the most important step in the power of the aircraft, but other minor changes included the installation of alternative float and ski undercarriages and small cabins to protect the crew.

To meet overseas requirements for a more robust aircraft, the wooden fuselage was replaced by a metal tubular structure resulting in the D.H.60M. The next major development in the power plant was to invert the Gipsy engine as the Gipsy III to give a cleaner line and better visibility for the pilot. With this engine installed in the wooden fuselage Moth, it became known as the Moth Major. For military training the D.H.60T Moth Trainer was developed with the metal tubular fuselage and the upright Gipsy II engine. It had provision for military equipment and the increased all-up weight required new wings to be designed. It was a combination of the Moth Major and Moth Trainer which led to the world famous D.H.82 Tiger Moth.

The first major development in the Moth range was the high-wing

Five D.H.60T Moth Trainers for Egypt at Stag Lane before delivery (*Hawker Siddeley*)

D.H.80 prototype, from which the Puss Moth was developed (*Flight*)

The sole Cierva C.24 Autogiro built by de Havillands in 1931 (*P. J. Birtles*)

Many D.H.82A Tiger Moths were converted for agricultural duties

The newly established airfield at Hatfield in 1932 (*Hawker Siddeley*)

D.H.75 Hawk Moth, which reversed the birth process of the Moth powerplant, by mounting two Gipsy engines in a V-8 layout on a common crankcase. This engine, known as the Ghost, gave insufficient power for the four-seat Hawk Moth to be suitable for air taxi work, so a more powerful Lynx engine was installed. Only eight Hawk Moths were built, but its smaller brother, the D.H.80A Puss Moth, was a far greater success.

The Puss Moth gave a pilot and two passengers the comfort and protection of an enclosed cabin, and the inverted Gipsy III engine improved the forward view from this welded steel fuselage high-wing monoplane. Significant numbers of the efficient Puss Moth were produced in Britain and Canada. It was a popular mount for long-distance record attempts, Jim and Amy Mollison being the star performers. It was possible to achieve 32 km (20 miles) to the gallon with three people at 169 km/h (105 mph). At the same time the Moth's power had doubled and the weight increased by 50 per cent, so an effort was made to return to the light aircraft with the D.H.81 Swallow Moth. Power came from a specially designed Gipsy IV engine, the aircraft being a tandem two-seat low-wing low cost monoplane. A canopy was fitted to improve crew comfort and reduce drag, but despite being a successful performer it arrived in the midst of the slump and the idea had to be shelved.

33

The Tiger Moth was evolved through the RAF requirement for a Moth trainer with the upper wing moved forward to give the front cockpit occupant room to abandon the aircraft by parachute. The Tiger Moth first flew on 26 October 1931, and eventually over 7,000 were built throughout the world. This universally popular aircraft used the Gipsy Major engine, the latest in the evolution of the D.H. engines.

By economising, short-time work, salary cuts, and unavoidable lay-offs, the company was able to survive the slump and sustain confidence in its products. The Tiger Moth began to attract important overseas sales and by the end of 1932 the company fortunes began improving significantly. The year 1932–33 was easily the best to date with greatly improved turnover and profit. The sale of the Stag Lane Aerodrome as building land helped pay for the new factory at Hatfield.

In 1931 the company co-operated with the Cierva Autogiro Company to combine the de Havilland cabin airframe experience with the autogiro principle. A sole prototype, the C.24, was built using the Puss Moth cabin as the basis, with short span low wings, and was first flown by Juan de la Cierva in September 1931. It not only came at a bad economic time, but it lacked somewhat in efficiency compared with the conventional aircraft and the whirling rotor only brought further complication. The aircraft continues to exist at the Mosquito Aircraft Museum on loan from the Science Museum.

Despite the failure of the Hawk Moth for charter purposes, the Puss Moth, although designed as a tourer, also found a use in air taxi and charter work. This idea was developed by using the Gipsy Major in a small low cost commercial aircraft which could carry a pilot and three or four passengers in an enclosed cabin. This highly economical biplane was the D.H.83 Fox Moth which pioneered many air routes in the Middle East and Asia, as well as some of the early feeder routes in the more sophisticated areas of Europe. It was this aircraft that opened the way to domestic unsubsidised air services.

The range of Moth developments continued with the D.H.85 Leopard Moth, which was a direct improvement of the Puss Moth. The higher power of the Gipsy Major allowed improvements all round,

Capt Geoffrey de Havilland, winner of the 1933 King's Cup in a Leopard Moth (*Flight*)

Hornet Moth production at
the new Hatfield factory
(*Hawker Siddeley*)

including better performance. On 8 July 1933, three of the new aircraft were entered for the King's Cup Air Race, on this occasion with Hatfield as the start and finish. The popular win was by de Havilland flying a Leopard Moth, while the others finished third and sixth. Highest average speed over the 1,295 km (804 miles) course was 224.5 km/h (139.51 mph). Of the 133 built one Leopard Moth was bought by Geoffrey de Havilland himself for touring and family flying.

The next stage in the Moth evolution was to produce the two-seat tourer D.H.87 Hornet Moth with the passenger seat beside the pilot and room for light luggage behind. This wooden tourer was probably responsible for introducing the thrill of flying an aircraft to many novice passengers. There had always previously been concern at putting the passenger within reach of the pilot in case of distraction. However, cars were being driven with passengers alongside, so why not aircraft as well? The 160 litre (35 Imp gallons) fuel tank gave a range of nearly 965 km (600 miles) at a cruising speed of 178.6 km/h (111 mph).

Since 1931 when the Swallow Moth had to be abandoned due to the depression de Havilland had wanted to return to a basic and economic light aircraft. It was to be a simple two-seat tandem layout low wing monoplane using the same sort of power as the original Cirrus engine in 1925. This ultimate Moth, the D.H.94 Moth Minor, was to be a design exercise for members of the technical department recently recruited

Early D.H.87 Hornet Moths were built with tapered wings (*Flight*)

from the de Havilland Aeronautical Technical School, which had been started in 1928 to provide a thorough theoretical and practical training to prospective engineers.

J. P. Smith was the leader amongst the younger designers, and John Cunningham was the principal pilot who had begun to assist Geoffrey de Havilland Jnr, the elder son of the founder.

Robust simplicity was the major characteristic of the Moth Minor which was powered by a specially designed Gipsy Minor engine. Although the aircraft was experimental, it was soon put into production with minor changes in the summer of 1939 at a fly away price of £575. A coupé-top version was available for £690. The main event during the development was when spinning tests were being conducted by Geoffrey Jnr and Cunningham with progressively aft-loaded ballast. The limit was reached rather dramatically when it would not recover from a spin and both pilots had to bale out of the Moth Minor test aircraft at 900 metres (3,000 ft) near Hatfield.

Orders for the Moth Minor poured in from clubs as part of the newly-formed Civil Air Guard and private owners thanks to the low operating costs. The first of a 111 Moth Minors to be built at Hatfield was delivered in the early summer of 1939 to the RAF Flying Club based on the company's airfield. However, with the outbreak of war on 3 September all production ceased and about a hundred sets of unfinished aircraft and the jigs were shipped out to Australia, where some of them were completed.

So ended the Moth era, apart from massive production efforts on the Tiger Moth for the Empire Air Training Scheme during the war. de Havillands were unable to recover the light aircraft market after the war was over, and so ended Britain's chance of ever again dominating this field of aviation.

The Growth of Commercial Business

5

The principal of a double Fox Moth as the basis for an economical transport aircraft seemed to answer the problems of the new Iraqi Air Force. At about the same time, a successful Romford coach company owner, Edward Hillman, arrived at Stag Lane, to announce that he intended to fly the masses in the same way as he had carried them by coach.

The D.H.84 Dragon was already on the drawing boards, with power from two Gipsy Major engines and Moth wings as extension planes. Hillman declared it ideal for his low cost unsubsidised London to Paris service at £5.10.0 (£5.50) return. Four months from start of design, the first aircraft was airborne and Hillman took delivery of his initial aircraft in December 1932, only a month after the maiden flight. Hillman operated a fleet of five throughout 1933 with a 100 per cent reliability. Iraq took delivery of six fitted with military equipment. Once again, the Royal seal of approval was given when the Prince of Wales purchased one for his personal use. The aircraft were built at the rate of one a week for operators all over the world. The Dragon was able to carry eight passengers more economically than ever before, allowing unsubsidised

One of three D.H.84M Dragons sold to Portugal (*Hawker Siddeley*)

commercial operation. In addition to the 115 produced in Britain, 87 were built in Australia after the start of the war in Europe.

The Dragon helped the company return to prosperity in 1932–3, although Canada and Australia were still operating at a loss. The Stag Lane airfield was sold for building land at £105,000, leaving the factory area for manufacturing activities, and work started on the new factory at Hatfield early in 1934.

As this move was being made to Hatfield, the first components of the new D.H.86 four-engined airliner were being manufactured to continue the England to Australia air route on the low demand last section from Singapore. The aircraft had to have the economics of the Dragon to make it profitable, but would need more power, and it was designed to use a six-cylinder version of the Gipsy Major. This engine became the Gipsy Six, developing 149 kW (200 hp), and the aircraft could continue to fly on only two engines, meeting the stringent but vital safety requirements. The international competition was keen, with foreign government subsidies for the modern larger metal aircraft, which had greater operating costs making them uneconomic on the less frequented routes.

The D.H.86 had to be produced in the short time of four months to meet the delivery date commencing September 1933 covering design, building and testing, to achieve a Certificate of Airworthiness (C of A) by 31 January 1934. The Gipsy Six engine proved to be most reliable and a good performer at 153 kW (205 hp), one of the tests being a 100-hour test bed run at full throttle without replacements or adjustments. First flight was by Hubert Broad on 14 January 1934 from the diminishing airfield at Stag Lane, and the C of A was achieved one day ahead of schedule, confirming the initial order by Qantas of Australia. Orders followed from Imperial Airways and many other airlines at home and abroad. A total of 62 were built, some serving with the

de Havilland Flying Club facilities at Hatfield in the mid-1930s
(*British Aerospace*)

RAF as aircrew trainers and communications aircraft, and the ultimate version, the D.H.86B, could carry up to 17 passengers.

Using the experience of the tapered wing, the faired undercarriage and the better engines of the D.H.86, the same improvements were applied to the Dragon layout to produce the very popular D.H.89 Dragon Rapide. It seated up to eight passengers and cruised at about 220 km/h (135 mph). The Dragon Rapide continued in production until 1945, the wartime needs of communications and aircrew training boosting production at Brush in Loughborough due to the de Havilland commitment to Mosquitoes.

One of the other developments in this family was the D.H.90 Dragonfly, which used the tapered wings on a smaller aircraft returning to the Gipsy Major engines. It was probably the first business aircraft, and could carry five passengers, but its monocoque shell of pre-formed ply was expensive to produce and difficult to repair. An attempt to develop a dual-control Dragon Rapide with a retractable undercarriage, the D.H.92 Dolphin, was abandoned due to high structural weight.

A significant aircraft was the D.H.88 Comet Racer produced for the challenging England to Australia air race. Britain had no suitable aircraft in production, and the competition from abroad was very strong, one of the major rivals being the Douglas DC-2. Time was very short to produce a new aircraft, but the de Havilland directors were determined to provide an aircraft capable of winning not only the £10,000 first prize, but the prestige of such an achievement.

When the two class prizes of speed and handicap were announced, it was decided to build a special long-range racing aircraft to aim for the speed prize only. Over 320 km/h (200 mph) had to be achieved and de Havillands undertook to build, in a period of nine months, a production batch of three of these aircraft with a guaranteed performance, for £5,000 each. This would by no means cover the actual cost, but orders

Hatfield paint shop filled with Rapides, Dragonflies, D.H.86 and Moth variants (*T. Greville*)

had to be placed quickly and technical details would initially even be withheld from the buyers to preserve the commercial confidentiality.

The airframe was of course a challenge. The Gipsy Six engines could be adapted for the task, but the propellers were a major problem. In Britain, only fixed-pitch were available, but for the heavy take offs at a high temperature and subsequent cruise, a variable-pitch propeller was essential. The only ones available were in America, with a further possibility in France. The opportunity of developing this type of propeller in Britain was invaluable as it would certainly be required for efficient airline operations in the future.

The ideal propeller appeared to be the American Hamilton Standard, but the range in production were too large for the proposed Racer, and cropping even the smaller blades would be inefficient. License production was discussed, but de Havillands had to join the queue, as offers had been made to other companies. An order was confirmed for Hamilton Standard propellers as an insurance against the unavailability of a suitable alternative.

Contact was then made with Ratier in France who were developing a smaller propeller, much more suitable in size and performance for the Comet Racer and with a very simple pitch change. The blades could be pre-set in fine pitch for take-off by air pressure and once airborne, the airflow on a disc on the hub pushed it back changing the blades to coarse pitch for the cruise. The major disadvantage was that it could not be returned to fine pitch for landing, making an overshoot hazardous. Another problem with the Ratier propellers was the impossibility of achieving synchronisation of the pitch change. However, since these propellers were readily available, they were ordered for the race.

Engine development was progressing to achieve the maximum power from the Gipsy Six with the minimum frontal area to reduce drag. Flight testing was undertaken with an adapted Leopard Moth, and as they became available, the two types of propeller were tried. For cooling and efficiency reasons, the Ratier was confirmed as the one to be selected.

The airframe itself was constructed by a novel process of stressed diagonal wood planking producing a strong slim cantilever wing and a fine fuselage housing the two crew in tandem to reduce drag. The wing was too thin to accommodate any fuel, so all the tankage to achieve up to the 4,200 km (2,600 miles) range was in the fuselage. To give the best performance for take off and landing, the slim wing was fitted with flaps, and to further reduce drag, the undercarriage was retractable. Not only were all these new features combined in this high performance aircraft, but time was also short to complete the aircraft to receive a C of A before the start of the race. The Comet Racer was the first British aircraft to combine variable pitch propellers, wing flaps and retractable undercarriage.

After the closing date of 1 June 1934, a total of 64 varied entries were published, including three Comet Racers, competing in an international field. The biggest threat appeared to come from the KLM-entered Douglas DC-2.

The Comet Racers were built at Stag Lane and moved to Hatfield for assembly, the first one being flown by Hubert Broad on 8 September, and soon proved its capabilities. The entrants had to be at Mildenhall by 1630 hours on Sunday 14 October. All three Comets were there in good time for the preparations and the inevitable dramas of last minute snags included damage to the propellers and undercarriage of one of the aircraft. The problems were cleared up just in time for the aircraft to take their position on 20 October amongst the 20 starters.

The next three days and nights were summed up as 'it was lousy – and that's praising it!', but it was Comet Racer G-ACSS flown by Tom Campbell Black and C. W. A. Scott who won the speed section in 70 hours 54 minutes and 18 seconds, closely followed by the DC-2. The Mollisons had to retire due to fuel problems, while the third Comet flown by Owen Carthcart Jones and Ken Waller finished fourth. This latter crew immediately turned round and flew back with newsreel film of the finish, arriving at Lympne on 2 November. They had covered the 18,840 km (11,700 miles) home in 61 hours 46 minutes flying time, and broken the round trip record with a time of 13 days 6 hours and 43 minutes.

One of the major results for de Havilland of building the Comet Racers was the setting up of license production of Hamilton Standard propellers by what was to become the de Havilland Propeller Company. The launch order was for the Bristol 142 twin-engined all-metal monoplane, later to be developed into the Blenheim bomber, and the license agreement was signed in June 1934. Production and expertise was gradually built up and an increased investment in the company was required to finance the new venture in the rapidly expanding organisation.

The first Air Ministry order was received early in 1935, and the first delivery was made to Bristol for a Pegasus engine test-bed on 30 July. The first airborne D.H. propeller drove a Whitley bomber from Baginton on 17 March 1936. That year, civil propeller business began to appear, as well as the first of many export orders.

Within two years of the signing of the license agreement, the British Government realised the defence need of a good supply of variable pitch propellers, and a new factory was started at Lostock, near Bolton, as a major manufacturing unit dispersed from other production areas. The new factory supplemented the production facilities at Stag Lane, which had become probably the biggest producer of variable pitch propellers in the world. Practically all the new aircraft entering service with the RAF were fitted with de Havilland propellers, including the Hurricane, Spitfire and Wellington. However, the smaller range for the civil market was not neglected, and propellers were also supplied for the large airliners in service with Imperial Airways.

During the war, Lostock manufactured 77,029 propellers and assembled 37,801 from American components, while Stag Lane produced 23,210. In addition to this effort, many more propellers were repaired and returned to service.

Following the success of the Comet Racer, de Havillands and many other people realised how close the challenge was from the American

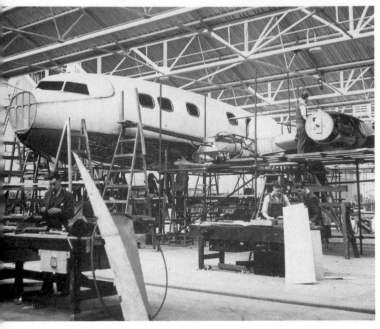

D.H.91 Albatross under assembly at Hatfield (*British Aerospace*)

Propellers were eventually to become a major part of the company business (*de Havilland*)

built commercial airliners. The Comet Racer was not likely to be a commercial proposition, but there was an undeniable need for a new airliner capable of achieving the competitive shorter flight times on the traditional British Empire routes. de Havillands put the case forcefully to the Government, requesting financial assistance, but the response was slow in coming. Eventually, fourteen and a half months after negotiations had been started, the American competition had further progressed, an order was placed for two D.H.91 Albatross airliners, with the company sharing about half the cost.

The Albatross was aerodynamically a very clean and graceful monoplane design, powered by four of the new close-cowled 335 kW (450 hp) Gipsy Twelve engines driving de Havilland controllable-pitch airscrews. The fuselage structure of the Albatross went a step further than the Comet Racer by using two skins of pre-formed plywood, stabilised by an interlayer of balsa wood, preparing the way for the Mosquito. The one-piece cantilever wing followed the example set by the Comet Racer, and was again used in the Mosquito.

The two prototypes were essentially high-speed Atlantic mail carriers, but this allowed the development of the airliner version to start. Imperial Airways ordered five for their short European routes, but these stages were by no means ideal for the long-range aircraft. However, just as de Havillands were hopeful of entering the world airline market, the war killed any further prospects and the Albatross airliners were allocated to wartime transport duties.

The de Havilland factories began to feel the effect of the rearmament programme in 1936 when they were equally busy in the commerical field. In addition to the growing manufacturing activities, the RAF

T.K.1, first design by the
D.H. Aeronautical
Technical School
(de Havilland)

T.K.2 modified for air
racing in 1938
(The Aeroplane)

The diminutive T.K.4
crashed at Hatfield killing
Bob Waight, the Chief Test
Pilot

Reserve School, the London Flying Club and the de Havilland
Aeronautical Technical School were all contributing to the activities at
Hatfield. The Technical School, with some 150 engineering students,
produced a series of interesting designs, some of which were built as
one-off exercises. The TK.1 was a modest biplane conversion of the
discarded Swallow Moth airframe, but the TK.2 was a more adven-
turous low-wing monoplane racer capable of speeds up to 306 km/h
(190 mph). The TK.2 in fact survived until after the Second World War,
but was eventually scrapped due to old age. The TK.4 was the next one
built, and was a very small high performance racer, but it crashed after a
very short career killing Bob Waight, the Chief Test Pilot. Following his
death, Geoffrey de Havilland Jnr was appointed Chief Test Pilot on
1 October 1937. The only other Technical School design to reach
the hardware stage was the tail-first TK.5 which refused to fly.

As the rearmament programme built up Hatfield became increasingly
busy with the Tiger Moth production, turning out practically one per

The overweight D.H.93 Don military trainer under construction (*Hawker Siddeley*)

day. The Australian and Canadian companies were also making their contribution and a small company was set up in New Zealand to build Tiger Moths locally.

In 1936, de Havillands were asked to produce a general purpose trainer to an ill-conceived Air Ministry specification. It was the D.H.93 Don, powered by a single Gipsy Twelve engine, and was to be able to undertake a wide range of training tasks. It had side by side dual controls, a cabin for navigation training and the added weight and drag of a rotatable gun turret. The weight of equipment grew so much that by the time it was ready for delivery it was barely able to fly, and many of the completed aircraft were allocated to ground instruction duties.

In the six years from 1934 to 1939, the issued capital had doubled to £800,000, the turnover had increased from £625,000 to £5 million, and profits had quadrupled. The build-up of military tasks, while good for business, were causing difficulties with the civil activities, where early deliveries were impossible. There were also complaints that the British Government were still neglecting the financial support of airliner development, particularly in comparison with the USA.

de Havillands had of course become very familiar with wood construction, but they realised the competitive edge of metal structures, and began to re-equip the factory with metal working tools. In early 1938, the D.H.95 Flamingo was announced as an all-metal airliner, smaller than and complementary to the Albatross. Even though new manufacturing techniques had to be mastered, the first aircraft was completed for its first flight right after Christmas in 1938. It was powered by two Bristol Perseus XIIC sleeve-valve radial engines and could seat up to 20 passengers in its 2.21 m (7 ft 4 in) wide cabin. The Flamingo entered service with Jersey Airways in July 1939, but all hopes of further development had to be abandoned with the outbreak of war on 3 September. Only 16 Flamingoes were built and used on wartime communication duties.

Tiger Moths of the RAF Reserve Flying School at Hatfield (*Hawker Siddeley*)

The Second World War

6

When war was declared the Hatfield factory was busy producing Tiger Moth trainers, Dominie trainers and communications aircraft, Airspeed Oxford trainers and was soon to be heavily committed to the repair of Hurricanes damaged during the Battle of Britain. Essential as these tasks were, the de Havilland directors felt that they could contribute more effectively to end the hostilities, despite their contempt of the war.

The Comet Racer and Albatross airliner had demonstrated that speed for relatively low power could be achieved very efficiently by cleanness of form based on close attention to detail. The Albatross and the Flamingo formed the basis of the early studies, but it soon became apparent that by removing the defensive guns speed could be increased to outpace the intercepting fighters. Therefore as the guns were only a defence against enemy aircraft they could be dispensed with and the weight of the gunners saved, together with the extra structure and fuel needed to carry them. The resulting smaller twin-engined aircraft could carry the same load as the bigger bomber, with just two crew, at higher speeds. Not only would its speed avoid enemy fighters, but each aircraft could fly two sorties in one night instead of only one. The ideal power plants were two of the newly developed Rolls-Royce Merlin liquid-cooled engines developing about 895 kW (1,200 hp) each.

Wooden construction was decided upon. The company had a long experience of using the material, it would save further demands on the overtaxed metal industries, and the aircraft could be in production much sooner. Timber was in plentiful supply, and an aircraft of wooden construction not only saved strategic materials for other purposes, but non-strategic labour could be used in its production. Despite these decisive points, the Government could not appreciate the logic or urgency, until Poland was invaded.

At the end of 1939 de Havillands were authorised to proceed with the unarmed, high-speed bomber, having an estimated range of 2,400 km (1,500 miles) and capable of carrying a 454 kg (1,000 lb) bomb load. At the same time provision was made for a reconnaissance role, and the company pointed out the possibilities of a long-range fighter.

With the Battle of Britain underway there was an urgency to supply large numbers of the aircraft types already in production, concentrating all capacity on immediate operational needs. The Mosquito, as the new aircraft was named, was not likely to be available for about 18 months,

The wartime factory and aerodrome at Hatfield (*Hawker Siddeley*)

and it was therefore omitted from the official programme, making the ordering of materials practically impossible. But de Havillands had no intention of giving up. By pointing out that demands for metal were minimal, the programme was finally reinstated on 19 July 1940, provided that it did not interfere with the work the company were doing on other important contracts. This was due in large measure to Sir Wilfred Freeman, Air Member of Development at the Air Ministry, who had supported the idea of an unarmed twin-engined high-speed bomber from late 1939.

The design office had meanwhile been moved to a moated country house called Salisbury Hall about 6.5 km (4 miles) from Hatfield, where construction of the Mosquito prototype commenced, R. E. Bishop was the Chief Designer and C. C. Walker the Chief Engineer. The prototype has since returned to its birthplace in 1958, which it shares with other de Havilland products in the Mosquito Aircraft Museum.

The factory at Hatfield was not too badly affected by the threat of bombing during the Battle of Britain, although there was much time lost due to air raid warnings. The only occasion bombs actually fell on the factory was on 3 October 1940, when a stray Ju 88 unloaded over the factory having missed its target in Reading. Its bombs killed 21 people and injured 70. Among the material losses was about nine months output of the Mosquito, representing about 80 per cent of the materials. The enemy aircraft was shot down by the Hatfield Aerodrome defences, crashing a few miles away near Hertford. As a result of this raid, the Mosquito production was dispersed so widely that no enemy action could possibly disrupt production in the future. The furniture industry was among the skills brought in to build the fuselages and wings, and the smallest sub-contractor was in a garden shed in Welwyn producing electrical components.

As an insurance, Tiger Moths were fitted with bomb racks during the invasion scare (*Hawker Siddeley*)

The Mosquito fuselage structure consisted of two thin plywood skins, stabilised by a sandwich of balsa wood, moulded and glued over concrete tools. The one-piece wing was a stressed double-ply skin with stringers in between, allowing clear space to be left between the spars for the fuel tanks. This form of construction made the wings lighter, stronger and simpler.

Having been completed at Salisbury Hall, the yellow painted prototype was dismantled and moved by road to Hatfield on 3 November to

Salisbury Hall, where the Mosquito was designed, and prototype built in a two-bay hangar
(*Hawker Siddeley*)

be prepared for its maiden flight by Geoffrey de Havilland Jnr, which took place only eleven months after start of detail design, on 27 November 1940.

The performance and manoeuvrability were immediately impressive, with no serious problems encountered during the development programme. Production at Hatfield started to build up on the Mosquito while Oxford production was returned to Airspeed. Tiger Moth production was taken over by Morris Motors at Cowley and that of Rapides by Brush at Loughborough. de Havillands had also been asked to build Wellington bombers, and for this purpose set up the D.H. Second

Mosquito prototype taking off from the grass at Hatfield
(*British Aerospace*)

**Mosquito bomber
production line at Hatfield**
(de Havilland)

**Canadian-built Mosquito
B.Mk.XX shortly after
arrival at Hatfield**
(Hawker Siddeley)

Aircraft Group at Leavesden near Watford, where adequate space and labour was available. However, Leavesden was soon allocated to Mosquito production, concentrating on the fighter versions, and also dispersing its work widely.

To save time in dismantling and re-assembly, the second Mosquito at Salisbury Hall, the fighter prototype, was flown out of an adjacent field, as were two subsequent aircraft. Before dawn on 13 May 1941, a German spy courier in civilian clothes landed by parachute in a field near Salisbury Hall. He was very soon captured, and found to have arrived some 80 km (50 miles) off course, and was therefore not a threat to the Mosquito. The fighter prototype flew out to Hatfield on 15 May, while the inexpert agent was executed at Wandsworth on 10 December.

First deliveries were made to the RAF in July 1941, and the demand for all versions of the aircraft began to increase rapidly. Such was this demand that plans were made for large scale production at de Havilland Canada, mainly of the bomber version. In Britain, additional production facilities were set up for the fighter versions with Standard Motors at Coventry.

The load of the bomber versions was doubled even before it entered service by cropping the vanes of the 227 kg (500 lb) bombs, allowing four to be carried, instead of just four 113 kg (250 lb) bombs. Later, two 227 kg (500 lb) bombs were fitted in the bomb bay behind the cannon in the fighter, making a very effective fighter-bomber. On both versions, a pair of 227 kg (500 lb) bombs could be carried under the wings, or alternatively, 454.6 litre (100 Imp gallon) fuel drop tanks. Later Mosquitoes could carry a single 1,814.4 kg (4,000 lb) bomb, an equivalent load to the American Boeing B-17 Flying Fortress, and high altitude developments included extended wing-tips and pressure cabins. The basic fighter version was used on intruder sorties, against targets of opportunity, whether in the air or on the ground, and when fitted with Airborne Interception (AI) radar, the Mosquito was a very potent night fighter. As an unarmed bomber, it was ideal for pathfinding and pin-pointing targets for the main bomber force, and both these and the fighter-bombers made a number of precision raids on special targets where the surrounding buildings had to remain undamaged. The bomber version was adapted to high and low level unarmed photo reconnaissance, giving greater range and accuracy than the single-seat Spitfires. Later on, the fighter-bombers were also adapted for anti-shipping strikes, delivering a hefty punch with rocket projectiles, equivalent to the broadside from a cruiser.

The high-speed unarmed formula proved itself in combat, with bomber losses remaining as low as one per cent, and many aircraft exceeding 150 sorties. Diversion raids, to take defending night fighters away from the main force, were a speciality, and at the same time causing a nuisance. In the bomber role, the small two-seater aircraft was able to carry a heavier bomb load than the large four-engined heavy bombers crewed by up to eleven men. The Mosquito was exposed to less risk, for a shorter time, and used less fuel and engineering support.

A more unusual role was as an airliner operated by BOAC on a regular courier service between Leuchars in Scotland and Stockholm in Sweden. It was known as the 'ball bearing run', because Britain used it in part to buy the total supply of ball bearings from Sweden, not only for our use but to deny them to Germany. The aircraft could carry up to 500 kg (half a ton) of urgent freight or mail, and on occasions also transported agents and other passengers, stowed on a mattress in the bomb bay.

Mosquitoes were also used to catch the elusive V-1 flying bombs, and some aircraft were fitted with a 57 mm (6-pdr) cannon weighing nearly 1,000 kg (1 ton) as an anti-shipping weapon. From September 1941 until early 1944, the Mosquito was the fastest operational aircraft on either side. Nearly 7,000 were built by VJ-day. Mosquitoes were used in all theatres of the war, with production lines also set up by de Havilland Australia, although the original glues selected were unsatisfactory in the hotter climate.

One sadness was the death of John de Havilland, third son of the founder, and three colleagues on 23 August 1943, when two Mosquitoes on test flights collided in cloud near St. Albans.

To support the vast Mosquito operations, a Mosquito repair organisation was set up, and was so successful that one in every four aircraft delivered came from a repair depot. The service department had to instruct a wide range of military and civilian personnel, a total of some 3,500 persons attending courses during the war.

The ultimate Mosquitoes, despite being very similar to the first aircraft, continued to advance in performance. The PR. Mk 34 for example could carry 5,760 litres (1,267 Imp gallons) of fuel, and had an operational range of 4,500 km (2,800 miles), cruising at 9,140 m (30,000 ft) at 507 km/h (315 mph). Its top speed was 676 km/h (420 mph).

Although the Mosquito was de Havilland's main contribution to the war effort, aircraft development continued to improve. The Hornet and the Vampire were two very different outstanding answers for the fighter role, but were not produced in time to see war service.

Major Halford had started designing a jet engine in 1941 for the Engine Division, and with the Mosquito established in production, senior design staff could be spared to consider a suitable single-jet powered interceptor. No detail could be worked out until more was known about the proposed engine, allowing a twin Napier Sabre-engined Mosquito project to be studied. This was abandoned when the Sabre engines were not available, and consideration was given to substituting them with Griffons, but the estimated performance was not very attractive.

In May 1942, permission was granted by the Government to proceed with the jet fighter, D.H.100 Vampire, powered by a single Goblin engine which had been running on the test bed since 13 April. To avoid interference with Mosquito production and development, suggestions were made for the jet fighter, code-named 'Spider Crab', to be built elsewhere. In December, the night bomber development of the Mosquito was dropped and every effort went into the interceptor.

By the end of January 1943, the mock-up of the twin-Merlin powered D.H.103 was complete. These engines were two specially-adapted Merlins with low frontal area, and to avoid swing of the aircraft on take-off or landing, they rotated in opposite directions. The D.H.103, named Hornet, was designed as a long-range escort fighter proposed for use in the South Pacific, but the go-ahead was not given by the Government until June 1943.

The jet fighter flew from Hatfield for the first time on 20 September 1943, sixteen months after the official go ahead, and exceeded 805 km/h (500 mph) in the spring of 1944. Series production was taken over by the English Electric factories at Preston, deliveries commencing in early 1945.

The Hornet flew thirteen months from the go ahead on 28 July 1944. It could achieve over 756 km/h (470 mph) and had a range of more than 4,023 km (2,500 miles) with drop tanks. It was the first aircraft to use the technique of bonding wood to metal, production being at Hatfield, from where deliveries commenced in February 1945.

In addition to the military aircraft produced in the war effort, in the latter stages the company also found time to design and produce the civil Dove, an all-metal light transport to replace the Rapides. This first flew on 25 September 1945, the 25th anniversary of the formation of the company.

Returning to jet engine development, with the decision by the Government to approve production of the Goblin early in 1941, de Havillands became the first company to commence quantity production of a

Vampire prototype, code named 'Spider Crab', de Havilland's first jet aircraft (*Hawker Siddeley*)

50

de Havilland Engine
Company, jet engine
production
(de Havilland)

jet engine. To maintain secrecy it was code-named 'Supercharger' and the first drawings were issued on 8 August 1941. The initial runs were very satisfactory, allowing the development programme to commence. On 5 May 1942, the engine seized due to the air intake ducts being sucked flat, but little damage was done, and on 2 June the engine ran at full speed for the first time. Production plans were being investigated by September.

Within two years of the start of design, the Goblin jet engine was sufficiently developed to install in an airframe for flight testing. The Vampire prototype was not so advanced, due to pre-occupation with Mosquito development and the Hornet, but an opportunity arose to install the new engines in the twin-jet Gloster Meteor. It first flew, powered by a pair of Goblin engines, on 5 March 1943, and in fact this was the first production standard jet-powered British aircraft to fly, powered by production standard engines. de Havillands were pioneering again. The Vampire began flight trials at Hatfield six months later.

The Americans were being kept fully informed on development of these jet engines, and on 30 October 1943 one of the early production examples was shipped to the Lockheed Company in California for installation in their new XP-80A aircraft, later to become known as the Shooting Star. It first flew in January 1944, and exceeded 805 km/h (500 mph) during the spring. Goblin type approval was achieved by January 1945, and it was in full production in a new specially built factory. The Goblin had changed little during its development, and was the most powerful jet engine in production, providing a reliable power source despite the relatively small effort which had been spent on it. The way was opened for the new jet age, leading to ever increasing speeds.

Piston engine development also continued during the war years, the main product being the Gipsy Queen, which was later to power the Dove and the Heron.

On 1 February 1944, the Engine Division was formed into the de Havilland Engine Company Limited with Frank Halford as Chairman of the board of directors, and its technical head. The new company was therefore not only able to support the activities of the Aircraft Company, but could more effectively provide engines to the other airframe manufacturers.

The Propeller Division was equally busy during the Second World War, building over 100,000 propellers from scratch, assembling nearly 38,000 from American supplied parts, and repairing nearly 41,000 damaged in war service. de Havilland variable pitch propellers were fitted to the earlier Spitfires and Hurricanes, and constant-speed propellers were supplied for a whole range of aircraft including the Wellington, Beaufighter, Stirling and Manchester bombers. The division undertook, at short notice, the conversion of the Spitfire propellers to constant-speed units, which greatly improved the performance all round. Following the urgent conversion of the Spitfires, the Hurricanes and Defiants were similarly converted, all in a very short space of time. The existing propellers could all be modified, but had to be dismantled to complete the conversion, and additional piping and controls had to be installed in the aircraft.

The de Havilland School of Flying became No.1 Elementary Flying Training School (EFTS) in August 1935 during the RAF expansion, and continued operating throughout the war and up to its 30th anniversary on 31 March 1953. De Havillands also formed No.13 EFTS in 1935 at White Waltham, near Maidenhead. The company located the site and developed it into an airfield, constructing a replica of the Hatfield School building, both of which still stand largely unaltered externally. On 11 January 1941, the school at White Waltham closed to become the base of the Air Transport Auxiliary, but in July the company were asked to operate No.17 EFTS at Peterborough until it closed in May 1942. From mid 1941, No.1 EFTS progressively moved out of Hatfield to Panshanger, about 6.5 km (4 miles) to the north-east, where previously a decoy factory had been built to draw off the enemy bombers.

During the war, the de Havilland companies had grown from light and commercial aircraft builders into a mammoth world-wide industrial organisation making a major contribution in aircraft, engines, propellers and training to the defeat of the enemy. The payroll increased in seven years from 5,000 to 38,000, with many thousands in other companies supplying the de Havilland production lines with components, assemblies and materials. Another measure was turnover. Before the expansion began in 1936, the turnover was nearly £1.5 million. In the last year of the war, it was £25 million, not including the shadow factory and associated companies at home and overseas.

The expansion had been carefully controlled, using sub-contractors wherever possible, and some 40 per cent of the workforce were women. The company was therefore well placed to enter the post-war commercial market, while still retaining a strong military capability.

The Jet Age

7

The de Havilland companies were far better prepared for peacetime work after the Second World War than Airco had been after the First. Aviation was also firmly established and advancing rapidly, spurred on by the performance gains attainable with jet propulsion.

The initial commercial product of the company after the war was the D.H.104 Dove, as mentioned in the last chapter. This was the first aircraft to use the metal to metal bonding process, known as Redux, which is still being used today in the BAe 146 airliner. This process, by avoiding weakening by drilling holes for rivets, gives a stronger, lighter joint.

Dove prototype outside the Hatfield Experimental Department
(*Hawker Siddeley*)

However, the Dove did not just appear so soon after the end of the war without a great deal of planning. As early as 1941, the Brabazon Committee had been considering the specifications of British airliners for post-war use. The Americans had continued to produce transport aircraft, the best examples being the Douglas DC-4 and Lockheed Constellation, while Britain concentrated on fighters and bombers. This meant that there was little point in producing anything close to the American specifications. To be competitive a greater step would have to be taken, either to produce more advanced aircraft using the jet engine, or aircraft in a category not being filled. Among the categories being considered were the jet-powered mail carrier or airliner; a Dakota replacement – attempted by the Airspeed Ambassador; and an eight-passenger light transport which emerged as the Dove.

The Dove was the most obvious one to start with, as it would fit into the market filled by the Rapide before the war, and would be financially and technically possible for the company to produce without the restrictions of government control.

Meanwhile, from 1943 the Airspeed Company, then part of the de Havilland Enterprise, had been at work on the design of the A.S.57 Ambassador.

The all-metal Dove, powered by a pair of de Havilland engines driving de Havilland propellers, soon demonstrated its efficiency and eventually some 540 were sold, making it the best-selling British commercial aircraft of its time.

Production and development of military aircraft continued, unlike after First World War. There were improvements to the Mosquito, in particular the ultimate night fighter developments, and a number of overseas air forces were re-equipped. The Hornet was adapted for naval use as the Sea Hornet, and Preston were producing Vampires in quantity, the first significant overseas order being placed by Sweden. The Goblin jet engines were produced under license by Flygmotor at Trollhattan in Sweden to power these aircraft.

To cope with all this future development it was decided to build a concrete runway across the grass airfield at Hatfield. A 1,830 m (6,000 ft) run was laid and came into use on 12 May 1947.

On 27 April 1946, the Propeller Division was formed into a separate company, de Havilland Propellers Ltd, situated in a new factory built on the north side of the Hatfield aerodrome. The new company had a good start by announcing the first propeller in the world to have a type approval for a prop-jet installation and the first reverse-pitch propeller for shortening the landing run.

The Engine Company activities continued to prosper, with the Gipsy Queen in demand for the Dove and Goblins required for the Vampires. The original Stag Lane factory was still occupied by the design and experimental departments while production was at Leavesden and Stone Grove near Edgware. Test beds and flight testing was at Hatfield. A more powerful jet engine for later fighters and the jet airliner, the Ghost, first ran at Hatfield on 2 September 1945, and was later flight tested in a pair of Lancastrian aircraft for low-altitude endurance work and a modified Vampire for high-altitude, high-performance testing.

The war effort had also increased the size and capability of the overseas companies. The Canadian company was given the task of design and development of a basic trainer to replace the Tiger Moth, and the D.H.C.1 Chipmunk was first flown from Downsview on 22 May 1946 by W. P. I. 'Pat' Fillingham, invited over from the home-based team. That day was also the 18th birthday of the Canadian company, and the Chipmunk was the first of many outstanding designs from this part of the organisation, which was to keep the de Havilland name in the forefront long after the parent company had been absorbed in mergers.

D.H. Ghost engines were flight developed in a Lancastrian for endurance testing (*British Aerospace*)

Post-war de Havilland aerodrome at Hatfield with the new perimeter track and runway (*Hawker Siddeley*)

The Australian company saw a need for a rugged light transport and produced the Drover three-engined aircraft for domestic services and 'flying doctor' operations. Not many were built, as the Drover was too similar in size to the more practical Dove. However, D.H. Australia produced a substantial number of Vampire jet fighters and trainers for the RAAF.

The Engine Company meanwhile had to decide on their best course of action to maintain prosperity. The continued range of small piston engines would provide good business for a number of years, without heavy investment in development. The centrifugal compressor in the jet engines was easier to develop, but less efficient than the axial type. The turbine-driven propeller was highly efficient for lower speeds, and by-pass jets offered better pure jet economy, but required far greater development. For very high-speed, high-altitude military purposes the rocket engine had great possibilities, as well as being a short duration boost engine for heavy-weight take-off.

Over 1,500 Gipsy Queen engines were produced for the Doves and Herons, the Dove using the geared, supercharged Queen 70; and the Heron, the direct-drive Queen 30. Nearly 30,000 Gipsy engines were built, of which about half were Gipsy Major series powering Tiger Moths, Chipmunks and many de Havilland and other British and foreign aircraft.

The Goblin jet engine, producing about 1,360 kg (3,000 lb) thrust, was best suited for single- or two-seat subsonic military aircraft, and sold widely as the power plant for the Vampire fighters and two-seat trainers. The similar, but larger and improved Ghost engine developed 2,268 kg (5,000 lb) thrust, which made it ideal for the more refined Venom single-seat and two-seat fighters. It brought a new standard of efficiency in power without the high development costs of the axial-flow jet engines. When adapted for civil use in the Comet jet airliner, some 80 per cent of the components were redesigned, in particular the intake was the more efficient direct-fronted entry, while on the Venom the air intake was in the wing-roots on either side of the fuselage nacelle. Not only was the Goblin the first military jet engine to pass a Government type test on 2 February 1945, but the Ghost broke entirely new ground in the very stringent civil requirement by gaining its civil type approval on 28 June 1948, making it the first jet engine approved for commercial operations. The civil Ghost engine also had to give sufficient excess power to provide cabin pressurisation for the comfort of the passengers and crew.

Late in 1950, the Engine Company commenced work on a private venture basis on a more advanced axial-flow engine, capable of providing sufficient power for supersonic flight. The development potential was some 11,340 kg (25,000 lb) thrust dry rating, or around 13,600 kg (30,000 lb) with reheat. This large engine, named the Gyron, first ran on the test bed on 3 January 1953, and after the successful initial runs a development contract was awarded by the Government, followed by a contract for a scaled-down version known as the Gyron Junior. The engines worked most efficiently by utilising the ram effect of the air entering the intake at high speed.

Meanwhile, the rocket engine programme was progressing using hydrogen peroxide fuel, which was relatively safe to handle but gave a very high thrust and was capable of some power control, unlike the solid fuel motors. The first rocket engine, known as the Sprite, was operated on the Hatfield test bed for the first time in November 1949. It developed about equal power to the 2,268 kg (5,000 lb) thrust of the Ghost jet engine for 11 seconds of take-off run. It was proposed in pairs for the Valiant jet bomber, in special jettisonable packs, but although test take-offs were made it was not adopted in service as adequate runways were already available. Provision was also made for the Sprite engines between the paired jet pipes on the Comet for improved performance at hot and high airfields, and test take-offs were made from Hatfield. However, as with the V-bombers, they were not used in practice, and fairings were attached between the jet pipes in place of the rocket packs. The production version known as the Super Sprite, with improved catalyst, was running by March 1953. It weighed only 227 kg (600 lb) and provided 1,814 kg (4,000 lb) thrust for 40 seconds.

A logical progression was to combine these two forms of power in one

Sprite rocket assisted
take-off of the Comet
prototype (de Havilland)

fighter aircraft. Known as the mixed-power plant formula, the rocket would blast an interceptor up to altitudes of 15,240 m to 18,290 m (50,000 ft to 60,000 ft), and it could then cruise on its jet engine, with additional power from reheat. Fuel consumption was the biggest problem, but it was still inexpensive in those days. However, due to technological advances, the high-altitude jet bomber became a thing of the past, and official interest waned. The guided missile systems took over, forcing the bombers to low level as their only chance of approaching below the defending radars. The rocket for the mixed-power plant formula was the variable-thrust Spectre, to be linked with the Gyron Junior engine, while the Saunders Roe Company were responsible for the airframe. Two SR.53 development aircraft were flown in 1957, but the larger P.177 production version was cancelled in December 1957 for economic reasons. The Spectre flew in a Canberra test bed, causing some alarm at Hatfield on its low-level runs along the runway. The Gyron was air-tested, beginning 7 July 1955, in the lower engine nacelles of one of the Short Sperrin interim jet bombers (of which only two development aircraft were built), the engine being intended for the subsequently abandoned Hawker P.1121 supersonic fighter.

Frank Halford, leader of de Havilland power-plant development, who had suffered some ill-health and then had appeared fit again, died suddenly on 16 April 1955. His tremendous experience was abruptly lost, but he left behind a strong, knowledgeable and dedicated team.

In the spring of 1955, the Gyron Junior made its first run, and following the disastrous 1957 Defence White Paper abandoning military aircraft projects in favour of missile systems, it was the only one of the three main de Havilland engine programmes with a future. Twelve years of work on the mixed-power plant formula had to be abandoned. The Gyron Junior was selected as the power plant for the Blackburn N.A.39 naval strike aircraft, two being fitted to what was to become the Buccaneer, ordered by the Fleet Air Arm. The engines in this case not only provided the source of motive power and pressurisation, but also furnished compressed air across the flying surfaces to improve low speed handling on take-off and landing from the restricting decks of aircraft carriers. The Gyron Juniors were used in the first 50 or so Buccaneer S.Mk 1s, but the Mk 2 was powered by the more powerful Rolls-Royce Spey engines.

Another aircraft to use the Gyron Junior in a somewhat modified state was the Bristol T.188 supersonic research aircraft. Two aircraft were built from stainless steel, but this material was so difficult to fabricate, and the construction so protracted that by the time they were ready to commence their test programme, the aircraft were outdated.

The Spectre rockets were adapted for use with the Vulcan and Victor bombers as assisted take-off units, and at least one test take-off was made from Hatfield with a Victor, but further work was abandoned.

To widen the range of engine products, de Havillands linked with the American General Electric Company to produce their lightweight T.58 engine in Britain. In less than 12 months the engine, which became known as the Gnome, had been run in the test bed on 5 June 1959, and provided a replacement turbine power plant for the Westland Whirlwind, and later the Wessex helicopters.

As the 1940s came to an end, the Propeller Company commenced work on the early development of guided weapons, while maintaining design development, testing and production of more advanced propellers. By 1948 they had secured the propeller business for about 85 per cent of all British transport aircraft built since the end of the war, but production runs were small, keeping the Lostock factory only half occupied. Propellers ranged from the '1,000' size on the Heron, as used on the Comet Racers, to the large six-blade contra-rotating type driven by the Rolls-Royce Griffon engines on the Shackleton. Special 5.0 m (16.5 ft) eight-blade contra-rotating propellers were supplied for the three Proteus-powered Saro Princess flying boats. These were the largest turbine propellers of their time, but only one Princess was ever flown. Various types of de Havilland propellers meanwhile were in use worldwide with more than one hundred civil operators and two dozen air forces.

In April 1952, the Government awarded de Havilland a development contract for an air-launched guided weapon known as Blue Jay, subsequently called Firestreak. Apart from the warhead and propulsion, the Propeller Company designed, developed and manufactured the entire missile, complete with infra-red homing head. Initial successful trials were made on the Aberporth ranges in South Wales, and during the mid-1950s the better facilities at Woomera in Australia were used to iron out the problems expected with such a new air-to-air system. Firestreak was adopted in 1958–9 as the standard air-to-air armament of the Lightning, Javelin and Sea Vixen jet fighters. In October 1958, it was announced that an improved missile was under development, later known as the Red Top. It was used to arm later versions of the RAF and RN fighters, and is still in service on the Lightnings.

On a rather larger scale, de Havilland Propellers were selected as the prime contractors for the Blue Streak long-range ballistic missile. They led a team including Rolls-Royce, the de Havilland Aircraft Company and Sperry Gyroscopes on this thermo-nuclear warhead carrier with a range of several thousand kilometres. Development towers were built at Hatfield, the rocket motors were tested in Cumberland, and firing trials were destined for Woomera. The Aircraft Company were naturally to build the light stainless steel airframe, which was so thin that when it was lifted from the horizontal to its vertical position it had to be pressurised to avoid distortion.

With the more mobile alternatives of submarine and air-launched deterrents, the vulnerable fixed-based ground-launched weapons were abandoned, including the Blue Streak. Having already completed significant development however, the Blue Streak was proposed as the lower stage of a rocket system capable of placing a payload into orbit around the earth. A number of test launches were made from Woomera, in which Blue Streak was a success, but other stages failed. The programme was eventually abandoned, leaving the successors of de Havillands in a very strong position in the missile and space satellite fields.

As the Mosquito production came to an end the Aircraft Company began to retrieve Vampire production from English Electric. Hatfield had parallel production lines for the Dove, Hornet and Vampire. Out of the Dove grew the four-engined Heron with a larger fuselage of the same cross section, but able to carry around 14 passengers. Heron production was also established at Hatfield, initially of the Mk 1 with a fixed undercarriage. The later Heron Mk 2 with retractable undercarriage and other refinements was selected by the Queen's Flight, giving four-engined security.

The Vampire fighters offered opportunities for development, following some of the experience with naval adaptations of the Mosquito and Hornet. The Mosquito was the first twin-engined aircraft to operate from a ship when it landed and took off from the Fleet carrier HMS *Indefatigable* on 25 March 1944, piloted by Capt Eric 'Winkle' Brown. The Hornet was adapted for naval use as the Sea Hornet, providing the Royal Navy with its first twin-engined long-range fighter.

A Vampire was modified for deck trials and made the first ever

The first Hatfield-built Chipmunk, in Dove assembly hangar
(*British Aerospace*)

Vampire was the first jet aircraft to operate from an aircraft carrier (*Hawker Siddeley*)

Ghost-engined high-altitude Vampire with pressure cabin and extended wing span (*Hawker Siddeley*)

landing by a jet aircraft on a carrier, HMS *Ocean*, on 3 December 1945, again flown by Capt Eric Brown. A small batch of interim Sea Vampires was produced for the Fleet Air Arm to gain jet experience.

As part of the Comet jet airliner development, the D.H.108 was a Vampire fuselage fitted with swept-back wings to provide information on the stability of the tail-less layout, and also the aerodynamics of the wing planform for later fighters. A Ghost-powered Vampire with extended wing-tips and a special pressure cabin achieved a record height of 18,119.14 m (59,446 ft) on 23 March 1948, flown by John Cunningham, the Chief Test Pilot.

The logical development was to give the Vampire layout thinner wings with sweep-back on the leading edges and wing-tip fuel tanks. This aircraft became the Venom, which has just been retired from the Swiss Air Force. Other developments of the Vampire, eventually also adopted for the Venom, was to provide a two-seat side by side cockpit, leading to the Vampire night fighter and later the popular Vampire Trainer.

With all these aircraft in high demand from Britain and overseas the production facilities were becoming overwhelmed at Hatfield, especially as plans were being made to build the Comet jet airliner, another first for de Havillands. Although sub-contracting could take up some of the excess work, an additional large assembly area was required. The large Government shadow factory was available at Broughton, near

Herons, Venoms and
Comets in production at
the Chester factory
(*Hawker Siddeley*)

Hornets, Chipmunks and
export Vampires on the
apron at Chester
(*Hawker Siddeley*)

Chester, which had just been vacated by Vickers Armstrong. de Havilland took possession on 1 July 1948, setting up jigs to complete Mosquito and Hornet production, and to establish a Vampire line. Dove and Heron production was moved to Chester from 1951, and after initial manufacture at Hatfield the British production of the Chipmunk was also moved to the Chester factory. This factory, covering over 92,900 sq m (1 million sq ft) was the most modern available in Europe, with its vast assembly hall fitted with overhead cranes capable of lifting whole aircraft to a new stage on the production line. It was a plant geared to aircraft production in the most efficient way, producing thousands of aircraft, many of which were for export. The factory is still in use today as a major part of British Aerospace, producing the D.H.125 business jets and wings for the European Airbus programme.

Like the Vampire, the Venom was also developed into a two-seat night fighter, and later an all-weather naval fighter, the Sea Venom. This development was undertaken at the old Airspeed factory at Christchurch, but the majority of the production was at Chester.

In 1950, the design office at Hatfield began work on a larger and more advanced all-weather jet fighter, the D.H.110. It was a completely new design of all-metal construction, powered by two paired Rolls-Royce Avon engines, with swept wings, twin tail booms and and a crew of two. The pilot was seated under a bubble canopy on the port side, while the

61

D.H.110 was developed
into the Sea Vixen
(*C. E. Brown*)

Maiden flight of the Comet
from Hatfield
(*Hawker Siddeley*)

navigator with his radar scope was located inside the fuselage on the starboard side. The fuselage nose was occupied by the latest AI radar and the swept-back wing was based on experience gained with the experimental D.H.108.

Originally designed to RAF Specification F.4/48, the D.H.110 lost out to the delta-wing Gloster Javelin. Two prototypes had been produced in the competition, one of which was lost tragically at the SBAC display at Farnborough in September 1952.

A requirement still existed for a more advanced replacement for the Sea Venom, the D.H.110 requiring considerable re-design to fit the task. This re-design was undertaken at the Christchurch factory, where the majority of the Sea Vixens were built until production was transferred to Chester on the closure of the old Airspeed factory. To navalise the D.H.110, folding wings had to be engineered, as well as the fitting of arrester gear and other naval equipment. The initial production order was placed in 1955 and the first pre-production naval Sea Vixen development aircraft flew on 20 June 1955.

The most important project for de Havilland was the Comet, the world's first commerical jet airliner borne out of the Brabazon Committee's Type IV specification. Many layouts were considered, including the tailless design, but finally the simple classic form was chosen, with modest swept wings and four engines buried in the wing roots.

The initial studies of what was to result in the Comet were completed on 2 March 1945, and envisaged seating for up to 36 passengers. The power was to come from four Ghost jet engines. There were many problems to overcome, including pressurising and air conditioning the large cabin, navigating at high speed, and satisfactory low-speed handling for approach and landing.

On Friday, the 27 September 1946, Sir Geoffrey de Havilland cleared the final major point with BOAC, to allow detail design of the Comet to commence. That evening, his elder son Geoffrey was killed when the second D.H.108 broke up at high speed over the Thames estuary while practising for a world speed record attempt. John Cunningham was then appointed Chief Test Pilot.

Five and a half years from the start of detail design the Comet entered commercial service with BOAC, a very fair time scale for a normal development, but the Comet had to go through the prototype phase and was a great pioneering step forward. Initial orders were for 16 aircraft. This number did not allow full production tooling to be made, which would have been the case for a larger order. These sixteen aircraft included the two prototypes, eight Comet 1s for BOAC and six for British South American Airways, who were later merged with BOAC, combining their Comet orders.

The first Comet made its maiden flight from the new runway at Hatfield on 27 July 1949, not only Sir Geoffrey de Havilland's birthday, but also John Cunningham's who commanded this epic flight. Flight trials in general were troublefree, with only minor adjustments required. The performance estimates suggested a load of 36 passengers, flying on stage lengths of up to 2,414 km (1,500 miles), cruising at just under 805 km/h (500 mph).

On 30 June 1950, Alan Butler retired from the chairmanship of de Havillands and his place was taken by Frank Hearle, who continued as chairman until 30 September 1954, having been in partial retirement since 1944.

The first of a number of Comet exports was to Canadian Pacific Airlines in December 1949, and from that time the airlines of the world began beating a path to Hatfield to place orders for the developments of the early Comets. The first of these major developments was the Comet 2

Comet Srs 1 production at Hatfield
(*Hawker Siddeley*)

with its Ghost engines replaced by four Rolls-Royce Avons, giving greater range and payload in a 0.914 m (3 ft) longer fuselage. Orders for the improved Ghost-powered Comet 1A came from Air France and UAT amongst other customers and Comet 2 customers included Japan Air Lines.

The even more powerful and stretched Comet 3, aimed at North Atlantic operations, was ordered by Pan Am in 1952, followed by BOAC in 1953, who had also ordered Comet 2s. As the aircraft went into service, commencing with the world's first jet passenger commercial flight on 2 May 1952 from London to Johannesburg, the experience gradually built up, extending the overhaul life of the engines and increasing the utilisation of the aircraft.

The Comet brought new standards of passenger comfort, and although the cost per flying hour was greater, its higher speed made it economically competitive with existing airliners.

Unfortunately, within two hours of completion of the first year of Comet operations, G-ALYV crashed in a storm shortly after take-off from Calcutta on 2 May 1953, with the loss of 43 lives.

With growing world airline interest including an order from Air India for two Comet 3s, additional production capacity had to be sought. Chester was an obvious choice for expansion and plans for a third production line were set up with Short Bros. of Belfast.

Then a major blow hit the Comet. On 10 January 1954, the BOAC Comet 1 G-ALYP took-off from Rome but soon afterwards crashed into the sea near Elba with the loss of all on board. The aircraft were temporarily withdrawn from service for inspection and a number of precautionary modifications were made. Comets resumed service on 23 March, but on 8 April, the BOAC Comet 1 G-ALYY was lost in similar circumstances in the sea off Naples. All Comets were grounded and the Certificate of Airworthiness withdrawn. All production was suspended, although the development of the long-range Comet 3 continued.

After an exhaustive investigation involving recovering and re-assembling the wreckage of G-ALYP, test flying and structural testing in water tanks, it was discovered that the pressure cabin had failed due to metal fatigue causing an explosive decompression. Not much was known about this phenomenon and de Havillands had suffered the

Comet 2 and Comet 3 in formation
(*Hawker Siddeley*)

results of pioneering. They had fully complied with all the testing required by the knowledge available, but the loss of the Comets highlighted the need for new requirements. The experience gained from the investigations was circulated to the international aviation industry to avoid similar disasters.

A few of the surviving Comet 1s and 2s were strengthened and flown mainly on development and testing, while others were operated by the RAF. From the Comet 3, which did not enter production, the more powerful Comet 4 series was developed, nineteen of which were ordered by BOAC. It could carry twice as many passengers twice as far as the Comet 1, with greatly improved economics. On 30 September 1958, a pair of Comet 4s inaugurated the first non-stop North Atlantic jet service from London to New York, beating the first crossing by the American Boeing 707 by a month.

Much of the competitive lead had been lost, but a number of significant orders were received from airlines in South America, Africa, Europe and the Middle East, establishing variants of the new Comet 4 with the airliners of the world. It brought new standards of speed and comfort at an economical level, and the basic Comet 4 airframe will still be in service in the next century, over fifty years after its predecessor was conceived, as the Nimrod jet-powered maritime reconnaissance aircraft.

In 1956, what was to become the last major de Havilland programme was started, with studies for the first 'second generation' airliner. The medium stages of airline operation, using an aircraft cruising a little below the speed of sound appeared to be the most fruitful area on which to concentrate. The rear engine layout was chosen, and the D.H.121, later to become the Trident, was selected by BEA for delivery from 1964, with Comets supplied earlier to provide jet experience. On 12 February 1958, the choice of the Trident was confirmed, to be built by a consortium consisting of de Havilland, Hunting and Fairey known as Airco, after the First World War company.

A delay with the Trident was caused by BEA, who experienced a drop in their passenger figures over one year, and asked for the size of the aircraft to be reduced by about 10 per cent. The fuselage was shortened and the less powerful Rolls-Royce Spey engines were selected. This reduction in size was to drastically curtail the sales prospects of this new airliner in competition with the larger Boeing 727. Modest sales were eventually achieved in the Middle East and Asia, and finally substantial orders in China. The ultimate Trident 3 was closer to the optimum size, although its performance on take-off had to be boosted by an extra engine for safe hot and high operations. BEA, later part of British Airways, were the major operator of Tridents, and even they acknowledged the error of specifying the original aircraft, which was too small, based on a very short-term market prediction. It also highlighted the problems of building an airliner for the specific needs of one operator, without taking into account the wider market requirements.

By mid-1959, the de Havilland Enterprise consisted of approximately

First four D.H.125s during flight development at Hatfield (*de Havilland*)

37,000 employees worldwide, with a turnover of £80m a year. Government policy decreed that there should be mergers of many of the individual companies into two major groups, but the new Airco consortium did not comply. de Havillands were therefore merged with the Hawker Siddeley Group at the end of 1959 to become a major part of Hawker Siddeley Aviation, while Hunting became part of the British Aircraft Corporation and Faireys merged their helicopter interests with Westlands, which like Shorts remained independent of the major grouping.

In the early days of Hawker Siddeley Aviation the de Havilland Division (as it became known) became the centre for commerical aircraft development, their initial product, started in the de Havilland days, being the D.H.125 business jet. It first flew in August 1962 and over the years has been progressively developed with sales exceeding 550 aircraft at the time of writing. The Hatfield/Chester Division, later to become part of British Aerospace during the nationalisation of April 1977, played a major part in the European Airbus programme by designing and building the high performance wings, initially under private investment. The Division also made a number of studies of short-range feeder airliners culminating in the BAe 146, which is set for a successful career into the next century.

Meanwhile, in the mergers, de Havilland Engines became part of Bristol Siddeley Engines (later to become part of Rolls-Royce) and the Propeller Company became Hawker Siddeley Dynamics, responsible for propellers, guided missiles, space and communications and other related products. Hawker Siddeley Dynamics in turn became part of the Dynamics Group of British Aerospace, but throughout Hatfield and Chester much of the de Havilland spirit lives on and will no doubt continue to do so for many years, even though the centenary of Sir Geoffrey's birth has been passed. The pioneer founder of the Company died on 21 May 1965, having spawned the development of aviation from the earliest days to the jet age.

BAe 146 Srs 200, the current Hatfield product (*British Aerospace*)

AIRCRAFT SECTION

AIRCO D.H.1

First flight: January 1915

Type: Two-seat fighter-reconnaissance

Notes: The D.H.1 was a two-seat pusher two-bay biplane, capable of carrying a machine gun in the front cockpit. The first D.H.1 was flown from Hendon by Geoffrey de Havilland, powered by a 54 kW (70 hp) Renault engine, as the planned Beardmore was in short supply. Despite the lack of power, the performance was still lively and stability was also very good. The structure was typical for the period, with the tail supported on booms. The design was simple, avoiding the use of special stampings, forgings, pressings and castings. Although not the most efficient layout, the pusher engine arrangement gave excellent visibility.

The prototype was delivered to Farnborough for testing in February 1915 and production started at Airco, Hendon of the Renault-powered D.H.1, but only about five of this version were built before the more powerful Beardmore engine became available. However, as Airco had more pressing requirements, an order for 100 of this improved version, known as the D.H.1A was placed with Savages Ltd, a Kings Lynn fairground equipment manufacturer.

Unfortunately, because the aircraft was largely ignored by the War Office, the contracts were reduced with only 73 aircraft of both versions being built. Of this total delivered to the RFC 43 were allocated to training units (where many were wrecked), and 24 to Home Defence units, including No. 35 Reserve Squadron RFC, where the D.H.1A was found to be an improvement over the contemporary F.E.2b, being lighter on the controls and more manoeuvrable. The D.H.1/1A remained on training duties until the late summer of 1918 when the last were withdrawn.

Overseas service was with the Middle East Brigade in July 1916 when six were issued to No. 14 Squadron RFC in Palestine for operations against the Turks. An early success was when a D.H.1A forced down an Aviatik two-seater on 1 August 1916 near Salmana, but a D.H.1A was shot down on 5 March 1917 whilst bombing Tel el Sheria, shortly before the type was withdrawn.

Data
Variant: D.H.1A
Power plant: One 89 kW (120 hp) Beardmore inline engine in pusher installation
Accommodation: Pilot and observer in two open tandem cockpits (pilot behind the observer)
Fuel capacity: 160 ltr (35.3 Imp gal) plus 25 ltr (5.5 Imp gal) in gravity tank. Oil tank capacity: 10 ltr (2.3 Imp gal)
Wing span: 12.5 m (41 ft)
Wing area: 33.65 sq m (426.25 sq ft)
Length: 8.82 m (28 ft 11¼ in)
Height: 3.4 m (11 ft 2 in)
Weight empty: 730 kg (1,610 lb)
Max t/o weight: 1,061 kg (2,340 lb)
Max level speed: 140 km/h (90 mph) at ground level
Service ceiling: 4,100 m (13,500 ft)
Armament: One Lewis machine gun mounted in front cockpit
Production Total of 73 built, of which 43 to training units, 24 to Home Defence and 6 to ME Brigade

D.H.1A prototype with pilot's cockpit behind the observer's (de Havilland)

AIRCO D.H.2

First flight: 1 June 1915

Type: Single-seat scout

Notes: The D.H.2 was smaller, but similar in layout to the D.H.1, designed as a two-bay pusher biplane scout with a swivelling Lewis gun mounted centrally in front of the pilot. The orthodox construction was of wood with fabric covering and power was from a rotary Gnome Monosoupape aircooled engine, or occasionally, a Le Rhône, in pusher installation between the tubular steel tail booms. Flight trials were completed in July 1915 and the following month orders were placed with Airco for the first of 452 production aircraft, of which 400 were built.

The initial production aircraft was delivered on 10 January 1916 to No. 24 Squadron RFC commanded by Major Lanoe Hawker, VC. They gained the distinction of becoming the first single-seat fighter squadron to enter the hostilities when its complement of twelve D.H.2s were flown from Hounslow to St Omer, France, on 7 February. Before the middle of the year two more squadrons had been formed, No. 29 on 25 March and No. 32 on 28 May, the strength of the units being increased to 18 aircraft in preparation for the Battle of the Somme.

Due to its more advanced flying characteristics over the aircraft which it replaced, the D.H.2 was looked upon initially with some suspicion. In inexperienced hands it was prone to spinning and then little was known about recovery. At times it also caught fire and gained the unwarranted appellation of 'spinning incinerator'. Experienced pilots found the sensitive controls and aerobatic capabilities a great advantage in combat against the Fokker monoplanes. The D.H.2 was of strong construction, although some fatalities were caused by cylinders blowing off and severing the tailboom.

Lt Tidmarsh was the first to score for No. 24 Squadron when he shot down an enemy aircraft near Bapaume on 2 April 1916, the pilots having decided to fix the gun and aim the aircraft at the target. Three months later Major L. W. B. Rees, the CO of No. 32 Squadron, won the VC while flying a D.H.2 on 1 July 1916. He attacked ten enemy two-seat bombers single handed, forcing two down and causing the remainder to abandon their attack. Successes continued, but as the year came to a close the D.H.2 became outclassed by the new Albatros D.II Scouts. Replacements in the form of the D.H.5s and Sopwith Pups did not start entering service until March 1917, and the D.H.2s remained in operational service until June. It was during this period of decline that Rittmeister Man-

Service D.H.2 armed with a Lewis machine gun

fred von Richthofen, flying an Albatros, shot down the famed CO of No. 24 Squadron, Major Hawker VC, on 23 November 1916, after one of the longest individual air combats of the war.

No. 29 Squadron was the first to re-equip in March 1917 and following their withdrawal some surplus D.H.2s were shipped out to the Middle East for service in Palestine where they were issued in small numbers to a variety of squadrons. By the end of 1917 it was outclassed even in that relatively quiet area, and its last duties were training in the UK before final retirement in 1918.

Data

Variant: D.H.2/Gnome Monosoupape

Power plant: One 75 kW (100 hp) Gnome Monosoupape or 82 kW (110 hp) Le Rhône rotary engine

Accommodation: Pilot in open cockpit

Fuel capacity: 140 ltr (26.3 Imp gal); oil 23 ltr (5 Imp gal)

Wing span: 8.6 m (28 ft 3 in)

Wing area: 23.1 sq m (249 sq ft)

Length: 7.68 m (25 ft 2½ in)

Height: 2.91 m (9 ft 6½ in)

Weight empty: 429 kg (943 lb)

Max t/o weight: 655 kg (1,441 lb)

Max level speed: 150 km/h (93 mph)

Service ceiling: 4,270 m (14,000 ft)

Endurance/range: 2¾ hours

Armament: One Lewis machine gun, normally fixed to fire forward

Production 400 built, of which 266 delivered to BEF, 32 to ME, 2 to Home Defence and 100 to training units

AIRCO D.H.3

First flight: 1916

Type: Three-seat twin pusher-engined fighter-bomber

Notes: Early in 1916, Airco produced their first twin-engined design to an ill-defined Farnborough specification for a fighter-bomber, which was a considerable advance over the previous two aircraft. The lower of the biplane wings was mounted on top of the fuselage with the two Beardmore engines fitted mid-way between the two. The short main undercarriage gave a low ground clearance and as a precaution against nosing-over in soft ground, twin nose wheels were fitted. The three-bay wings could be folded back to save hangar space, and the elegant single fin and rudder were the first of the classical de Havilland shape.

Construction was of wood with mainly fabric covering, and the front half of the fuselage was covered with stressed plywood. Accommodation was for three crew in open cockpits, the pilot just forward of the leading edge of the wing, with a gunner in the nose and a second gunner well behind the line of the propellers. Each gunner was armed with a Lewis gun and had basic flight controls in case of emergency.

The prototype was modified to the D.H.3A with the installation of more powerful Beardmore engines driving four-blade propellers. To avoid the use of extension shafts, cut-outs were made in the wing trailing edges and the rudder area was increased.

The testing squadron at Upavon recommended the adoption of the D.H.3A as it had sufficient endurance to bomb the industrial centres of the Rhine from bases in Northern France. The bomb load was carried externally under the wings.

Work commenced on an initial batch of 50, but when the first machine was almost finished the D.H.3 was cancelled in favour of smaller bombers. The completed aircraft were stored at Hendon behind the Airco sheds until burnt in 1917.

Data
Variant: D.H.3A
Power plant: Two 119 kW (160 hp) Beardmore inline engines
Accommodation: Pilot and two gunners in open tandem cockpits
Fuel capacity: 540 ltr (155 Imp gal); oil 51 ltr (12 Imp gal)
Wing span: 18.54 m (60 ft 10 in)
Wing area: 71.5 sq m (770 sq ft)
Length: 11.23 m (36 ft 10 in)
Height: 4.42 m (14 ft 6 in)
Weight empty: 1,805 kg (3,980 lb)
Max t/o weight: 2,610 kg (5,776 lb)
Max level speed: 153 km/h (95.1 mph) at ground level
Service ceiling: 3,050 m (10,000 ft)
Endurance/range: 8 hours
Armament: Two Lewis machine guns
Production Prototype D.H.3, and D.H.3A 7744

D.H.3 prototype, de Havilland's first twin-engined design
(de Havilland)

AIRCO D.H.4

First flight: August 1916

Type: Two-seat day bomber
Notes: The D.H.4 was not only the first aircraft designed specifically for day bomber duties, but was one of the most outstanding aircraft of the First World War. A wide range of engines were offered for this aircraft, the prototype making its maiden flight powered by a BHP engine and piloted by Geoffrey de Havilland. However, this engine was not suited to mass production so the excellent Rolls-Royce Eagle liquid-cooled V-12 engine was adopted for the production aircraft.

Construction was conventional fabric and ply-covered wood. The two crew were in open cockpits separated by the main fuel tank, the resulting communications difficulty being the main criticism of the aircraft.

To minimise delays in production an order was placed for an initial batch of 50 aircraft before the first flight of the prototype. The confidence was well rewarded by the excellent test report compiled at Upavon.

Standard armament was a synchronised forward-firing Vickers gun for the pilot mounted on top of the fuselage, and single or twin Lewis gun on a Scarff ring for the observer.

The first D.H.4s entered service in France with No. 55 Squadron RFC on 6 March 1917, and with the increased demand following German raids on London on 13 June 1917, Westlands took their share in production. Its excellent performance made the D.H.4 superior to its contemporaries and it surpassed most of the fighters in service. Safe escape could usually be made with its high rate of climb and top speed.

During the summer and autumn of 1917, further squadrons on the Western Front were re-equipped with D.H.4s using a variety of engines, many of which were unsatisfactory. However, the most successful combination was found in August 1917 with the Eagle VIII, giving a maximum speed without bomb load of 215 km/h (133.5 mph) at 3,050 m (10,000 ft). In addition to flying with the RFC as a day bomber, it also was used by the RNAS and later the combination of the two, as the RAF, on fighter-reconnaissance, photography, anti-Zeppelin and anti-submarine operations. The first operation was by No. 55 Squadron using six aircraft to bomb railway sidings at Valenciennes on 6 April 1917, which was highly successful and avoided the defending fighters.

The RNAS received their first D.H.4s from Westland production in the spring of 1917, and they were used mainly on coastal and home defence. The German coastal submarine *UB 12* was sunk on 12 August 1918 and Zeppelin *L 70* was shot down on 5 August 1918 during the last Zeppelin raid of the war on Britain.

In October 1917, No. 55 Squadron was withdrawn from the Western Front to form one of three units of the 41st Wing, which became the Independent Force, RAF, on 6 June 1918, to undertake the first organised programme of strategic bombing. This commenced on 17 October 1917, with a raid on Saarbrücken and continued right up to the Armistice.

The D.H.4 also has the rare distinction of being a British aircraft adopted by the American Government. On 6 April 1917, when the USA declared war on Germany, their aircraft strength did not include a single suitable combat aircraft. The chosen power plant was the American V-12 Liberty engine which suffered from initial teething troubles before becoming very reliable. Produc-

D.H.4 in military service (*Hawker Siddeley*)

tion of the airframe was entrusted to three motor manufacturers who had considerable difficulty adapting their techniques to aircraft construction. A total of 12,348 D.H.4s were ordered, but only 4,846 were built in the USA and less than 200 reached the battle front before the end of hostilities. The first aircraft arrived unassembled in France on 11 May 1918, and flew six days later. The first mission was delayed until 2 August due to the lack of combat readiness of the aircraft.

The main American development was the D.H.4B on which the whole fuselage covered with stressed plywood and the pilot moved back, exchanging places with the increased capacity fuel tanks. This redesign not only improved communications, but also the pilot's view and his safety in a crash.

The surplus aircraft available after the war were modified for a variety of duties including transport, training, crop dusting, engine testing and racing, keeping a number of the pioneer American aircraft manufacturers in work during the post-war period. A more radical conversion was by the Boeing Company who were awarded a contract for 180 D.H.4s with welded steel tube fuselage structure, known as the D.H.4M, and a further 100 were produced by the Atlantic Aircraft Corporation. The most interesting conversions of the D.H.4 in America was for the pioneer US Mail service which commenced operation on 15 May 1918. The normal cockpit area was used for the carriage of the mail, with the pilot located further aft. These aircraft flew in all weather conditions, a few D.H.4s remaining in service until 1931.

In Britain, the D.H.4 was soon retired from active service at the end of the First World War, but a number were modified for civil use, making a

useful contribution to communications and the start of operations with the emerging airlines. Initially, four aircraft were converted for No. 2 (Communications) Squadron by modifying the rear cockpit to give a small sheltered cabin for two passengers. These were designated D.H.4A and operated from Kenley on communications flights to Paris and Brussels for the negotiation and signing of the Peace Treaty on 28 June 1919. The squadron was disbanded in September 1919, and the surplus aircraft bought by Handley Page Ltd for their pioneer airline operations. Four new D.H.4s on the Airco production line were also converted and delivered to Aircraft Transport & Travel who commenced commercial services from London (Hounslow) to Paris (Le Bourget) on 25 August 1919. The first airmail flight was scheduled for 11 November, but was delayed for one day by bad weather. Instone Air Line entered D.H.4A, G-EAMU, in the first King's Cup Air Race in September 1922, Captain Barnard flying it to first place.

Instone Air Line D.H.4A, winner of the first King's Cup Air Race in 1922 (*Flight*)

High-speed D.H.4R powered by a Napier Lion engine
(*de Havilland*)

Not only were some of the surplus D.H.4s converted to civil use, but a number were given to developing countries who wished to form an air force, including New Zealand, Greece and Spain. Canada used the aircraft on government duties for forestry patrols, geological survey and photo reconnaissance. The US supplied some of the South and Central American governments with their surplus aircraft. In Australia, as in the UK, D.H.4s were amongst the aircraft used to pioneer communications and mail flights in the more difficult and remote regions.

Probably one of the crudest modifications was the D.H.4R produced in less than 15 days for the Aerial Derby of 1919. The alterations included the installation of a Napier Lion engine, the drastic reduction in span of the lower wing to just outboard of the first bay, and the deletion of the rear cockpit. The D.H.4R was flown for the first time on 20 June, the day before the race, and achieved a top speed of 240 km/h (150 mph). It would have flown faster, but the radiator overheated. Not only did it win the Aerial Derby, flown by Captain Gathergood at an average speed of 208 km/h

(129.5 mph), but it also set up a new British closed circuit record.

Data
Variant: D.H.4/Rolls-Royce Eagle VIII inline engine
Power plant: One 172 kW (230 hp) BHP, or 186 kW (250 hp) R-R Eagle, or 280 kW (375 hp) R-R Eagle VIII, or 298 kW (400 hp) Liberty 12, or 324 kW (435 hp) Liberty 12A inline engine, and many experimental installations
Accommodation: Pilot and observer/gunner in two open tandem cockpits
Fuel capacity: 298 ltr (65.75 Imp gal); oil 25 ltr (5.5 Imp gal)
Wing span: 12.92 m (42 ft 4⅝ in)
Wing area: 40.32 sq in (434 sq ft)
Length: 9.35 m (30 ft 8 in)
Height: 3.3 m (10 ft 1 in)
Weight empty: 1,082.7 kg (2,387 lb)
Max t/o weight: 1,575 kg (3,472 lb)
Max level speed: 230 km/h (143 mph)
Service ceiling: 6,700 m (22,000 ft)
Endurance/range: 3¾ hours
Armament: One or two forward-firing fixed Vickers machine guns, plus single or double Lewis gun on Scarff ring in the rear cockpit. Bomb load consisted of two 103.5 kg (230 lb) and four 50.8 kg (112 lb) bombs
Production Total of 1,449 in Britain and 4,846 in the USA.
D.H.4 sub-contractors in Britain were F. W. Berwick & Co Ltd/London; Glendower Aircraft Co Ltd/London; Palladium Autocars Ltd/London; The Vulcan Motor & Engineer Co Ltd/Southport; Warring & Gillow Ltd/London and Westland Aircraft Works/Yeovil.

D.H.4 license-manufacturers in the USA were Dayton-Wright Airplane Co/Dayton (3,106); The Fisher Body Corp (1,600) and Standard Aircraft Corp/New Jersey (140).

AIRCO D.H.5

First flight: Late 1916

Type: Single-seat scout
Notes: The availability of a reliable gun interrupter gear allowed an aircraft to be designed with the more efficient tractor layout to replace the out-classed D.H.2s. This new scout was powered by a Le Rhône rotary engine and armed with a fixed forward-firing Vickers machine gun. For the hazardous ground attack task four 11 kg (25 lb) bombs could be carried under the fuselage.

The structure was typical: wood with fabric covering, while the use of plywood panels in the fuselage aided its strength. During the official trials the performance was found to be poorer than the lower powered Sopwith Pup but despite this, 400 D.H.5s were ordered on 15 January 1917 shared equally between Airco and the Darracq Company as an insurance against failure of the Sopwith Camel. Deliveries commenced with No. 24 Squadron RFC on 1 May 1917, followed by No. 32 Squadron, both being fully equipped by the end of June. Only a total of five squadrons were to use the aircraft on the Western Front where the unconventional layout was viewed with some suspicion by the pilots. There were poor results in the air-to-air combat role, but much improved performance was achieved in ground attack to assist the infantry, starting during the Battle of Ypres. To support this effort, a further 150 aircraft were ordered, but it is doubtful if all were finally built. Losses with the D.H.5s in ground attack were not unnaturally very high, and all were withdrawn by the end of 1917 to be relegated to home based training duties, and replaced by more suitable aircraft.

D.H.5 featured sharp backward stagger of the wings

Data

Variant: D.H.5
Power plant: One 82 kW (110 hp) Le Rhône or one 82 kW (110 hp) Clerget rotary engine
Accommodation: Pilot in open cockpit
Fuel capacity: 119 ltr (26 Imp gal); oil, 18.1 ltr (4 Imp gal)
Wing span: 7.82 m (25 ft 8 in)
Wing area: 19.7 sq m (212.1 sq ft)
Length: 6.7 m (22 ft)
Height: 2.78 m (9 ft 1½ in)

Weight empty: 458 kg (1,010 lb)
Max t/o weight: 677 kg (1,492 lb)
Max level speed: 175 km/h (109 mph)
Service ceiling: 4,880 m (16,000 ft)
Endurance/range: 2¾ hours
Armament: One fixed forward-firing Vickers machine gun. Four 11 kg (25 lb) bombs could be carried on underfuselage racks.
Production Total of 550 ordered from Airco/Hendon (200), British Cauldron Co Ltd/Cricklewood (50); The Darracq Motor Engineering Co Ltd/Fulham (200) and March, Jones & Cribb/Leeds (100), but not all built.

AIRCO D.H.6

First flight: 1917

Type: Two-seat basic trainer
Notes: Towards the end of 1916 it was realised that if the necessary expansion of the RFC was to continue, a simple training aircraft was essential, which would be capable of rapid construction by non-skilled labour as well as being safe but demanding to fly. The Airco answer was de Havilland's D.H.6. The design was rugged and simple, with the two crew in a single large cockpit.

The angular design was hardly attractive, but ease of production was paramount, and construction was conventional fabric-covered wood with ply covering of the forward fuselage for added strength. The standard power plant was an uncowled RAF 1a engine, but when D.H.6 airframe production outstripped supplies of these engines, Curtiss OX-5 or Renault units were substituted.

The first production contract of the total of 2,950 D.H.6s was for 700 placed on 13 January 1917 with the Graham White Aviation Company and as numbers rapidly came into service, they were widely used on training duties at home, in the Middle East and Australia. Because of its viceless characteristics, the D.H.6 was considered too safe by some instructors for elementary training. Its landing speed was about 56 km/h (35 mph), and it was virtually unspinable. The controls were heavy and stability poor, and it was felt that the aircraft would not provide enough preparation for the more advanced aircraft.

Training accidents on all types of aircraft were claiming more casualties than those killed in action, but in 1918 the D.H.6 suffered a number of unexplained accidents. During the subsequent investigations it was found that the aircraft was

D.H.6 training and observation aircraft (*J. M. Bruce & Stuart Leslie collection*)

unstable in a loop: when it reached the inverted position, even with full power, it would not continue over, but simply fell out of the sky. Recovery could be achieved by cutting the engine, but the novice pilot could not be expected to know this. By giving the wings a reverse stagger, the problem was overcome, but the aircraft became unsuitable for training, especially as the more practical Avro 504K had been adopted by this time.

With the alarming loss of coastal shipping, the D.H.6 was pressed into service on maritime patrol to try and frighten off the enemy U-boats. The D.H.6s were eventually allocated to over 30 coastal patrol flights ranging from the South West coast at Padstow right round Scotland to Machrihanish. Due to their poor load carrying capability the D.H.6s had to fly unarmed, but carried an observer who could signal with an Aldis lamp. The only recorded action was on 30 May 1918, when a D.H.6 bombed the German minelayer submarine *UC 49* after it had torpedoed one of our ships, but it crash dived and escaped.

A total of 71 D.H.6s were allocated to Home Defence units in 1918, but their only use was as communications aircraft.

With the end of the war, over 1,000 D.H.6s were still on charge and many were acquired by civil operators in the UK, Australia and South Africa, where they were used for joy-riding. It was a D.H.6 owned and raced by Airco which was allocated the first civil registration, K-100, in the spring of 1919.

Following the sale of surplus D.H.6s to Spain, a further 60 were produced under license by Hispano-Suiza from 1921 onwards and remained in use as military trainers until the early 1930s. Some D.H.6s were used for civil training at Hendon, Cambridge and Bournemouth, and one with the de Havilland School of Flying survived until 1923. Rebuilt and improved versions in America were used by the barnstormers in the late 1920s. One of the last operators of the D.H.6 was Giro Aviation at Southport, who had an approval to carry two joy riding passengers in a converted front cockpit, flying thousands of passengers in this manner from 1921 to 1933.

Data
Variant: D.H.6/RAF 1a
Power plant: One 67 kW (90 hp) RAF 1a, or 67 kW (90 hp) Curtiss OX-5, or 60 kW (80 hp) Renault inline engine
Accommodation: Two crew in tandem in communal open cockpit
Fuel capacity: 114 ltr (25 Imp gal); oil, 18.1 ltr (4 Imp gal)
Wing span: 10.95 m (35 ft 11⅛ in)
Wing area: 47.6 sq m (512.3 sq ft)
Length: 8.3 m (27 ft 3½ in)
Height: 3.3 m (10 ft 9½ in)
Weight empty: 662.25 kg (1,460 lb)
Max t/o weight: 919.5 kg (2,027 lb)
Max level speed: 106 km/h (66 mph)
Service ceiling: 1,860 m (6,100 ft)
Endurance/range: 2¾ hours
Armament: On anti-submarine patrols a maximum load of 45 kg (100 lb) bombs could be carried
Production Total of 3,013 built: Airco/Hendon (202 incl. prototypes); The Gloucestershire Aircraft Co Ltd/Cheltenham (150); The Graham-White Aviation Co Ltd/Hendon (750); Harland & Wolf Ltd/Belfast (300); The Kingsbury Aviation Co Ltd/Kingsbury (150); Morgan & Co/Leighton Buzzard (200); Ransome, Sims & Jeffries Ltd/Norwich (400); Savages Ltd/Stroud and King's Lynn (100); Canadian Aeroplanes Ltd/Toronto (1) and Hispano-Suiza SA/Spain (60 under license).

AIRCO D.H.9 and D.H.9A

First flight: D.H.9 – July 1917, D.H.9A – March 1918

Type: Two-seat day bomber

Notes: The sudden demand for expansion of the bomber force following an unexpected daylight attack on Britain by German bombers on 13 July 1917 had to be answered urgently. The most rapid response was an extensively modified D.H.4 with a top speed of 180 km/h (112 mph) and an extended range to reach further into enemy territory. To make use of existing tooling and minimise delays in getting the new type into service, the D.H.4 wings and tail were attached to a new fuselage with the pilot and observer in adjoining cockpits to improve communications. This new aircraft was the D.H.9 and it was substituted in all outstanding D.H.4 contracts.

The other major change was the power plant, the new 224 kW (300 hp) Siddeley Puma engine. However, this choice of the engine proved to be a mistake due to major production difficulties. Although these difficulties were eventually cleared up, the power was reduced to 172 kW (230 hp) and there was no suitable substitute engine available. This was reflected in poorer performance which made the aircraft more vulnerable to attack from enemy fighters, so operational range was limited to the endurance of the escorting scouts, while planned attacks were reduced in effect by aircraft dropping out due to defective engines. The D.H.9 altitude was also limited in practice to around 3,960 m (13,000 ft) and the advantage of having the crew closer together was lost by the lack of performance.

Eventually an alternative engine was tried, the Fiat A-12, tested on the second Airco production D.H.9, C 6052. The power was only a minor increase at 194 kW (260 hp) and the rate of production was so slow that it was too late to be of any use.

The internal bomb bay was another change, capable of holding two 100 kg (230 lb) or four 50 kg (112 lb) bombs, but the service trials only released the aircraft as suitable for day bombing because the pilot's vision was restricted by the lower wing.

Deliveries began to build up at the end of 1917 and No. 103 Squadron was the first unit to commence re-equipment at Old Sarum in December. It moved to France in May 1918, joining a number of other squadrons which were also equipped with D.H.9s, forming the VIII Brigade, of the Independent Force of the RAF.

Losses were high, both due to enemy action and technical problems, and although they were no longer regarded as frontline combat aircraft by June 1918, production continued to replace the superior D.H.4s. The combat attrition is shown by a raid flown on 31 July 1918, when twelve D.H.9s of No. 99 Squadron set out to attack Mainz. Three soon had to return with engine trouble and one was shot down. Over Saarbrücken another three were shot down by a large force of defending scouts. Whilst the five survivors dropped their bombs on the railway station, one of them crashed on the town. Two more D.H.9s were shot down on the way home, leaving only the CO, Captain Taylor and one other crew to return to Azelot. The enemy had also suffered casualties, but the squadron was unable to continue operations until replacement crews were available.

With plentiful stocks of D.H.9s, they were used more effectively in the Middle East and the Mediterranean area, where they did not have to contend with defending aircraft. Some were flown on reconnaissance duties, while others were used in their intended role of bombing. Other D.H.9s were allocated to Home Defence and coastal patrols replacing some of the D.H.6s, but no successes were claimed.

In early 1918, a further engine was tried in the D.H.9. This was the very much more successful Napier Lion, developing 224 kW (300 hp) at 3,050 m (10,000 ft), and proved ideal, although it came too late for active service. During trials at Martlesham, a new altitude record of 9,296 m (30,500 ft) was reached on 2 January 1919 in 66 minutes and 15 seconds by Captain A. Lang.

The United States planned to power their 14,000 D.H.9s on order with the Liberty 12A engine, but all contracts were cancelled with the Armistice, and only the RAF D.H.9s continued in limited service in the Middle East. Further surplus batches were supplied to Belgium, Holland,

Puma-engined D.H.9 with crew cockpits close together
(*F. N. Birkett*)

Canada, South Africa, New Zealand and Australia, where they remained in service until 1925.

D.H.9A

With the availability of the new Liberty engine and because of the poor performance of the Puma, it was decided to adapt the D.H.9 to take this new American engine. In early 1918, work on what was to become the D.H.9A was entrusted to Westlands at Yeovil. Completely new wings were designed, and among other changes was wire bracing of the fuselage.

However, the expected high production rate of Liberty engines was not achieved, and the first D.H.9A, a conversion of the D.H.9, was fitted with an Eagle engine in order that airframe development could proceed. When sufficient numbers of Liberty engines became available, one was installed in prototype C6122 which first flew on 19 April 1918.

Deliveries of the initial aircraft soon commenced, equipping No. 110 (Hyderabad) Squadron which reached France on 31 August to become part of the Independent Force. Only five raids were made, starting on 14 September, before the Armistice. No. 205 Squadron was the only other unit to use D.H.9As on active service and other squadrons were beginning to receive new aircraft. In the USA, production of 4,000 D.H.9As was planned, but with the end of hostilities in Europe only 13 modified examples were completed.

However, the D.H.9A did become the standard RAF day bomber, serving for many years both at home and in overseas territories as far away as

India for policing duties, ending its career as initial equipment of the Auxiliary Squadrons and as an advanced trainer.

With the cessation of hostilities in Europe, the D.H.9A units became part of Allied Occupation Force, mainly on communication duties, but were soon disbanded. Most of the day bomber squadrons were based overseas on active duties on the infamous North West Frontier in India, supporting the White Russians against the Bolsheviks and operating in Greece against Turkey. Policing duties in the Near and Middle East included the vast featureless areas of Iraq (then Mesopotamia) where four D.H.9A squadrons were based and used on active duty, as well as communications which helped to prove the routes for future commercial air transport. D.H.9As also played a vital part in the evacuation of the British Legation under siege at Kabul in Afghanistan in extremely bad weather conditions in December 1928. The last of the venerable 'Ninaks', as they were known, was retired from active duties in April 1930, and by the end of the year they had also been retired from the UK-based Auxiliary Squadrons.

Civil aircraft

Civil conversions of the D.H.9 were fairly plentiful, especially because with the military equipment removed performance was much improved. The first post-war civil aircraft flight was with D.H.9 G-EAAA which left Hendon on 1 May 1919 carrying newspapers, but it crashed in fog at Portsmouth failing to reach its destination of Bournemouth. In a number of cases the rear cockpit was enlarged to take two or even three passengers, initially without the protection of a cabin, and used for charter throughout Europe and joyriding. The cabin conversion was known as the D.H.9C and three were used by SNETA, the forerunner of Sabena, to commence European operations from Brussels in March 1920. Qantas commenced their scheduled services in Australia with D.H.9Cs in November 1922, and G-EAQM became the first single-engined aircraft to fly from England to Australia in August 1920 crewed by Parer and McIntosh.

On 1 March 1923, de Havillands were awarded a contract for the training of RAF reservists. Seven Puma-engined D.H.9s were used for this task and

No. 8 Squadron D.H.9A based at Hinaidi in Iraq in 1924

Civil conversions of the D.H.9 for passenger charter (*Hawker Siddeley*)

their life extended in 1926 when they were converted to D.H.9Js with the installation of the Jaguar III radial engine, continuing in service until 1933.

A small number of D.H.9s were converted for racing as single-seaters, and three competed in the 1922 King's Cup Air Race gaining third, fourth and tenth places. In 1923, Alan Cobham flew a Lion-powered D.H.9 to second place in the King's Cup at an average speed of 233 km/h (144.7 mph). A civil racing conversion of a D.H.9A was the D.H.9R with a Lion engine, similar to the D.H.4R. Despite more care taken in the conversion, the D.H.9R was slower, but it did capture a number of closed circuit records at an average speed of nearly 240 km/h (150 mph).

Jaguar-engined D.H.9J (*Westland Aircraft*)

Data
Variant: D.H.9/Puma
Power plant: one 172 kW (230 hp) Siddeley Puma, or 321 kW (450 hp) Napier Lion inline engine
Accommodation: Pilot and observer/gunner in two open tandem cockpits
Fuel capacity: 318 ltr (70 Imp gal); oil 20.5 ltr (4.5 Imp gal)
Wing span: 12.92 m (42 ft 4⅝ in)
Wing area: 40.3 sq m (434 sq ft)
Length: 9.3 m (30 ft 5 in)
Height: 3.44 m (11 ft 3½ in)
Weight empty: 1,012 kg (2,230 lb)
Max t/o weight: 1,500 kg (3,325 lb)
Max level speed: 176 km/h (109.5 mph)
Service ceiling: 4,730 m (15,500 ft)
Endurance/range: 4½ hours
Armament: 2 × 103.5 kg (230 lb) or 4 × 50.8 kg (112 lb) bombs
One forward-firing synchronised Vickers machine gun, one or two Scarff-mounted Lewis guns in rear cockpit
Production 3,204 built in Britain

Variant: D.H.9A/Liberty
Power plant: one 298 kW (400 hp) Liberty 12, or 336 kW (450 hp) Napier Lion inline engine
Accommodation: Pilot and observer/gunner in two open tandem cockpits
Fuel capacity: 500 ltr (107 Imp gal); oil 53.5 ltr (15 Imp gal)
Wing span: 14 m (45 ft 11⅜ in)
Wing area: 45.2 sq m (486.75 sq ft)
Length: 9.2 m (30 ft 3 in)
Height: 3.45 m (11 ft 4 in)
Weight empty: 1,270 kg (2,800 lb)
Max t/o weight: 2,100 kg (4,645 lb)
Max level speed: 184 km/h (114.5 mph)
Service ceiling: 5,100 m (16,750 ft)
Endurance/range: 5¼ hours
Armament: 2 × 103.5 kg (230 lb), but up to 300 kg (660 lb) could be carried
One forward-firing synchronised Vickers machine gun, one or two Scarff-mounted Lewis guns in rear cockpit
Production Total 2,300 produced in Britain and 13 in the USA.

AIRCO D.H.10 Amiens

First flight: 4 March 1918

Type: Twin-engined three-seat day bomber
Notes: Designed to Air Board Specification A2b of April 1917, the D.H.10 was planned to have a capability of carrying a bomb load of 230 kg (500 lb) at a cruising speed of over 177 km/h (110 mph) and a ceiling of around 5,800 m (19,000 ft). The construction was almost identical to the earlier D.H.3, and despite their unreliability, two pusher Siddeley Puma engines were used for power.

The crew complement and equipment was the same as for the D.H.3, but major changes included an internal bomb bay and non-folding wings. Soon after the maiden flight from Hendon of the first of four prototypes it was delivered to Martlesham Heath for service trials, but was down on performance due to the choice of engines. The second prototype was therefore fitted with a pair of tractor

Rolls-Royce Eagle VIII engines and orders were placed for 800 D.H.10s to be built by five sub-contractors.

With the availability of the Liberty engines, one was fitted to the third D.H.10 prototype built to a revised specification for a long-range day bomber. The fourth prototype was to the full production standard, powered by two Liberty engines, and further production contracts were let for another 475 aircraft. A further improvement was to lower the engines to the top of the lower wing, to become the D.H.10A.

Due to the delays with the supply of Liberty engines, the D.H.10 entered service too late to participate in the First World War and was unable to be proven in active service. As an insurance against Liberty engine problems, a further version was built mainly by Mann, Egerton and Company, powered by two Rolls-Royce Eagle VIII engines and known as the D.H.10C. Only a small number of this type were completed.

As with many other aircraft types at the end of the war, the production contracts were drastically cut back, so it is not clear how many D.H.10s were actually produced. The Independent Force was to have a total of eight D.H.10 units of which No. 104 Squadron was just equipping at the Armistice, and two D.H.10s were modified for possible use as escort fighters by fitting a 37 mm (1½ pdr) Coventry Ordnance Works gun in the nose.

After the war, the relatively small number of D.H.10s continued in peace time service, initially on airmail services for the British Army of Occupation. On these duties, No. 120 Squadron flew the first ever night mail flight on 14 May 1919. No. 216 Squadron used D.H.10s on similar duties in the Middle East, flying between Cairo and Baghdad from June 1921 until 1923.

No. 97 Squadron, renumbered No. 60 Squadron on 1 April 1920, used D.H.10s from August 1919 over the North West Frontier between India and Afghanistan. Due to lack of spares and support from home, the aircraft strength was gradually reduced to one, and this was withdrawn in 1923.

Aircraft Transport and Travel used converted D.H.10 G-EAJO for a civil mail service between Hendon and Renfrew during the rail strike of October 1919. Other proposed civilian developments did not progress for economic reasons.

The last D.H.10 to remain in service was E6042 used by the A and AEE at Martlesham Heath and RAE Farnborough for experiments in controllability with one engine failed. Various tail configurations were tried, including twin fins and rudders, the tests continued until mid-1926 before the aircraft was retired.

Liberty-engined production D.H.10A (*Flight*)

Data

Variant: D.H.10 Amiens Mk IIIA
Power plant: Mk.I two 172 kW (230 hp) pusher Siddeley Puma inline engines, Mk II two 269 kW (360 hp) R-R Eagle VIII inline engines, Mk III two 298 kW (400 hp) Liberty 12 inline engines, Mk IIIC two 280 kW (375 hp) R-R Eagle VIII inline engines
Accommodation: Pilot and two gunners in open tandem cockpits
Fuel capacity: 1,000 ltr (215 Imp gal); oil 53 ltr (14 Imp gal)
Wing span: 19.96 m (65 ft 6 in)
Wing area: 77.8 sq m (837.5 sq ft)
Length: 12.07 m (39 ft 7½ in)
Height: 4.4 m (14 ft 6 in)
Weight empty: 2,608 kg (5,750 lb)
Max t/o weight: 4,082 kg (9,000 lb)
Max level speed: 200 km/h (129 mph)
Service ceiling: 5,340 m (17,500 ft)
Endurance/range: 5¾ hours
Armament: Either single or double Scarff ring-mounted Lewis machine guns in front and mid turrets. About 410 kg (900 lb) of bombs could be carried internally and on external racks
Production 4 prototypes and approx 170 series-production aircraft built by December 1918 out of a total of 1,294 ordered (194 cancelled).
Contracts included Airco/Hendon (219); British Cauldron Co Ltd/Cricklewood (100); The Siddeley-Deasy Motor Car Co Ltd/Coventry (150); The Daimler Co Ltd/Coventry (150); National Aircraft Factory No. 2/Stockport (200?); The Alliance Aeroplane Co Ltd/London (200?) and Mann, Egerton & Co Ltd/Norwich (75).

AIRCO D.H.11 Oxford

First flight: January 1920

Type: Long-range day bomber
Notes: The D.H.11 Oxford was designed to an Air Ministry contract for a long-range day-bomber replacement for the D.H.10. The three-seater had a deep fuselage filling the gap between the wings, giving a very aerodynamically clean design. Power was from a pair of the new ABC Dragonfly engines and the enclosed bomb bay was capable of carrying a load of 450 kg (1,000 lb). The pilot's seat was offset to starboard in the roomy cockpit, the mid-upper gunner was located on top of the fuselage with a 360° field of fire, and a second gunner was positioned in the nose.

Both gunners were equipped with Scarff ring-mounted Lewis guns. Although the prototype H5891 was under construction at the time of the Armistice, the lack of urgency after the war delayed its completion until January 1920.

Like a number of promising aircraft using the air-cooled nine-cylinder Dragonfly, the D.H.11 was not able to fully demonstrate its capabilities due to major problems with the engine, which was eventually abandoned. The Oxford did in fact fly with two of these engines, and took part in the Martlesham trials.

Due to the uncertainties of the postwar period and failure of the power plant, the construction of the two further prototypes was cancelled, as well as the projected Mk II powered by a pair of 216 kW (290 hp) Siddeley Puma engines.

Data
Variant: D.H.11 Oxford Mk.I
Power plant: Two 239 kW (320 hp) ABC Dragonfly radial engines

D.H.11 Oxford long-range day bomber prototype

Accommodation: Pilot and two gunners
Fuel capacity: 555 ltr (170 Imp gal)
Wing span: 18.3 m (60 ft 2 in)
Wing area: 66.8 sq m (719 sq ft)
Length: 13.8 m (45 ft 2¾ in)
Height: 4.1 m (13 ft 6 in)
Weight empty: 1,721 kg (3,795 lb)
Max t/o weight: 3,175 kg (7,000 lb)
Max level speed: 188 km/h (117 mph) (est); climb to 3,050 m (10,000 ft) 13½ min (est)
Endurance/range: 3¼ hours (est)
Armament: Two Scarff ring-mounted Lewis machine guns and up to 455 kg (1,000 lb) of bombs
Production One prototype H5891 completed, two further prototypes H5892–H5893 cancelled

AIRCO D.H.14 Okapi

First flight: Autumn 1919

Type: Two-seat day bomber
Notes: The D.H.14 was the last wartime design by Airco and was intended as a replacement for the D.H.4, D.H.9 and D.H.9A. Power for this large biplane came from a single Rolls-Royce Condor engine. Three prototypes were ordered, but construction was slowed down during the immediate postwar period. The two crew were accommo-dated in open tandem cockpits, behind the two-bay equal-span wings. The pilot was armed with a fixed synchronised forward-firing Vickers machine gun, and the observer with a pair of Scarff ring-mounted Lewis guns. A total of eight 50 kg (112 lb) bombs could be carried internally, the apertures being covered with brown paper, so that the bombs could fall through.

The third prototype, J1940, was completed first, but in a modified form as the civilian D.H.14A G-EAPY. It was planned to use it as a high speed, long-range mail carrier, powered by a Lion engine.

D.H.14 Okapi day bomber prototype J1938 (*IWM*)

Its first operation was to be flown by F. S. Cotton to Australia to claim a £10,000 prize, but before it was ready Ross and Keith Smith won the prize in a demilitarised Vickers Vimy bomber. F. S. Cotton then set off to claim the London to Cape Town record, but the aircraft turned over during a forced landing in Italy. It was returned to Britain for repair, but was wrecked on 24 July 1920 in a forced landing at Hertford.

When Airco closed down, the two partly built military prototypes were moved to Stag Lane for completion by the new de Havilland Aircraft Company. The first prototype was allocated to Farnborough for Condor engine trials, and both prototypes took part in service trials at Martlesham in the spring of 1921, but no further development was undertaken.

Data
Variant: D.H.14A Okapi
Power plant: D.H.14 one 391 kW (525 hp) R-R Condor inline engine; D.H.14A: one 336 kW (450 hp) Napier Lion inline engine

Accommodation: Pilot and observer/gunner in open tandem cockpits
Wing span: 15.4 m (50 ft 5 in)
Wing area: 57.3 sq m (617 sq ft)
Length: 11.46 m (37 ft 7 in)
Height: 4.27 m (14 ft)
Weight empty: 1,817 kg (4,006 lb)
Max t/o weight: 3,209 kg (7,074 lb)
Max level speed: 196 km/h (122 mph)
Service ceiling: approx 3,050 m (10,000 ft)
Armament: One synchronised forward-firing Vickers machine gun for the pilot and one Scarff ring-mounted Lewis gun for the observer. Eight 50.8 kg (112 lb) bombs could be carried internally, six in the lower wings and two in the fuselage
Production Three prototypes: J1938, J1939 and D.H.14A J1940/G-EAPY

AIRCO D.H.15 Gazelle

First flight: December 1918

Type: Engine test bed
Notes: The D.H.15 was basically a D.H.9A airframe modified to accommodate the water-cooled V-12 BHP Atlantic engine developed by the Galloway Engineering Company. It is possible that it was a more conventional insurance against failure of the D.H.14. The Galloway Atlantic combined two 172 kW (230 hp) BHP Atlantic engines on a single crankcase and two D.H.15s were ordered, although only the second was completed.

The new engine was selected for mass production before being fully developed and some 25 had been delivered by the end of October 1918. However, when aluminium cylinder blocks were fitted, the engine in effect became a double Puma and was named the Siddeley Pacific.

The D.H.15 looked very similar to the D.H.9A with a Liberty engine type of radiator and it retained its standard armament of a forward-firing synchronised fixed Vickers gun and a Lewis gun mounted on a Scarff ring for the observer. The main differences externally were the long horizontal exhaust pipes and the forward centre section struts were nearer the vertical in side elevation. Despite being an experimental aircraft it was named Gazelle, and completed extensive testing of the engine throughout 1919 and 1920.

Data
Variant: D.H.15 Gazelle
Power plant: One 373 kW (500 hp) BHP
(Galloway) Atlantic inline engine
Accommodation: Two crew in open tandem
cockpits
Fuel capacity: 500 ltr (108 Imp gal); oil 53 ltr
(14 Imp gal)
Wing span: 14 m (45 ft 11⅜ in)
Wing area: 45.2 sq m (486.75 sq ft)
Length: 9.1 m (29 ft 11 in)
Height: 3.45 m (11 ft 4 in)
Weight empty: 1,049 kg (2,312 lb)
Max t/o weight: 2,165 kg (4,773 lb)
Max level speed: 221 km/h (139 mph)
Service ceiling: 6,100 m (20,000 ft)
Armament: One synchronised forward-firing
Vickers gun and one Scarff ring-mounted Lewis
gun
Production J1936 not built; J1937

The Atlantic-engined Gazelle, developed from the D.H.9A
(*Flight*)

AIRCO D.H.16

First flight: March 1919

Type: Four-seat communication aircraft
Notes: The D.H.16 was Airco's first purely civilian
aircraft, a D.H.9A adapted by C. C. Walker during Geoffrey de Havilland's absence due to illness.
The pilot's cockpit was moved forward to under
the centre-section and the widened rear fuselage
had a cabin built to take two pairs of passengers
sitting side by side. Initially power came from an
Eagle VIII engine, with plans to replace it later
with a Napier Lion.

The prototype, registered K-130, started its
career with Aircraft Transport & Travel Ltd in
May 1919 on joy-riding, but on 25 August 1919, it
inaugurated civil air operations when it flew the
first London to Paris scheduled service, carrying
the registration G-EACT.

Only nine D.H.16s were produced, used mainly
by AT & T from Croydon during 1920, and the last
three were powered by the Lion engine, improving
both reliability and performance.

KLM, the Royal Dutch Airline, was formed in
May 1920, but as they were without any aircraft of
their own, they chartered D.H.16 G-EALU flown
by Capt Jerry Shaw to operate their inaugural
service on 17 May 1920.

With the closing down of AT & T, their assets
were taken over by Daimler Airline, but the
D.H.16s were stored until all but two were scrapped at Croydon in 1922. The surviving pair were
operated by the de Havilland Aeroplane Hire

Service starting on 3 July 1922, and continued
until one was destroyed in a crash in January 1923.
The surviving aircraft was then retired.

One D.H.16 that did not serve with the AT & T
was sold to the River Plate Aviation Company in
Buenos Aires in April 1920, and continued in
service until about 1925.

Data
Variant: D.H.16/Napier Lion
Power plant: One 239 kW (320 hp) R-R Eagle
VIII, or 336 kW (450 hp) Napier Lion inline
engine
Accommodation: Pilot in open cockpit and
enclosed passenger cabin with four seats
Wing span: 14.17 m (46 ft 5⅞ in)

Aircraft Transport & Travel D.H.16, Airco's first civil
aircraft (*de Havilland*)

Wing area: 45.5 sq m (489.75 sq ft)
Length: 9.7 m (31 ft 9 in)
Height: 3.45 m (11 ft 4 in)
Weight empty: 1,431 kg (3,155 lb)
Max t/o weight: 2,155 kg (4,750 lb)
Max level speed: 220 km/h (136 mph)

Service ceiling: 6,400 m (21,000 ft)
Endurance/range: 685 km (425 miles)
Production Nine aircraft: K-130 (later G-EACT); G-EALM; G-EALU; G-EAPM; G-EAPT; G-EAQG; G-EAQS; G-EARU and G-EASW

AIRCO D.H.18

First flight: February 1920

Type: Eight-seat airliner
Notes: The D.H.18 was the first Airco airliner, and in the event the last aircraft before liquidation. The passenger cabin was located in the centre section to avoid centre of gravity problems, with the pilot in an open cockpit behind. Power came from a Napier Lion engine.

The prototype was completed at Hendon, the structure being conventional wood with ply and fabric covering. The passenger door was watertight in case of landing on water, and with the seats removed, 7.2 m³ (256 ft³) of space was available for up to 1,000 kg (2,205 lb) of freight.

The prototype entered service with AT & T in April 1920 on the Croydon to Paris route, but it was damaged beyond repair on a forced landing in November. Two improved D.H.18As were started at Hendon but completed by de Havillands and entered service with AT & T until closure due to lack of subsidy and the economic situation in December 1920. The two aircraft, with the addition of a third were later operated by Instone Air Line until they were withdrawn at the end of 1921.

Two improved D.H.18Bs were then introduced with all-ply fuselage covering and used by Instone. In early 1922, Daimler Hire was formed and

leased a surviving D.H.18A to commence their services. Unfortunately, this was short lived as G-AEWO collided head on with a Farman Goliath at Grandvilliers in France on 7 April 1922 when both aircraft were following the same railway line in opposite directions in bad weather.

The two surviving D.H.18s were used for rather contrasting tasks. G-EARO undertook fuel consumption tests at Farnborough in the latter half of 1924, and was employed on further tests until November 1926. G-EAWW had only one test, and that was to check flotation after ditching. It was stripped of all unnecessary equipment and ditched off Felixstowe on 2 May 1924 where it floated for about 25 minutes.

Data
Variant: D.H.18B
Power plant: One 336 kW (450 hp) Napier Lion inline engine
Accommodation: Pilot in open cockpit and eight passengers in an enclosed cabin
Wing span: 15.6 m (51 ft 2¾ in)
Wing area: 57.7 sq m (621.25 sq ft)
Length: 11.9 m (39 ft)
Height: 4 m (13 ft 0½ in)
Weight empty: 1,955 kg (4,310 lb)
Max t/o weight: 3,228 kg (7,116 lb)
Max level speed: 200 km/h (128 mph)
Service ceiling: 4,880 m (16,000 ft)
Endurance/range: 645 km (400 miles)
Production Six aircraft: one D.H.18 (G-EARI), three D.H.18As (G-EARO, G-EAUF, G-EAWO) and two D.H.18Bs (G-EAWW and G-EAWX)

D.H.18 prototype later entered service with AT & T
(Surrey Flying Services)

82

DE HAVILLAND D.H.27 DERBY

D.H.27 Derby was de Havilland's first military aircraft

First flight: 13 October 1922

Type: Three-seat long-range day bomber
Notes: The de Havilland Company's first military design was a large single-engined long-range day bomber built to Air Ministry Specification 2/20. It was powered by a Rolls-Royce Condor III engine driving a four-blade wooden airscrew. The pilot was situated in a large open cockpit ahead of the wing with a fairing behind him joining the fuselage to the top wing containing the fuel tank. The navigator/bomb aimer was in an enclosed cabin in the fuselage. A gunner was located mid-way down the fuselage armed with a Lewis gun on a Scarff ring. The fuselage had a smooth plywood covering and the two-bay wooden structure wings were fabric covered, and capable of being folded back to save hangar space.

Its novel features included a variable incidence tailplane, oleo-damped rubber shock absorbers and a wide track split-leg undercarriage, allowing the bombs to be carried under the fuselage.

The D.H.27 was taken up on its maiden flight by Hubert Broad from Stag Lane, and two prototypes were ordered in competition with Avro Aldershot, but the latter won the contract for the re-

equipment of No. 99 Squadron at Bircham Newton. The two D.H.27s were then allocated to experimental flying at Martlesham Heath and the Isle of Grain. The last recorded flight of a Derby was by the first prototype from the Isle of Grain to Farnborough on 1 February 1924.

Data
Variant: D.H.27 Derby
Power plant: One 485 kW (650 hp) R-R Condor III inline engine
Accommodation: Pilot and rear gunner in open cockpits, and navigator in cabin
Fuel capacity: 960 ltr (212 Imp gal)
Wing span: 19.6 m (64 ft 5 in)
Wing area: 104 sq m (1,120 sq ft)
Length: 14.4 m (47 ft 4 in)
Height: 5.1 m (16 ft 10 in)
Weight empty: 3,056 kg (6,737 lb)
Max t/o weight: 5,236 kg (11,544 lb)
Max level speed: 169 km/h (105 mph)
Armament: One Lewis machine gun mounted on Scarff ring
Production J6894 and J6895

Civil prototype of the D.H.29 Doncaster airliner (*Flight*)

DE HAVILLAND D.H.29 DONCASTER

First flight: 5 July 1921

Type: Long-range transport aircraft

Notes: Following their success with the D.H.18, de Havilland were awarded a contract by the Air Ministry to build two prototypes of a long-range transport aircraft. The resulting Doncaster was the first British transport to be produced with monoplane cantilever wing, set high on the fuselage and of thick section. Construction was of spruce with plywood-covered fuselage and fabric-covered wing.

Ten passengers could be carried in the enclosed cabin, with an alternative freight capacity of 9.8 m³ (345 ft³). The two pilots were located in an open cockpit ahead of the wing. Power was from a single Lion 1B engine, and Capt de Havilland made the first flight from Stag Lane on 5 July 1921. Due to handling problems, the engine installation had to be raised 51 cm (20 in) and the fuel system modified.

Following trials at Martlesham Heath on the first prototype in January 1922, it was used for photographic and wireless developments. Later, a gunner's cockpit with a Scarff ring was installed on top of the fuselage. The modified prototype completed its testing at Farnborough after moving there on 17 April 1924.

The second Doncaster was completed as civil airliner G-EAYO in August 1921. Its efficiency was demonstrated by carrying ten passengers and two crew on the same power as the D.H.18 and same wing area as the D.H.4. However, poorly understood longitudinal and control problems caused by the high wing layout resulted in it not entering service, and further development was abandoned. The second Doncaster joined the first prototype at Martlesham Heath in November 1922 to have further tests on thick wing sections.

Data
Variant: D.H.29 Doncaster
Power plant: One 336 kW (450 hp) Napier Lion 1B inline engine
Accommodation: Two crew in open cockpit and 10 passengers in cabin
Wing span: 16.5 m (54 ft 1¼ in)
Wing area: 41 sq m (440 sq ft)
Length: 13 m (42 ft 7½ in)
Height: 5 m (16 ft 5 in)
Weight empty: 1,982 kg (4,370 lb)
Max t/o weight: 3,402 kg (7,500 lb)
Max level speed: 188 km/h (116 mph)
Service ceiling: 3,050 m (10,000 ft)
Production J6849 and G-EAYO

DE HAVILLAND D.H.34

First flight: 26 March 1922

Type: Eight-seat airliner

Notes: The D.H.34 made a significant contribution to the development of civil aviation in Britain despite the modest number of only eleven produced, as it consolidated the desirable features of earlier aircraft. Economics were being better understood, and the quest for greater speed and capacity had begun.

It was a wooden two-bay biplane airliner with an enclosed cabin for the passengers; the two crew were exposed to the elements in front of the wing. Apart from its biplane layout, it was very similar in structure to the D.H.29, but a unique feature was the capability of detaching the Lion power unit for servicing. A spare engine could also be transported in the cabin.

The D.H.34 was built to an Air Council Specification 17/21 for use by Daimler Hire and Instone Air Line, the first aircraft being delivered to Croydon for Daimler on 31 March, only five days after its maiden flight. It entered service two days later, carrying newspapers to Paris. The second aircraft made its maiden flight, was delivered and entered service with Instone all before lunch on 2 April 1922. Daimler subsequently used six, and Instone four D.H.34s; one other was built to Dobrolet order and shipped to the Soviet Union in July 1922.

These aircraft flew with great reliability and regularity over a number of European routes, achieving very high utilisation, and being assisted by the modest subsidies then available.

One of the criticisms of the aircraft was its high stalling speed, and this was highlighted in a crash at Ivinghoe, Bucks on 14 September 1923 when the two crew and three passengers were killed. To overcome this problem the wing area was increased resulting in an 11 km/h (7 mph) reduction in landing speed, but two further crashes followed, with the second and fatal one at Croydon on 24 December 1924 under similar circumstances to the first.

Imperial Airways was formed on 1 April 1924 as a merger of the existing airlines, and seven surviving D.H.34s were absorbed into the fleet, two more of which were converted to D.H.34B standard with increased wing area. However, as Imperial Airways decided to only use multi-engined airliners for greater safety, the remaining

Imperial Airways D.H.34 (*P. T. Capon*)

D.H.34s were withdrawn from service by 31 March 1926 and scrapped at Croydon.

Data
Variant: D.H.34
Power plant: One 336 kW (450 hp) Napier Lion inline engine
Accommodation: Three crew, including a cabin boy, and eight passengers
Wing span: 15.65 m (51 ft 4 in)
Wing area: 54.8 sq m (590 sq ft)
Length: 11.89 m (39 ft)
Height: 3.66 m (12 ft)
Weight empty: 2,075 kg (4,574 lb)
Max t/o weight: 3,266 kg (7,200 lb)
Max level speed: 206 km/h (128 mph)
Service ceiling: 3,050 m (10,000 ft)
Endurance/range: 587 km (365 miles)
Production Eleven aircraft: G-EBBQ; G-EBBR; G-EBBS; G-EBBT; G-EBBU; G-EBBV; G-EBBW; G-EBBX; G-EBBY; G-EBCX; one to Dobrolet order. G-EBCY not completed

DE HAVILLAND D.H.37

First flight: June 1922

Type: Three-seat touring aircraft
Notes: The D.H.37 was designed for Alan S. Butler as a three-seat touring aircraft for his travelling around Europe. At the same time as he ordered it, his investment gave the company the chance to purchase its premises thereby gaining the much needed security for the future. Alan Butler subsequently became chairman of the com-

pany, a post he retained until his retirement in 1950.

The D.H.37 was powered by a Rolls-Royce Falcon III engine acquired from the Aircraft Disposal Company. Construction was of wood with ply-covered fuselage and fabric flying surfaces. The two passengers were located in a cockpit in front of the pilot, with a sliding hatch which could be closed when it was unoccupied.

Alan Butler's D.H.37 was named *Sylvia* after his sister, and it performed well with an endurance of 5½ hours, a cruising speed of 168 km/h (105 mph) and it could climb to 3,050 m (10,000 ft) in 11 minutes. The aircraft was therefore also suitable for sporting events as well as touring, gaining fifth place in the 1922 King's Cup and third place in 1924 and 1925 in the same race.

The Falcon engine was replaced in 1926 by a 13.6 kg (30 lb) lighter ADC Nimbus engine which developed an additional 19 kW (25 hp). In this form it became the D.H.37A, named *Lois* after Butler's wife, and its performance in races was much improved. Regrettably it was written off in a crash near Bournemouth on 4 June 1927 while practising for a race, killing the passenger and injuring the pilot. Alan Butler was not flying it that day.

A second D.H.37 was built for the Controller of Civil Aviation in Australia, and left Britain by ship on 14 April 1924. It was also used for touring and racing, becoming the first aircraft on the Australian register as VH-UAA in 1928. This aircraft then commenced flying on busy communications routes around New Guinea, but finally crashed in New South Wales on 25 March 1932.

Data
Variant: D.H.37A
Power plant: One 205 kW (275 hp) R-R Falcon III, or (D.H.37A) 224 kW (300 hp) ADC Nimbus inline engine
Accommodation: Pilot and two passengers in open cockpits
Wing span: 11.28 m (37 ft)
Wing area: 36.97 sq m (398 sq ft)
Length: 8.99 m (29 ft 6 in)
Height: 3.4 m (11 ft 2 in)
Weight empty: 1,112 kg (2,452 lb)
Max t/o weight: 1,690 kg (3,725 lb)
Max level speed: 214 km/h (133 mph)
Service ceiling: 6,400 m (21,000 ft)
Endurance/range: 805 km (500 miles)
Production Two aircraft: G-EBDO became D.H.37A, G-AUAA became VH-UAA.

First of two D.H.37 touring aircraft (*P. T. Capon*)

DE HAVILLAND D.H.42
DORMOUSE AND DINGO

First flight: 25 July 1923

Type: Two-seat reconnaissance fighter and army co-operation

Notes: The three D.H.42 prototypes either differed in the intended role or construction. The first prototype, named Dormouse, was a high performance, two-crew, reconnaissance fighter to Air Ministry Specification 22/22 powered by a single Armstrong Siddeley Jaguar II radial engine. The structure was the typical wood with ply-covered fuselage and fabric-covered flying surfaces. The first public showing was in Hendon New Types Park on 28 June 1924, after which its engine was replaced by a Jaguar IV for testing a variety of airscrews at different all-up weights. In March 1925 it was delivered to the RAE Farnborough for wireless and magneto screening tests before being withdrawn from use at the end of the year.

The second prototype was the D.H.42A Dingo Mk I built to Army Co-operation Specification 8/24. It was first flown on 12 March 1924 powered by a Jupiter III engine. As in the first aircraft, the pilot had two forward-firing Vickers machine guns and the observer had a Scarff ring-mounted Lewis gun. While on tests at Martlesham Heath the aircraft crashed on 5 June 1924, and the wreck was returned to Stag Lane where it was scrapped.

The final prototype was the first aircraft de

D.H.42 Dormouse J7005 was one of three similar aircraft (*de Havilland*)

Havilland built with fabric-covered steel tube fuselage, and it was known as the D.H.42B Dingo Mk II. Also intended for army co-operation, it first flew in September 1924 powered by a Jupiter IV engine. This prototype was delivered to Farnborough on 16 November 1926 for experimental flying. No production order was forthcoming, but at least the company had gained experience in the latest developments and had some work during the difficult economic times.

Data
Variant: D.H.42 Dormouse
Power plant: D.H.42: One 269 kW (360 hp) A.S. Jaguar II or 313 kW (420 hp) Jaguar IV radial engine; D.H.42A: One 306 kW (410 hp) Bristol Jupiter III radial engine; D.H.42B: One 325 kW (436 hp) Bristol Jupiter IV radial engine
Accommodation: Pilot and one observer in open tandem cockpits
Wing span: 12.5 m (41 ft)
Wing area: 36.14 sq m (389 sq ft)
Length: 8.6 m (28 ft 3 in)
Weight empty: 1,140 kg (2,513 lb)
Max t/o weight: 1,768 kg (3,897 lb)
Max level speed: 201 km/h (125 mph)
Service ceiling: 4,880 m (16,000 ft)
Production Three aircraft: D.H.42 Dormouse J7005, D.H.42A Dingo Mk I J7006 and D.H.42B Dingo Mk II J7007

DE HAVILLAND D.H.50

First flight: 3 August 1923

Type: Four-seat cabin communication aircraft
Notes: The D.H.50 was designed as a replacement for the D.H.9C and proved a reasonable success

with export sales and overseas production. The pilot was in an open cockpit above and behind the passenger cabin, and like the D.H.9C it was powered by a Puma engine.

Only four days after its maiden flight, Alan J. Cobham flew the prototype to the Göteborg Exhibition in Sweden, where it won the commer-

Imperial Airways D.H.50 at Croydon (*Hawker Siddeley*)

cial aircraft competition for its high standards of economy, reliability, speed and structure. A year later on 12 August Cobham flew the same aircraft (G-EBFN) to victory in the King's Cup at an average speed of 170 km/h (106.6 mph) and the prototype eventually joined Qantas in 1926 bringing cabin comfort to the passengers for the first time.

The second prototype, G-EBFO, was very much in the public eye with a number of epic long-distance flights by Cobham. As a result of being exhibited at the Prague Aero Exhibition in May 1924, seven D.H.50s were built under license by Aero in 1926; these were operated by the Czech airline CLS.

The second prototype was then delivered to Imperial Airways for a series of survey flights, commencing with a 14,480 km (9,000 miles) flight to Rangoon with Sir Sefton Brancker. On return, following a minor accident, the Puma engine was replaced by a Jaguar radial, and during repairs preparations were made for the next long-distance flight by fitting additional fuel tanks. With these modifications the aircraft was redesignated D.H.50J.

This survey flight was from London to Cape Town, flown by Alan Cobham with A. B. Elliot as engineer and B. W. G. Emmett as photographer. The flight was sponsored by Lord Wakefield, departing on 16 November 1925, and returning the following 13 March. Plans were immediately made for the third flight in the series, this time to Australia. Because much of the route was over water, floats were fitted by Short Bros. at Rochester and the aircraft took off from the Medway on 30 June 1926. The 45,060 km (28,000 miles) round trip to Melbourne was only marred by the unfortunate death of Elliot, who was shot by a stray bullet while flying over the deserts of Iraq.

Following the return on 1 October 1926, when Cobham landed on the River Thames by the Houses of Parliament, he received a knighthood from His Majesty, King George V.

Imperial Airways subsequently opened up the surveyed routes with larger aircraft and G-EBFO was sold in Australia, although two further D.H.50s were used on other routes. Another two were registered in Britain, but most of the remainder of the Stag Lane production were sold in Australia, a total of nine being delivered. One also joined the RNZAF for photographic survey duties, until it also went to Australia.

So successful was the D.H.50 in commercial service with Qantas that four D.H.50As, with slightly longer cabins and other minor changes, and three D.H.50Js were built by the airline, and others by West Australian Airways and Larkin Aircraft Supply. Qantas used the aircraft to link the inland railheads in eastern Australia. Another aircraft was modified to carry a stretcher, doctor and nurse, to inaugurate the famous Flying Doctor Service in August 1927, and continued in service until replaced by a Fox Moth in 1934. In addition to commercial use other D.H.50s were operated by the RAAF for communications and survey flights.

Three other D.H.50As were license built by SABCA at Brussels in 1925 for use by Sabena in the Belgian Congo between 1925 and 1928, but their ultimate fate is unknown.

Data
Variant: D.H.50J
Power plant: D.H.50/D.H.50A: One 172 kW (230 hp) Siddeley Puma inline engine; D.H.50J: One 287 kW (385 hp) A.S. Jaguar III or various Jupiter radial engines
Accommodation: Pilot in open cockpit and four passengers in an enclosed cabin
Wing span: 13 m (42 ft 9 in)
Wing area: 40.32 sq m (434 sq ft)
Length: 8.76 m (28 ft 9 in)
Height: 3.35 m (11 ft)
Weight empty: 1,148.5 kg (2,532 lb)
Max t/o weight: 1,905 kg (4,200 lb)
Max level speed: 219 km/h (136 mph)
Service ceiling: 6,100 m (20,000 ft)
Endurance/range: 1,062 km (660 miles)
Production Total of 38 built:
D.H.50: de Havilland/Stag Lane (17); Aero/Czechoslovakia (7).
D.H.50A: Qantas/Australia (4); West Australian Airways (3); SABCA/Belgium (3); The Larkin Supply Co Ltd/Australia (1).
D.H.50J: Qantas/Australia (3).

DE HAVILLAND D.H.51

First flight: July 1924

Type: Three-seat open cockpit tourer

Notes: The D.H.51 was the first attempt to produce an economical and practical tourer for the private owner. Construction was conventional wood with ply and fabric covering, and power came from a war surplus 67 kW (90 hp) RAF 1a engine. However, this engine had to be replaced due to its single ignition not achieving the required airworthiness standards, and an Airdisco was substituted. The two passengers sat in the open cockpit facing each other, with the pilot just behind in a separate cockpit.

The change of engine removed the main advantage of cheapness, resulting in only three D.H.51s being built. Towards the end of 1924 the prototype was modified by having short-span single-bay wings fitted, becoming the D.H.51A. This aircraft eventually found its way to Australia in 1927. Fitted with wooden floats in 1929 it became the D.H.51B, but was destroyed in January 1931 when it overturned on forced landing in Sydney Harbour.

The second aircraft was an unsuccessful entry in the 1925 King's Cup Air Race. It was used for training at Renfrew and joy-riding in Somerset, until being scrapped in 1933.

The third and most significant D.H.51 was flown by Geoffrey de Havilland from Stag Lane on 11 September 1925, and six days later it was shipped to East Africa. It became the first aircraft on the Kenyan register as G-KAA, later VP-KAA. Passing through the hands of a number of owners, it spent long periods in storage between bursts of flying, and the occasional minor accident. It last flew in Nairobi in March 1962, bringing the flying time to just over 143 hours in thirty-six and a half years.

Subsequently the third D.H.51 was returned to Hatfield in 1965, and donated to the Shuttleworth Trust at Old Warden after rebuilding to flying condition by the apprentices at Rolls-Royce Leavesden and Hawker Siddeley Aviation, Chester. Not only is it the oldest D.H. aeroplane flying, but it is also the oldest on the British civil register.

Data
Variant: D.H.51
Power plant: One 89 kW (120 hp) Airdisco inline engine
Accommodation: Pilot and two passengers in open tandem cockpits
Wing Span: 11.28 m (37 ft)
Wing area: 30.19 sq m (325 sq ft)
Length: 8.08 m (26 ft 6 in)
Height: 2.97 m (9 ft 9 in)
Weight empty: 609 kg (1,342 lb)
Max t/o weight: 1,016 kg (2,240 lb)
Max level speed: 174 km/h (108 mph)
Service ceiling: 4,570 m (15,000 ft)
Endurance/range: 580 km (360 miles)
Production Three aircraft: G-EBIM/G-AUIM, G-EBIQ, and G-EBIR/G-KAA/VP-KAA/ G-EBIR

D.H.51 following its restoration for the Shuttleworth Trust

DE HAVILLAND D.H.52

First flight: 5 October 1922

Type: Ultra-light glider

Notes: The only glider to be built by de Havillands was the D.H.52 entered for the *Daily Mail* £1,000 Gliding Competition held at Itford, on the Sussex Downs in 1922. Two of these ultra-light gliders were completed at Stag Lane using traditional wood construction, with the high monoplane wing wire-braced to a central kingpost.

After adjustments following flight trials, the two gliders were taken to Itford ten days after the first flight, to compete with 33 other British and overseas entries.

The first glider was entered by de Havilland and flown by the diminutive Hubert Broad, while the second D.H.52 was privately entered and flown by E. D. C. Herne. Both launched successfully, flying for over two minutes each, but they were damaged on landing due to flexibility of the wings neutralising the aileron operation. During repairs, it was decided to try to improve control by locking the ailerons and resorting to wing warping. Unfortunately, immediately after release on its next launch, the flexible structure of the wing began to warp uncontrollably and at an altitude of some

First of two D.H.52 gliders just after launch (*de Havilland*)

10 m (30 ft) the wings failed at the root end and folded back. Luckily the pilot escaped without serious injury, but no further flights were made with the other glider, and both were scrapped.

Data
Variant: D.H.52
Accommodation: Pilot in open cockpit
Wing span: 15.24 m (50 ft)
Wing area: 20.44 sq m (220 sq ft)
Length: 8.53 m (28 ft)
Height: 2.44 m (8 ft)
Weight empty: 113.4 kg (250 lb)
Max t/o weight: 181.44 kg (400 lb)
Landing speed: 29 km/h (18 mph)
Production Racing No. 4 *Sibylla* and Racing No. 33 *Margon*

DE HAVILLAND D.H.53 HUMMING BIRD

First flight: September 1923

Type: Single-seat ultra-light tourer

Notes: In 1923 a prize of £500 was offered by the Secretary of State for Air to encourage the building of an economical light aircraft suitable for club and private flying. The aircraft was to be a single-seater, powered by an engine not exceeding 750 cc. The main object of the competition was to achieve the greatest distance on 4.5 ltr (1 Imp gal) of petrol and the event was to be held at Lympne in October of that year.

Amongst a number of other manufacturers, de Havillands entered two prototypes of the D.H.53 Humming Bird, a low-wing monoplane powered by a single two-cylinder, horizontally opposed, air-cooled 750 cc Douglas motorcycle engine. Although 95.5 km (59.3 miles) was flown using 4.5 ltr (1 Imp gal) of fuel, neither of the Humming

D.H.53 Humming Bird prototype at Stag Lane (*Flight*)

Birds won a prize, but they were the most robust and practical aircraft entered. The power specification was too low for practical touring and the engines were generally unreliable. Despite the lack of a prize the Humming Bird was the only aircraft to gain an order, when eight were purchased by the RAF for light communications duties.

Without the impractical requirements of the competition, the aircraft were powered by a more reliable two-cylinder Tomtit inverted-V engine and the fuel tankage was doubled to 18 ltr (4 Imp gal).

The eight RAF aircraft were built to Specification 44/23, and upon completion one was allocated to Northolt, three to the Central Flying School (CFS) at Upavon, and two to Netheravon. The other two were delivered to the RAE at Farnborough for some interesting experiments in aerial launching from beneath the airship *R 33*. On 15 October 1925, the first launch and recovery was made successfully from near Pulham, Norfolk, but on the second attempt the Humming Bird propeller was broken and the aircraft had to make a forced landing. To improve these operations a more powerful Bristol Cherub engine was installed, and modifications made to the trapeze gear. Despite a further successful re-engagement, the trials were abandoned.

There were no further civil orders from Britain, but three were shipped to Australia in 1924, one of them flying 3,138 km (1,950 miles) across the continent from Wyndham to Perth in May 1937. The six and a half day journey was completed in a flying time of 30 hours and 5 minutes.

Only two other Humming Birds were built, one exhibited in Prague in June 1924 and the other sold to the Soviet Union in January 1925. The eight RAF aircraft were disposed of to civil buyers in 1927, six gaining C of A's, and became popular with private owners and flying groups up to the outbreak of the Second World War.

The original prototype, G-EBHX, still survives with the Shuttleworth Trust, having been found derelict in a Kent garden in 1955. All that remained was the fuselage, wings, port aileron and undercarriage. None of the original drawings existed, resulting in much redesign by the students of the de Havilland Aeronautical Technical School, followed by rebuilding to flying condition as a training exercise. It was flown again from Hatfield on 4 August 1960 powered by a 30 kW (40 hp) ABC Scorpion engine.

More recently, one of the ex-RAF Humming Birds has been found which was converted to the Martin Monoplane. With new wings built by the apprentices at Hatfield, using the drawings prepared for G-EBHX, it is expected that this aircraft will soon take to the air. A replica was also built in Canada using the same drawings and flew for the first time on 7 May 1967.

Data
Variant: D.H.53 Humming Bird/Tomtit
Power plant: One 750 cc Douglas or one 19 kW (26 hp) Blackburn Tomtit engine
Accommodation: Pilot in open cockpit
Fuel capacity: 5 ltr (2 Imp gal)
Wing span: 9.15 m (30 ft 1 in)
Wing area: 11.61 sq m (125 sq ft)
Length: 5.99 m (19 ft 8 in)
Height: 2.21 m (7 ft 3 in)
Weight empty: 148 kg (326 lb)
Max t/o weight: 256 kg (565 lb)
Max level speed: 117.5 km/h (73 mph)
Service ceiling: 4,570 m (15,000 ft)
Endurance/range: 2½ hours/241 km (150 miles)
Production 15 aircraft plus one Canadian replica

DE HAVILLAND D.H.54 HIGHCLERE

First flight: 18 June 1925

Type: 14-seat passenger airliner
Notes: In 1924 de Havillands commenced design of the Highclere to Air Ministry Specification 40/22 to replace the successful D.H.34. The new aircraft was similar in layout to its predecessor, but had increased power from a Rolls-Royce Condor IIIA engine. Construction was of wood, with the passengers carried in an enclosed cabin in the fuselage centre-section. The two crew, equipped with dual controls, were in an open cockpit just forward of the top biplane wing. To reduce landing speed, full-span, automatic camber-changing flaps were fitted. As a precaution against ditching, the undercarriage could be jettisoned and the fuselage was made buoyant.

So successful was the first flight that passengers were carried later the same day, and its public debut was in the New Types Park at the RAF display at Hendon on 27 June 1925.

The D.H.54 was to be used by Imperial Airways on their cross-Channel routes, but by the time the C of A was granted on 23 April 1926 the airline had decided to concentrate on multi-engined passenger aircraft.

No further Highcleres were built and the prototype was flown to Farnborough on 7 March 1926 for trials with the Acoustics Department. On 9

The sole D.H.54 Highclere airliner evaluated by Imperial Airways (*de Havilland*)

November 1926 it returned to Imperial Airways at Croydon for conversion to the D.H.54A as a freighter. Its cabin was to be cleared to allow the carriage of a load of up to 1,360 kg (3,000 lb) of 6 m (20 ft) long pipes loaded through a rear cabin door. However, before this conversion could be completed the aircraft was wrecked when the hangar roof fell in under the weight of snow on 1 February 1927.

Data
Variant: D.H.54 Highclere
Power plant: One 485 kW (650 hp) R-R Condor IIIA inline engine
Accommodation: Two pilots in open cockpit and 14 passengers in cabin
Wing span: 20.78 m (68 ft 2 in)
Wing area: 93.27 sq m (1,004 sq ft)
Length: 15.54 m (51 ft)
Height: 5.36 m (17 ft 7 in)
Weight empty: 3,070 kg (6,768 lb)
Max t/o weight: 5,103 kg (11,250 lb)
Max level speed: 177 km/h (110 mph)
Service ceiling: 3,050 m (10,000 ft)
Endurance/range: 644 m (400 miles)
Production Prototype G-EBKI.

DE HAVILLAND D.H.56 HYENA

First flight: 17 May 1925

Type: Two-seat army co-operation aircraft
Notes: The Hyena was developed from the D.H.42B Dingo Mk II to Specification 33/26 for army co-operation duties. It featured a steel tube fuselage with fabric covering and the two-bay unequal span biplane wings were fabric-covered wood structure. The first prototype was powered by a Jaguar III radial engine, but before delivery to Martlesham Heath for official trials this was replaced by a Jaguar IV. The pilot was armed with a forward-firing synchronised Vickers machine gun, and the gunner seated behind the pilot had a similar gun mounted on a Scarff ring. The aircraft carried a range of equipment including bomb racks below the lower port wing, a message pick-up hook between the undercarriage legs, and supplies could be dropped down a chute in the observer's cockpit.

The first prototype was shown in the New Types Park at Hendon on 3 July 1926, and was joined at Martlesham Heath by the second prototype which first flew in June. Both Hyenas were used on competitive trials with the Armstrong Whitworth Atlas, Bristol Boarhound and the Vickers Vespa. The production contract was awarded to Atlas, and the Hyenas were flown to Farnborough for further evaluation with No. 4 Army Co-operation Squadron. In August 1926 one of the Hyenas spent some time with the School of Army Co-operation at Old Sarum. In September 1927, the second prototype joined the Engine Flight at Farnborough, where tests on the exhaust system continued until mid-1928.

First of two prototype D.H.56 Hyenas (*de Havilland*)

Data
Variant: D.H.56 Hyena
Power plant: One 314 kW (422 hp) Armstrong Siddeley Jaguar IV radial engine
Accommodation: Pilot and observer in open tandem cockpits
Fuel capacity: 455 ltr (100 Imp gal)
Wing span: 13.11 m (43 ft)
Wing area: 39.13 sq m (421.25 sq ft)

Length: 9.07 m (29 ft 9 in)
Height: 3.28 m (10 ft 9 in)
Weight empty: 1,088 kg (2,399 lb)
Max t/o weight: 1,905 kg (4,200 lb)
Max level speed: 209 km/h (130 mph)
Armament: One forward-firing synchronised Vickers machine gun and one similar Scarff ring-mounted gun
Production J7780 and J7781

DE HAVILLAND D.H.60 MOTH

First flight: 22 February 1925

Type: Two-seat tourer
Notes: The Moth was the major turning point of de Havillands, bringing great prosperity and fame to the company. The Moth provided the foundation stone for a whole range of highly successful private owner and club aircraft. When de Havilland designed the aircraft, he realised what was needed was a reliable, practical and economical aircraft, and he avoided the pitfalls of producing a cheap ultra-light, which had been the aim of the officially sponsored competitions. The aircraft had to be a two-seater suitable for touring and training, and powered by a reliable, but inexpensive engine.

From these ideas, the D.H.60 Moth was born as a rugged biplane with wooden structure, covered with ply on the fuselage and fabric on the tail and single-bay biplane wings. The two open cockpits were placed in tandem with room for luggage in the front one, and a gravity fuel tank holding 68.2 ltr (15 Imp gal) was faired into the centre-section of the upper wing.

The Moth was an instant success and the first for the new Air Ministry subsidised flying clubs was delivered to the Lancashire Aero Club at Woodford on 21 July 1925. The eighth built, G-EBLV, was delivered to the same club on 29 August, and is the oldest Moth to survive, being preserved in flying condition at British Aerospace, Hatfield. Amongst the other clubs to receive Moths was the London Aeroplane Club at Stag Lane.

Production soon began to build up, and the aircraft started selling overseas. One of the early improvements was to relocate the luggage into a locker behind the rear cockpit. One Moth, J8030, was purchased by the Air Ministry for trials which led to the adoption of later versions as standard RAF trainers.

Moths were later to feature in many long-dis-

tance flights, but early successes included winning the King's Cup Air Race for three consecutive years. In 1926, Hubert Broad flew G-EBMO at an average speed of 145.48 km/h (90.4 mph); Wally Hope flew G-EBME to win in 1927 at 149.34 km/h (92.8 mph); and in 1928 the same pilot flew G-EBYZ to first place at 169.78 km/h (105.5 mph).

In 1927, an improved model was produced with increased power known as the Cirrus II Moth or D.H.60X. The engine was lowered to improve the view, the gap between the wings reduced, and span increased by 0.30 m (1 ft). The first success for this version was to capture the altitude record for light aircraft of 5,267.86 m (17,283 ft) on 5 July 1927 flown from Stag Lane by Lady Bailey. She later flew a solo 28,967 km (18,000 miles) round trip to Cape Town.

It was also in 1927 that six Genet-engined Moths were supplied to the RAF for service at the CFS. The following year, 20 Cirrus II Moths were supplied to the RAF for instruction at the CFS and communications with No. 24 Squadron at Hendon.

By 1927 the world market was building up, with the overseas companies operating demonstrators to increase sales, and many new countries added to the list of exports. Assembly had commenced in

Cirrus-powered D.H.60 Moth prototype (de Havilland)

Gipsy Moth bought by HRH The Prince of Wales (*Flight*)

South Africa, Canada, and Australia. By the end of 1928 a total of 403 Moths had been built and within two months the production rate at Stag Lane had increased to 16 aircraft per week. In 1929 a further improvement was the introduction of the 67 kW (90 hp) Cirrus III engine. The Royal Singapore Flying Club ordered a special batch of Moths powered by Hermes I engines and fitted with floats. Hermes-powered D.H.60X Moth G-EBWD is part of the de Havilland collection of flying aircraft at the Shuttleworth Trust.

D.H.60G Gipsy Moth
The first major improvement to the Moth family was the installation of the Halford-designed de Havilland Gipsy engine which was not only a more efficient and reliable power plant, but also avoided reliance on a dwindling stock of the First World War vintage components. The first Gipsy Moth was G-EBQH and was to continue a very successful line with many records for speed and distance. de Havilland broke the altitude record on 25 July 1928 by reaching 6,090 m (19,980 ft) and Alan Butler broke the 100 km closed circuit record at an average speed of 192.86 km/h (119.84 mph).

Sales continued to grow on all continents of the world with assembly commencing in India, and Gipsy Moths inaugurated commercial flying in South Africa in July 1929. By the end of that year production rate at Stag Lane was three every day at an ex-works price of £650.

Probably the record which will be best remembered is the epic flight from England to Australia by Amy Johnson in Gipsy Moth G-AAAH *Jason*, now preserved in the London Science Museum. She left Croydon on 5 May 1930 and arrived at Port Darwin on 24 May to become the first woman to fly the route solo. Sir Francis Chichester was the first man to fly a Moth from England to Australia, and the aircraft was shipped to New Zealand for his flight back to Australia, calling in at the tiny and remote Norfolk and Lord Howe Islands to refuel.

Some Moths were converted to have coupé cabins, but as payload was reduced by some 11.3 kg (25 lb) only those in the colder climates retained this protection. The production of Gipsy Moths continued until 1934 when a total of 595 had been built at Stag Lane, including two by the students of the Aeronautical Technical School.

D.H.60M Moth
The next major variant was the 'Metal Moth', which was externally similar to the earlier Moth, but had a fabric-covered, welded steel tubular fuselage for greater ruggedness. This added 28.12 kg (62 lb) to the weight, but following an evaluation in Canada on wheel, ski and float undercarriages, a launch order for 50 was received from the RCAF in 1929. A further 90 were assembled in Canada, some with clear view canopies to protect against the extreme cold, and the air forces of China, Australia and Iraq adopted the type. The RAF ordered D.H.60Ms for training and com-

D.H.60M Metal Moth training aircraft (*The Aeroplane*)

One of the last D.H.60G III Moth Majors (*de Havilland*)

munications to Specification 4/29 and 8/30, and over 60 were sold in Britain to flying schools and private owners. The two Royal Moths were shared by the Prince of Wales and the Duke of Gloucester, a prelude to the formation of the King's Flight.

D.H.60G III Moth

The most visually obvious change to the basic Moth was caused by the inversion in 1931 of the Gipsy II engine, to become the Gipsy III. This gave the pilot a very much better view with the cylinders and oil sump under the propeller shaft. The prototype G-ABUI, with a return to a wooden fuselage, was first flown from Stag Lane in March 1932. The third aircraft was fitted with an uprated engine, known initially as the Gipsy IIIa, achieving an average speed of 211.37 km/h (131.34 mph) in the 1932 King's Cup Air Race. This engine was later developed into the Gipsy Major which powered the Tiger Moth, Dragon, Chipmunk and many other light aircraft. The new engine was introduced in the 48th aircraft in February 1934, to become the D.H.60G III Moth Major, although both versions were externally identical. A further 87 were built, production continuing until May 1935, with many going for export.

A number of fuselages were built and fitted with the later Tiger Moth wings and tail to become radio control Queen Bee target drones.

D.H.60T Moth Trainer

The final Moth variation before the step to the Tiger Moth was the Moth Trainer, powered by an upright Gipsy II engine and equipped for flying and operational training. It was fitted with full dual control with provision for a camera gun, a rack for four 9 kg (20 lb) practice bombs, radio and cameras. This additional equipment increased the all-up weight to 825.5 kg (1,820 lb) and new wings were fitted to retain the desirable handling charac-

teristics. Flight trials commenced at Stag Lane in April 1931, the first order coming from the Swedish Air Force for 10 aircraft. The air forces of China, Egypt and Iraq also ordered this version and the largest sale was for 40 to the Government of Brazil.

Data
Variant: D.H.60G Gipsy Moth/Gipsy I inline engine
Power plants: D.H.60 Moth alternatives: one 45 kW (60 hp) ADC Cirrus I, or 56 kW (75 hp) Armstrong Siddeley Genet I, or 63 kW (85 hp) Cirrus II, or 67 kW (90 hp) Cirrus III, or 78 kW (105 hp) Cirrus Hermes I inline engine; D.H.60G Gipsy Moth: one 75 kW (100 hp) D.H. Gipsy I, or 89 kW (120 hp) Gipsy II, or 89 kW (120 hp) Gipsy III inline engine; D.H.60M: one 67 kW (90 hp) Cirrus III, or 75 kW (100 hp) D.H.Gipsy I, or 89 kW (120 hp) Gipsy II inline engine; D.H.60G III: one 89 kW (120 hp) D.H.Gipsy III, or 99 kW (133 hp) Gipsy IIIA, or 97 kW (130 hp) Gipsy Major inline engine; D.H.60T: one 89 kW (120 hp) Gipsy II, or 89 kW (120 hp) Walter Major inline engine
Fuel capacity: 69 ltr (15 Imp gal)
Wing span: 9.14 m (30 ft)
Wing area: 22.57 sq m (243 sq ft)
Length: 7.29 m (23 ft 11 in)
Height: 2.68 m (8 ft 9½ in)
Weight empty: 417 kg (920 lb)
Max t/o weight: 748 kg (1,650 lb)
Max speed: 164 km/h (102 mph)
Ceiling: 4,420 m (14,500 ft)
Range: 515 km (320 miles)
Production Two prototype Cirrus Moths G-EBKT and G-EBKU.
D.H.60: Total 425 built, including both prototypes, one D.H.60X and license production by General Aircraft Co Ltd, Australia (9); Qantas, Australia (3, assembled from D.H. parts); Valton Leutokonetehdas (10) and Veljekset Karhumäki O/Y, Finland (2).
D.H.60G: Total 685, including aircraft built under license by Larkin Aircraft Supply Co Ltd, Australia (32); Aeroplanes Morane-Saulnier, France (40); and The Moth Corporation, USA (18).
D.H.60M: Total 748, including aircraft sub-contracted/built under license by de Havilland Aircraft Pty Ltd, Australia; de Havilland Aircraft of Canada Ltd (36); The Moth Corporation, USA (161); and Haerens Flyvesmaskinefabrik, Norway (10).
D.H.60 III: Moth Major: 134
D.H.60T: Moth Trainer: 64

DE HAVILLAND D.H.61 GIANT MOTH

First flight: December 1927

Type: Six to ten-seat passenger airliner

Notes: Rather surprisingly, the next airliner by de Havillands was still a single-engined aircraft, despite the rejection of the formula by Imperial Airways. The Giant Moth was built to an Australian requirement for an enlarged D.H.50J replacement, and a total of nine were produced mainly for Australia and Canada. Construction was standard de Havilland practice with the passengers in an enclosed cabin in the centre-section, between the biplane wings. As on the D.H.50, the pilot was in an open cockpit halfway down the fuselage, but to improve his view, it was offset to port.

Power for the prototype G-EBTL was from a Jupiter VI engine pending the availability of the Jupiter XI for the production aircraft. The prototype was shipped to Australia and commenced service in 1928. Three more D.H.61s were shipped to Australia, two for Qantas where they were used to carry mail on the last part of the Britain to Australia route, while the other aircraft was used on internal mail flights with the Larkin Aircraft Supply Company.

Two more Giant Moths were fitted with floats at Rochester and delivered to Canada in mid-1928 to carry men and equipment to forest fires. A third was shipped to Canada the following year, where its engine was changed for a Pratt & Whitney Hornet and floats were fitted. It flew in this form in June 1932 and joined the Ontario Provincial Government on forest fire duties.

The two other Giant Moths were initially sold in Britain, one to the *Daily Mail* in August 1928, equipped with typewriters, a darkroom, and carrying a motorcycle for a reporter. It was sold for joy-riding in January 1932 and shipped to New Guinea. The other British aircraft, delivered in May 1929, was used by Sir Alan Cobham's Flying Circus to encourage the establishment of municipal aerodromes. It was later transferred to Imperial Airways for survey flying in Africa, but was written-off in a crash after only two weeks.

Data

Variant: D.H.61 Giant Moth/Jupiter XI F radial engine

Power plant: One 373 kW (500 hp) Bristol Jupiter XI F, or 373 kW (500 hp) A.S. Jaguar VI C or 391 kW (525 hp) Pratt & Whitney Hornet radial engine

Accommodation: Pilot in open cockpit and 6–10 passengers in cabin

Wing span: 15.85 m (52 ft)

Length: 11.89 m (39 ft)

Height: 3.66 m (12 ft)

Weight empty: 1,656 kg (3,650 lb)

Max t/o weight: 3,175 kg (7,000 lb)

Max level speed: 212.4 km/h (132 mph)

Service ceiling: 4,880 m (16,000 ft)

Endurance/range: 1,046 km (650 miles)

Production Nine aircraft: G-EBTL (later G-AUTL); G-CAJT; G-CAPG; G-AUHW *Canberra*; G-AAAN *Geraldine*; G-AUJC *Diane*; G-AUJB *Apollo*; G-AAEV *Youth of Britain*; G-CARD; and CF-OAK.

Sir Alan Cobham's D.H.61 Giant Moth (*de Havilland*)

DE HAVILLAND D.H.65 HOUND

First flight: 17 November 1926

Type: General purpose aircraft
Notes: In 1926 de Havillands decided to produce a private venture general purpose aircraft without the restrictions usually imposed by military requirements. The work on two prototype D.H.65 Hounds was commenced keeping the structure as simple as possible, with the minimum number of parts, and construction was mainly of wood. The D.H.65 was powered by a Lion VIII engine, although any similar power plant could be fitted, and by attention to detail in design and construction a very good performance was achieved.

The prototype was prepared for trials at Martlesham Heath to Specification 12/26 with a Lion XA engine, which changed the designation to D.H.65A. Although it was a two-seater, its performance was noticeably better than the contemporary fighters, but it was not adopted mainly because it was not a metal airframe. Meanwhile, the construction of the second prototype had been abandoned. The first prototype was then flown on a series of speed with load records, covering 100 km with a 1,000 kg load, achieving 261.164 km/h (162.284 mph) and 500 km with the same load at 255.325 km/h (158.656 mph). The aircraft was returned to Martlesham Heath in September 1928, but was withdrawn from use due to deterioration in the wooden fuselage.

A much modified Hound, the D.H.65J, was completed in 1928. The front fuselage was steel tubing, the wing spars duralumin and the interplane struts were steel. Armament for the two crew was a forward-firing Vickers machine gun and a Lewis gun on a low-drag ring mount in the observer's cockpit. Power came from a Jupiter VIIIF, and a load of 200 kg (450 lb) of bombs

D.H.65A Hound, first prototype (*de Havilland*)

could be carried under the wings, or a torpedo between the undercarriage. Following official tests at Martlesham Heath it was selected by the RAAF, but then rejected at the last moment in favour of the Westland Wapiti to standardise with the RAF.

Data
Variant: D.H.65A Hound
Power plant: D.H.65: one 395 kW (530 hp) Napier Lion XIII inline engine; D.H.65A: one 403 kW (540 hp) Lion XA or XI inline engine; D.H.65J: one 388 kW (520 hp) Bristol Jupiter VIIIF radial engine
Accommodation: Pilot and observer/gunner in two open tandem cockpits
Wing span: 13.72 m (45 ft)
Wing area: 42.87 sq m (461.5 sq ft)
Length: 9.45 m (31 ft)
Height: 3.51 m (11 ft 6 in)
Weight empty: 1,352 kg (2,981 lb)
Max t/o weight: 2,238 kg (4,934 lb)
Max level speed: 259 km/h (161 mph)
Service ceiling: 7,800 m (25,600 ft)
Armament: One forward-firing synchronised Vickers machine gun and one ring-mounted Lewis gun for the observer (on D.H.65J).
Production G-EBNJ/J9127 converted to D.H.65A; c/n 332 D.H.65J for RAAF

DE HAVILLAND D.H.66 HERCULES

First flight: 30 September 1926

Type: 7–14-seat passenger airliner
Notes: In 1925, Imperial Airways drew up a specification for a multi-engined aircraft to operate the government-subsidised commercial service from Cairo to Karachi, as part of the Empire route to India, flown every two weeks.

de Havillands proposed a large two-bay biplane design with an enclosed cabin accommodating seven passengers, a wireless operator and up to 13.16 m³ (465 ft³) of freight or mail. The two pilots sat side-by-side in an open cockpit ahead of the wings. Power came from three Jupiter VI engines, and although the wings were fabric-covered wooden structures, the fuselage was fabric-covered tubular steel. The cabin and rear baggage compartments were two large plywood boxes suspended inside.

D.H.66 Hercules airliner (*Flight*)

Despite its complexity and size the D.H.66, named Hercules following a competition in the *Meccano Magazine*, was designed, built, tested and delivered in less than twelve months, with the first of five initial order for Imperial Airways leaving for Cairo on 18 December 1926. Two more had arrived in Cairo before the end of the year, and services commenced on 12 January, later extending to Delhi. To cope with the extra work a further D.H.66 was ordered.

In 1928, West Australian Airways were awarded a contract by the Australian Government to fly subsidised commercial services between Perth and Adelaide. Due to the success of the Hercules in the Middle East, four were ordered in June 1928 for service in Australia. These D.H.66s differed from the earlier aircraft in seating 14 passengers, and the crew had the protection of an enclosed cabin. Canopies were later fitted to the Imperial Airways aircraft. Following acceptance at Stag Lane in March 1929, the four aircraft were shipped to Perth, and reassembled in time for the inaugural service on 2 June 1929.

The first accident was to Imperial Airways G-EBMZ on 6 September 1929 when it stalled and crashed on the approach to landing at Jask in Iran killing a pilot and two passengers. As a replacement, an eleventh and final aircraft was built. Then, in February 1930, G-EBNA force-landed on rough ground at Gaza, Egypt and broke up, fortunately without casualties. As the type was now out of production, West Australian Airways sold their fourth aircraft to Imperial Airways.

In 1931, the Hercules was used experimentally to extend the airmail services between Croydon and Darwin, but the original Hercules was wrecked in a forced landing on 19 April 1931 near Koepang, Indonesia on the inaugural flight. The mail was retrieved by the Australian Captain Charles Kingsford-Smith in the Fokker F.VI-IB/3m monoplane *Southern Cross*, and he also flew the first part of the return journey.

Imperial Airways again approached Australia to make up their fleet strength, the third WAA aircraft being handed over on 18 May 1931. This aircraft was used on a proving flight to South Africa, arriving at Cape Town on 22 December 1931, with regular flights following.

In October 1932, Sir Alan Cobham flew this same aircraft in an air pageant, giving free rides sponsored by the South African newspaper *Cape Times*. One of the remaining two Australian aircraft was flying joy-rides from Maylands Aerodrome, Perth, until sold in New Guinea in 1936 for transport around the gold fields. Both these aircraft were lost during the Second World War, one crashing on 6 February 1941 and the other destroyed by Japanese action in 1942.

Of the remaining six, one D.H.66 was damaged beyond repair during an anti-locust sortie near Salisbury, Southern Rhodesia on 23 November 1935, three were bought by the South African Air Force, and the other two were retired in 1935.

Data
Variant: D.H.66 Hercules
Power plant: Three 313 kW (420 hp) Bristol Jupiter VI radial engines
Accommodation: 7 to 14 passengers in enclosed cabin and two pilots, initially in an open cockpit, later provided with canopy
Wing span: 24.23 m (79 ft 6 in)
Wing area: 143.72 sq m (1,547 sq ft)
Length: 16.92 m (55 ft 6 in)
Height: 5.56 m (18 ft 3 in)
Weight empty: 4,110 kg (9,060 lb)
Max t/o weight: 7,103 kg (15,660 lb)
Max level speed: 206 km/h (128 mph)
Service ceiling: 3,960 m (13,000 ft)
Production Eleven aircraft: G-EBMW *City of Cairo*; G-EBMX *City of Delhi*; G-EBMY *City of Baghdad*; G-EBMZ *City of Jerusalem*; G-EBNA *City of Teheran*; G-AUJO *City of Perth* (later VH-UJO); G-AUJP *City of Adelaide* (later VH-UJP); G-AUJQ (later G-ABMT *City of Cape Town*); G-AUJR (later G-ABCP *City of Jodhpur*); G-AAJH *City of Basra*; and G-AARY *City of Karachi*

DE HAVILLAND D.H.67

First flight: June 1929

Type: Aerial survey aircraft

Notes: The D.H.67 was the first of three military designs to be started by de Havillands, but passed on to the Gloster Aircraft Company for completion and development. It was a scaled-down Hercules powered by two Jupiter VI engines and the rugged metal structure was fabric covered. The aerial survey specification, issued by the Aircraft Operating Company, included provision for a photographer and his equipment to be in an enclosed cabin with a good view and within easy contact of the pilot. Beneath the open tandem cockpit for the pilot and navigator, the photographer had a prone position with floor-mounted cameras.

By November 1927, the design had been revised in a number of ways to become the D.H.67B. Among these changes were side-by-side seats for the pilot and navigator, and the photographer was moved to an open cockpit in the nose, retaining his cabin. To improve the performance the aircraft was to have two Jupiter VIII engines. It was at this design stage that the project was passed to Glosters who made drastic changes, redesigning the aircraft for the alternative carriage of up to eight passengers, as a flying ambulance, or a bomber with an armament of three machine guns. It then became the AS.31 and bore only superficial resemblance to the original aircraft.

Two prototypes were built, powered by a pair of Jupiter XI engines, the first for the Aircraft Operating Company, and the second for the Air Ministry, who used it at Farnborough for wireless experiments until retirement on 17 September 1936. Alan Butler delivered the first aircraft to Cape Town, arriving on 11 April 1930, where its initial task was a survey of the Zambezi Basin, followed by 163,160 sq km (63,000 sq miles) of Northern Rhodesia.

It flew further surveys in Central Africa, achieving 500 hours with great reliability, until being bought by the South African Air Force which operated it on photographic duties until retirement in 1942.

Data
Variant: D.H.67B
Power plant: Two 391 kW (525 hp) Bristol Jupiter XI radial engines
Accommodation: Pilot and navigator side-by-side in open cockpit, photographer in cabin
Wing span: 18.59 m (61 ft)
Wing area: 95.22 sq m (1,025 sq ft)
Length: 14.78 m (48 ft 6 in)
Height: 5.72 m (18 ft 9 in)
Weight empty: 2,546.5 kg (5,614 lb)
Max t/o weight: 3,887 kg (8,570 lb)
Max level speed: 211 km/h (131 mph)
Service ceiling: 7,070 m (23,200 ft)
Endurance/range: 6½ hours/796.6 km (495 miles)
Production (by the Gloster Aircraft Company) G-AADO/250, K2602

Gloster-built AS.31, developed from D.H.67

DE HAVILLAND D.H.71 TIGER MOTH RACER

D.H.71 Tiger Moth Racer served as Gipsy engine test-bed
(*Flight*)

First flight: 24 June 1927

Type: Racer and engine test-bed
Notes: The monoplane D.H.71, named Tiger Moth, bears no similarity with the later illustrious biplane trainer of the same name, but was a significant development aircraft for the famed Gipsy engine, which benefited light aviation before and after the Second World War. In addition to being an engine test-bed, it also demonstrated the efficiency of the monoplane with an inline engine over the existing radial engine powered biplanes.

Two prototypes were constructed in great secrecy for the 1927 King's Cup Air Race, the slim fuselage being plywood-covered, and the wings fabric-covered with wire bracing through the undercarriage. Both racers were entered for the King's Cup, but as the combination of a new airframe and engine created greater risk, the initial flight was powered by a Cirrus II engine. The new Gipsy engine, at the time developing 101 kW (135 hp) was then installed in the first aircraft, but development problems could not be cleared up in time for the race, and the second aircraft participated on its own. However, the weather caused the sensitive aircraft to be unsteady and the pilot was forced to retire, even though an average speed of 267 km/h (166 mph) had been achieved. The 100 km Light Aeroplane Category closed circuit record was broken at 300 km/h (186.47 mph) on 24 August 1927, and five days later an unsuccess-

ful attempt was made on the altitude record, the pilot suffering from the lack of oxygen at over 5,800 m (19,000 ft). The aircraft was still climbing at 305 m (1,000 ft)/min when the pilot was forced to give up.

In 1930, the first aircraft was shipped to Australia, but crashed at take-off on 17 September that year, killing the pilot. The second aircraft was powered by a Cirrus II engine throughout, and was used for airframe development. It was withdrawn from use in 1928, stored first at Stag Lane, and then hung in the roof of the factory at Hatfield, without its engine, in 1933. It was destroyed on 3 October 1940, when the factory was damaged by bombs from a German Ju 88A.

Data
Variant: D.H.71/Cirrus II
Power plant: One 63 kW (85 hp) ΛDC Cirrus II or 101 kW (135 hp) D.H. Gipsy inline engine
Accommodation: One pilot in partially enclosed cabin
Wing span: 6.86 m (22 ft 6 in)
Wing area: 7.11 sq m (76.5 sq ft)
Length: 5.68 m (18 ft 7½ in)
Height: 2.13 m (7 ft)
Weight empty: 280 kg (618 lb)
Max t/o weight: 410.51 kg (905 lb)
Max level speed: 311 km/h (193 mph)
Service ceiling: over 5,800 m (19,000 ft)
Production G-EBQU/D.H. Gipsy (later VH-UNH) and G-EBRV/Cirrus II

DE HAVILLAND D.H.72 CANBERRA

First flight: 28 July 1931

Type: Night bomber

Notes: Designed to Air Ministry Specification B.22/27, the Canberra was another of the trio of military aircraft passed on to the Gloster Aircraft Company for completion. Design and construction of the single prototype was practically completed at Stag Lane, leaving Glosters to complete the engine installation, final assembly and flight testing. The Canberra was a three-engined night bomber, to be powered by 321 kW (430 hp) Jupiter VIII engines to compete with the Boulton and Paul P.32.

The fuselage was of tubular steel construction, built in three main sections, with the 8.5 m (28 ft) front section containing the front gunner's and pilot's cockpits, the radio compartment, fuel tanks and wing attachment. The two portions of rear fuselage contained cockpits for a centre gun position and rear gunner. The six-bay folding wings of this large biplane had main spars of duralumin plate, with duralumin tube ribs. Construction was delayed due to lack of structural strength of the wing under static test. The centre engine was mounted on the top wing centre-section and the other two on the lower wings. The bomb load was to be carried externally under the fuselage and wings.

Engine development continued while the airframe was being built, making progressively more powerful ones available. In June 1930, the unfinished aircraft was moved to Glosters, and finally the day dawned for the first flight, almost four years after design had commenced.

Howard Saint, Gloster's Chief Test Pilot, made the maiden flight. The controllability was so poor he seriously considered abandoning the aircraft, but managed to make a safe landing. Various adjustments to control gearing and ballast followed, but even its delivery flight to Martlesham Heath for official trials was fraught with problems. It took five days to accomplish, arriving after various landings due to bad weather and difficulties with starting the engines. The official trials were soon abandoned and no more was heard of this aircraft.

Data
Variant: D.H.72 Canberra
Power plant: Three 444 kW (595 hp) Bristol Jupiter XFS radial engines
Accommodation: One pilot, three gunners (nose, dorsal and tail) and radio operator
Fuel capacity: 877 ltr (193 Imp gal) main tanks plus 273 ltr (60 Imp gal) gravity tank
Wing span: 28.96 m (95 ft)
Wing area: 179.30 sq m (1,930 sq ft)
Length: 21.03 m (69 ft)
Height: 6.25 m (20 ft 6 in)
Weight empty: 6,139 kg (13,535 lb)
Max t/o weight: 10,333 kg (22,781 lb)
Max level speed: 195 km/h (121 mph)
Service ceiling: 4,570 m (15,000 ft)
Endurance/range: 1,529 km (950 miles)
Armament: Three Lewis machine guns on Scarff rings. Max load of 1,179.4 kg (2,600 lb) bombs
Production One prototype J9184

The sole D.H.72 bomber was completed by Gloster Aircraft *(Hawker Siddeley)*

DE HAVILLAND D.H.75 HAWK MOTH

First flight: 7 December 1928

Type: Light transport and air taxi

Notes: de Havillands first cabin Moth did not prove to be a great success due to it being too large, and initially under powered. The Hawk Moth was a four-seat high-wing monoplane with a tubular metal fuselage structure and wooden wings, all covered with fabric. The power plant was the specially developed D.H. Ghost engine, but its power of 148 kW (198 hp) was so inadequate that the prototype was retired in 1930, less than two years after it first flew.

Only seven more Hawk Moths were built, mainly for Australia or Canada, and six were D.H.75As with increased wing span and chord, powered by A.S. Lynx geared radial engines. The first of these was shipped to Canada in December 1929 as a demonstrator and for trials on ski and float undercarriages. As a result, an order for three was placed, including the demonstrator, but float operations proved unsuccessful in practice, and only wheel and ski undercarriages were used. Even these were not a success as one aircraft was destroyed in 1931 after flying only 18 hours 30 minutes, and the remaining two were withdrawn from use in 1934 after flying infrequently.

Two Hawk Moths went to Australia, the first as a demonstrator, which was badly damaged in a forced landing in Tasmania on 10 January 1935. During the repair, the engine was replaced by a 224 kW (300 hp) Wright Whirlwind J-5 radial and in 1943 a 261 kW (350 hp) A.S. Cheetah IX was installed. Having passed through a number of owners it was finally withdrawn in 1951. The second Australian aircraft flew commercially until it crashed in May 1935.

One other D.H.75A (G-AAUZ) was built and entered in the 1930 King's Cup Air Race by HRH Prince George, gaining seventh place at an average speed of 203.09 km/h (126.2 mph). This aircraft was sold overseas in 1938.

In a further attempt to improve the performance the Hawk Moth was re-engined with a 224 kW (300 hp) Wright Whirlwind R-975 radial in May 1930 to become the D.H.75B. However, further development was abandoned in favour of the Puss Moth.

Data

Variant: D.H.75A Hawk Moth
Power plant: One 179 kW (240 hp) Armstrong Siddeley Lynx VI A radial engine
Accommodation: Four-seat cabin for pilot and passengers
Wing span: 14.33 m (47 ft)
Wing area: 31.03 sq m (334 sq ft)
Length: 8.79 m (28 ft 10 in)
Height: 2.84 m (9 ft 4 in)
Weight empty: 1,080 kg (2,380 lb)
Max t/o weight: 1,656 kg (3,650 lb)
Max level speed: 204 km/h (127 mph)
Service ceiling: 4,420 m (14,500 ft)
Endurance/range: 901 km (560 miles)
Production Eight aircraft: prototype G-EBVV, six D.H.75As, and one D.H.75B

D.H.75A Hawk Moth light transport (*Flight*)

DE HAVILLAND D.H.77

First flight: December 1929

Type: Single-seat low-wing monoplane interceptor

Notes: Air Ministry Specification F.20/27 called for a high-speed fighter capable of intercepting hostile aircraft in the coastal areas, while other parts of the home defence would be by longer-endurance patrol fighters. The interceptor was to operate in daylight against high-performance day bombers, and would normally be held at readiness on the ground, climbing rapidly when hostile aircraft were detected. Although four 0.303-in (7.7 mm) machine guns were specified all the submissions had only two guns. The aircraft was to be light, with short endurance, but high performance.

de Havillands submitted their D.H.77 as a private venture, powered by a new experimental Halford air-cooled 'H' engine. This engine had two parallel crankshafts with four banks of four cylinders, and was called Rapier. The low monoplane wing was braced with streamlined tubular struts, the undercarriage was fixed, and the pilot sat in a high placed open cockpit. Composite construction was used with steel tube in the fuselage and fabric over wood fairings. The wings consisted of a single spruce mainspar with three-ply skin.

In its official trials at Martlesham Heath the D.H.77 performed generally very well proving the greater efficiency of the monoplane layout, and achieving equivalent results to the biplane Hawker Fury using only 60 per cent of the power. The main criticism was of the ailerons, which were heavy and ineffective close to the stall, but the aircraft missed the main competitive trials due to teething troubles with the new engine. The D.H.77 was also unsatisfactory in a spin. No doubt all the problems could easily have been cured, but the Fury biplane had already been chosen.

On completion of the official trials, the D.H.77 became the third and last military aircraft to be transferred to Glosters, where the armament was removed and it was flown on engine development until going to Farnborough in December 1932 for further engine testing. While at Farnborough, a 220 kW (295 hp) Rapier II was installed and a crash guard was fitted over the cockpit. In this form the D.H.77 continued flying at the RAE on engine and spinning trials until disposal in June 1934.

Data
Variant: D.H.77
Power plant: One 224 kW (300 hp) Napier Halford Rapier I (later 220 kW/295 hp Rapier II) H-type engine
Accommodation: Pilot in open cockpit
Fuel capacity: 136 ltr (30 Imp gal)
Wing span: 9.8 m (32 ft 2 in)
Wing area: 15.14 sq m (163 sq ft)
Length: 7.44 m (24 ft 4¾ in)
Height: 2.29 m (7 ft 6 in)
Weight empty: 751 kg (1,655 lb)
Max t/o weight: 1,036 kg (2,285 lb)
Max level speed: 328 km/h (204 mph)
Service ceiling: 7,315 m (24,000 ft)
Armament: Two synchronised Vickers machine guns faired into cither side of the fuselage
Production One prototype J9771

Only one D.H.77 interceptor was built (*de Havilland*)

DE HAVILLAND D.H.80A PUSS MOTH

Jim Mollison's long-range D.H.80A Puss Moth
(*de Havilland*)

First flight: 9 September 1929

Type: Private owner touring aircraft

Notes: Following the success of the basic Moth, many owners began venturing farther afield, highlighting the need for a two to three-seat cabin tourer with room for overnight luggage. The initial attempt at this requirement was the all-wood D.H.80 with ply-covered fuselage and fabric-covered high monoplane wing. This was the first aircraft to feature the inverted Gipsy III engine giving a better view and reduced drag. Despite the good performance of the unnamed prototype it did not enter production, as the more robust metal structure was essential for successful sales and longer life. The new version, known as the D.H.80A Puss Moth, had a welded steel tube fuselage, and the fabric-covered wooden-structured wings folded back to save hangar space. Airbrakes had to be fitted on the undercarriage fairings to increase drag for landing.

The Puss Moth soon became popular with private owners and flying clubs, as well as being used to open up regular passenger and mail services, charter, business flying, survey and military communications. Fry's Chocolate used one for business, Hillman Airways started services with three, and the Iraqi Air Force fitted racks for four 9 kg (20 lb) bombs to their three D.H.80As.

Early in its career there were a number of unexplained fatal accidents to Puss Moths, often in remote areas, which were caused by structural failure of the wings. After a thorough investigation, it was found that a combination of high speed and turbulence could cause wing failure, which was easily cured by adding a strut connecting the forward wing strut with the rear wing root.

Some notable long distance flights were made including the crossing of both the North and South Atlantic. For the first, Jim Mollison flew a specially modified Puss Moth named *The Hearts Content* with a 341 ltr (75 Imp gal) tank in the front part of the cabin and a 191 ltr (42 Imp gal) tank in the rear, giving a range of 5,793 km (3,600 miles), or duration of 33 hours. A suitably long take-off site was found in Ireland, commencing the flight on 18 August 1932 against the prevailing winds to the USA. After landfall, Mollison flew on hoping to reach New York, but had to land in New Brunswick due to shortage of fuel and exhaustion. He had flown 4,184 km (2,600 miles) in an elapsed time of 30 hours and 15 minutes.

Bert Hinkler, the Australian pioneer flew from New York to London via the South Atlantic in a Puss Moth, landing in England on 7 December 1931. He set off again from London on 7 January 1933, to attempt a record-breaking flight to Australia, but crashed in the Apennine Mountains, a victim of wing failure. Another Australian, C. J. Melrose, flew his Puss Moth to Britain for the MacRobertson Air Race leaving Mildenhall on 20 October 1934. Despite the strong competition he gained third place in the handicap section at an average speed of 165.76 km/h (103 mph).

HRH the Prince of Wales was one of many Puss Moth owners, and altogether he owned four over a period of time. A total of 259 Puss Moths were built at Stag Lane, plus a further 25 by de Havillands Canada, 13 of which were for the RCAF. These RCAF aircraft were equipped for blind flying and navigation training. The Puss Moth was replaced on the production lines by the improved Leopard Moth, and a number of the D.H.80As were impressed with many other civilian aircraft for wartime communications duties. A small number survived, and a handful are still airworthy as valued vintage aircraft.

Data
Variant: D.H.80A Puss Moth
Power plant: One 89 kW (120 hp) D.H. Gipsy III
or 97 kW (130 hp) Gipsy Major inline engine
Accommodation: Two- to three-seat cabin
aircraft, including pilot
Fuel capacity: 91 ltr (20 Imp gal)
Wing span: 11.2 m (36 ft 9 in)
Wing area: 20.44 sq m (220 sq ft)
Length: 7.62 m (25 ft)

Height: 2.13 m (7 ft)
Weight empty: 522 kg (1,150 lb)
Max t/o weight: 862 kg (1,900 lb)
Max level speed: 209 km/h (130 mph)
Service ceiling: 5,340 m (17,500 ft)
Endurance/range: 724 km (450 miles)
Production Prototype D.H.80 G-AAHZ, total of
259 D.H.80A Puss Moths built at Stag Lane; 25
D.H.80A Puss Moths assembled in Canada

DE HAVILLAND D.H.81 SWALLOW MOTH

First flight: 21 August 1931

Type: Light trainer and tourer
Notes: With the increase in weight and power from
the original Moth in its most developed form as the
D.H.60T, de Havillands felt that it would be a
worthwhile exercise to return to the original practical light aeroplane formula, started by the Moth.
Using the gathered experience, and more up to
date techniques, the resulting aeroplane was a
low-wing monoplane, with a two-seat open tandem cockpit. Its construction was customary
timber throughout, with ply-covered fuselage and
fabric-covered wings. Power came from a specially
designed Gipsy IV inverted four-cylinder engine
which gave the aircraft a top speed of 188.29 km/h
(117 mph).

Following its initial test flying from Stag Lane,
modifications were made, including thickening the
wings, reducing the fin area, and a sideways hinged
canopy was fitted to give greater protection from

the elements to the occupants. The canopy also
reduced the drag significantly, increasing the top
speed to 208 km/h (129 mph), and in this form the
aircraft became the D.H.81A.

The aircraft was eventually allocated the Class B
markings E-7 in January 1932 but it made its final
flight of 10 minutes on 3 February. It remained
unregistered.

Despite being a promising aircraft, further
development of the D.H.81 was abandoned due to
the effects of the slump, so that efforts could be
concentrated on existing types. However, the principle was later revived as the D.H.94 Moth Minor.

Data
Variant: D.H.81 Swallow Moth
Power plant: One 60 kW (80 hp) D.H. Gipsy IV
inline engine
Accommodation: Two-seat open cockpit in
tandem (later with canopy, as D.H.81A)
Wing span: 10.82 m (35 ft 6 in)
Wing area: 13.84 sq m (149 sq ft)
Length: 7.16 m (23 ft 6 in)
Height: 2.54 m (8 ft 4 in)
Max t/o weight: 603 kg (1,330 lb)
Max level speed: 208 km/h (129 mph)
Production One protoytpe c/n 1992 E-7

Only known picture of D.H.81A Swallow Moth
(*Alec Davis*)

DE HAVILLAND D.H.82 TIGER MOTH

First flight: 26 October 1931

Type: Two-seat basic trainer

Notes: One of the greatest training aircraft of all time, the Tiger Moth evolved directly from the metal tube fuselage D.H.60M Moth, but with the inverted Gipsy III engine for power. The existing layout was unable to comply with the Air Ministry Specification 15/31 due to an inadequate escape route if the occupant of the front cockpit had to abandon the aircraft. Consequently, the centre section struts and fuel tank were moved forward to improve the clearance, and to balance this move, the wings were swept back. All these changes were made on the existing airframe without drawings, and the first eight aircraft were known as D.H.60T Tiger Moth. However, with the introduction of dihedral on the lower wing to improve ground clearance, the D.H.82 was born.

Following its maiden flight from Stag Lane, an initial order for 35 Tiger Moth Mk Is was placed by the RAF to Specification T.23/31 leading to the eventual adoption of the aircraft as the standard RAF trainer. The first was delivered to No. 3 Flying Training School (FTS) in November 1931, while others went to the CFS, and Singapore and Hong Kong where they were fitted with floats.

The Tiger Moth was offered as an all-round trainer, capable not only of teaching flying skills, but also gunnery, bombing, photographic reconnaissance and wireless operation. As a result, a number of overseas air forces placed orders, with license production in Norway and Sweden. Of the total 114 of the initial D.H.82s built at Stag Lane

Prototype D.H.82 Tiger Moth basic trainer
(*via A. J. Jackson*)

only three were for civil use, of which two, including the prototype, were flying in Sir Alan Cobham's Flying Circus.

In 1934 an improved Tiger Moth was produced powered by a Gipsy Major engine and amongst other detailed modifications, featured a smooth plywood fuselage top decking replacing the fabric-covered wooden stringers. In this form it became known as the D.H.82A and 50 were ordered initially by the RAF to Specification T.26/33 as the Tiger Moth Mk II. To adapt the aircraft for instrument training, a blind-flying hood could be pulled over the rear cockpit, and as volume production built up, the manufacture was moved to the new factory under construction at Hatfield. This increased production also allowed de Havillands to satisfy the growing demand from civilian customers at home and overseas, and a number of foreign air forces.

The threat of war increased the training needs, and by August 1939 there were over 40 Reserve Flying Training Schools, all but two equipped with Tiger Moths. In 1938, to supplement the RAFVR Schools, the Civil Air Guard was formed to teach all suitable men and women between the ages of 16

Standard D.H.82A Tiger Moth trainer in RAF service
(*Hawker Siddeley*)

Pilotless D.H.82B Queen Bee catapulted from a warship for AA gunnery training (*Keystone*)

and 60 to fly to provide a pool of pilots. More Tiger Moths were needed for this although the Civil Air Guard was disbanded at the outbreak of war on 3 September 1939, when all civil flying ceased.

One of the early developments of the Tiger Moth was the expendable D.H.82B Queen Bee radio controlled target aircraft to Air Ministry Specification 18/33. This was a combination of the Moth Major wooden fuselage, with all the other components from the Tiger Moth. Most were fitted with floats as they were to be used to train land- and sea-based gunners, with the radio equipment fitted in the rear cockpit, although it could be flown by a pilot in the front cockpit. First manual flight was on 5 January 1935 and radio control development was undertaken at Farnborough beginning June 1935. A total of 320 Queen Bees to Specification 20/35 were built by de Havillands and a further 100 by Scottish Aviation, deliveries ending in July 1944.

Among the overseas production was an initial batch of 25 from de Havilland Canada, the first flying in December 1937, and after 227 had been built, a new D.H.82C version was produced featuring a cockpit canopy, main wheel brakes and a tailwheel instead of the usual skid. Power was increased by fitting a 108 kW (145 hp) Gipsy Major 1C, but when these were in short supply, the American 89 kW (120 hp) Menasco Pirate engine was used.

Following the Dunkirk evacuation various ideas were put forward for arming the Tiger Moth, the most practical being the fitting of racks under the fuselage and wings to carry eight 9 kg (20 lb) or 11.3 kg (25 lb) bombs. 1,500 sets of these racks were manufactured and distributed in case of invasion of Britain by the enemy, which fortunately did not come. Tiger Moths were also pressed into service on coastal duties, like the D.H.6 in the First World War. One U-boat was in fact spotted and later destroyed by the alerted naval forces.

A total of 1,975 Tiger Moths were built at Stag Lane and Hatfield before the move to Morris Motors in 1940, where a further 3,508 were completed by 15 August 1945 when the factory ceased aircraft production. Much re-organisation had to be done to adapt the aircraft to mass production, with some additional drawings, but production rate eventually reached some 40 aircraft per week.

The need for pilots was so great that the Empire Air Training Scheme was started in Canada, South Africa and Rhodesia, while Australia, New Zealand and India also contributed to the massive effort. This allowed training away from the threat of attack and required more Tiger Moths, which were built in the countries concerned to spread the load. By far the greatest training effort was in Canada where 19 flying schools were operated by the RCAF and six by the RAF. Tiger Moths were also used by four wireless schools in Canada.

The Australian and New Zealand de Havilland factories built 1,085 and 345 Tiger Moths respectively for their own use and the Empire Training Scheme. By the time the war came to an end, over 9,000 Tiger Moths had been built, many of which were declared surplus with the reduction in the need for pilot training.

These surplus aircraft formed a cheap basis for the equipment of the reforming civil flying clubs and schools, but many continued in RAF service for elementary training, in the RAFVR Schools

Jackaroo four-seat cabin conversion of Tiger Moth
(*P. J. Birtles*)

and University Air Squadrons. In 1950, the Chipmunk began to replace the venerable Tiger Moth, and in the autumn of 1955 the last RAF Tiger Moths were put up for disposal at Cosford.

Large batches of Tiger Moths were bought by civilian organisations such as Rollasons and Whittemores at Croydon, while more went to Hants and Sussex Aviation. Many of these arrived stacked on trucks and following conversion were sold in Britain and Europe at about £700 each. When the war finished it was possible to buy a Tiger Moth for £5, but it was usually somewhere inaccessible like the Canal Zone, and the cost of return transport was uneconomic, so they were just scrapped. The Tiger Moth was finally retired from military service by the Fleet Air Arm in mid 1972.

In civilian use, one of the most beneficial duties performed by the Tiger Moth was crop spraying, particularly in New Zealand. When used for top dressing a hopper was fitted in the front cockpit, while for insecticide spraying a tank fed underwing pipes. The life of these aircraft was short, not only due to accidents from low flying but also corrosion of the airframe by the chemicals.

The Tiger Moth proved a fairly adaptable aircraft, but one conversion to a four-seat cabin aircraft, known as the Thruxton Jackaroo was not approved by de Havillands. In late 1958, the Wiltshire School of Flying decided to adapt the Tiger Moth, widening the fuselage from 60.96 cm (24 inches to 93.98 cm (37 inches). The first conversion flew from Thruxton on 2 March 1957, only nine months after the go-ahead, but lack of interest resulted in only 26 conversions, including the mock-up and six spares.

The Tiger Moth is now a much sought after vintage aircraft, with many still flying. Just after the war, if a Tiger Moth needed re-covering with fabric, it was cheaper to scrap it and buy another. Now, Tiger Moths are restored from a collection of motley parts to flying trim, and in good condition fetch a high price. With enough in existence, it is even worthwhile making spares to keep the current ones airworthy for probably as long as petrol is available.

Data
Variant: D.H.82A Tiger Moth/Gipsy Major I
Power plant: One 97 kW (130 hp) D.H. Gipsy Major 1, or 108 kW (145 hp) Gipsy Major 1C, or 89 kW (120 hp) Menasco Pirate D.4 inline engine
Accommodation: Two crew in tandem open cockpits
Fuel capacity: 86 ltr (19 Imp gal)
Wing span: 8.94 m (29 ft 4 in)
Wing area: 22.2 sq m (239 sq ft)
Length: 7.29 ft (23 ft 11 in)
Height: 2.66 m (8 ft 9½ in)
Weight empty: 506 kg (1,115 lb)
Max t/o weight: 828 kg (1,825 lb)
Max level speed: 167.37 km/h (104 mph)
Service ceiling: 4,270 m (14,000 ft)
Endurance/range: 483 km (300 miles)
Production D.H.82: Total of 134: de Havilland/UK (114); Haerens Flyvemaskinefabric, Norway (17); and AB Svenska, Sweden (3).
D.H.82A: Total of 8,706: de Havilland/UK (1,849); Morris Motors Ltd/Cowley (3,509); de Havilland Aircraft Canada Ltd (1,747); de Havilland Aircraft New Zealand Ltd (345); de Havilland Aircraft Australia Ltd (1,125); Harens Flyvemaskinefabric, Norway (20); AB Svenska, Sweden (20); and OGMA, Portugal (91).
D.H.82B: Total of 420: de Havilland/UK (320); and Scottish Aviation Ltd/Glasgow (100)

DE HAVILLAND D.H.83 FOX MOTH

First flight: 29 January 1932

Type: Light airliner and air taxi

Notes: The Fox Moth was designed in 1932 to fulfil an urgent need for a light commercial transport capable of profitable operations without a subsidy. To reduce initial costs, Tiger Moth wings and a combination of Puss Moth and Gipsy Moth tail were attached to a new plywood-covered fuselage which carried up to four passengers in an enclosed cabin in the centre-section. The pilot was in an open cockpit above and behind the cabin. Power came initially from a Gipsy III engine, and the wings could be folded.

Although originally intended as a family tourer, the Fox Moth could be used as an air ambulance and also for photographic survey, air freighter with loads up to 272 kg (600 lb), air taxi, business aircraft, or joy-riding.

The prototype was shipped to Canada after its early flight trials, and was evaluated on floats and skis. A total of 98 Fox Moths were produced at Stag Lane, and an early sporting success was when Wally Hope won the 1932 King's Cup Air Race at an average speed of 200 km/h (124.25 mph). HRH Prince of Wales also owned a Fox Moth for a short while and many others initiated domestic routes in Britain.

Fox Moths from British production helped to open up local scheduled services in India and Burma, while others were used by the air forces of Australia and Brazil.

Canada was the most important overseas market, where the aircraft was ideal for bush flying. After the Second World War there was such a shortage of suitable aircraft that de Havilland Canada put the Fox Moth back into production as the D.H.83C, fitted a clear-view canopy for the pilot and an enlarged loading door. A total of 52 were built in Canada from 1946 powered by a Gipsy Major 1C engine, giving much useful service to the economy and opening up the pioneer air services.

Data

Variant: D.H.83 Fox Moth
Power plant: One 97 kW (130 hp) D.H. Gipsy Major inline engine (D.H.83C: one 108 kW/145 hp Gipsy Major 1C)
Accommodation: Pilot in open cockpit and four passengers in a cabin
Fuel capacity: 114 ltr (25 Imp gal)
Wing span: 9.41 m (30 ft 10⅝ in)
Wing area: 24.29 sq m (261.5 sq ft)
Length: 7.85 m (25 ft 9 in)
Height: 2.56 m (8 ft 4¾ in)
Weight empty: 499 kg (1,100 lb)
Max t/o weight: 939 kg (2,070 lb)
Max level speed: 198 km/h (123 mph)
Service ceiling: 3,990 m (13,100 ft)
Endurance/range: 668 km (415 miles)
Production Total of 154: prototype G-ABUO and 97 production aircraft at de Havilland/Stag Lane; de Havilland Canada Ltd (54); and de Havilland Australia Ltd (2).

The D.H.83 Fox Moth was a popular aircraft for joy-riding (*P. J. Birtles*)

DE HAVILLAND D.H.84 DRAGON

First flight: 24 November 1932

Type: Six to eight passenger local service airliner
Notes: The Dragon was an equal span two-bay biplane with twin Gipsy Major 1 engines and fixed undercarriage, designed to fulfil the requirements of local airlines and military patrol. Hillman Airways of Romford were the first to start commercial services when their inaugural flight was made to Paris on 1 April 1933, and so successful was this service that it was able to profit and expand despite competition from the subsidised national airlines.

The military D.H.84M could carry sixteen 9 kg (20 lb) bombs on external racks, two machine guns in the nose and a dorsal Scarff ring-mounted Lewis gun. To balance this extra load, the fin area was increased by the addition of a curved dorsal portion. The first of eight for the Iraqi Air Force left Hatfield on 13 May 1933, and other military orders came from Denmark (five delivered in March 1934) and Portugal (three delivered in 1937).

Not only were British companies using Dragons, but a number of major international airlines also initiated operations with this aircraft. Misrair of Egypt, now Egyptair, is one example, commencing operations in July 1933; and Aer Lingus commenced services with a Dragon on 27 May 1936.

Jim and Amy Mollison had a Dragon modified to attempt to beat the 8,544 km (5,309 miles) long-distance record, flying from the east coast of Canada to Baghdad. The three extra tanks in the cabin increased the weight to 3,326.7 kg (7,334 lb), giving an estimated range of 10,500 km (6,525 miles). To arrive at their starting point, they had first to fly the Atlantic from Britain to North America against the prevailing winds. On the first attempted take-off from Croydon the undercarriage collapsed due to the extra weight, but after repairs a more successful departure was made from Pendine Sands in South Wales. However, the aircraft was wrecked on landing at Bridgeport, Conn. in the USA injuring both the crew. Fortunately, a replacement sponsored by Lord Wakefield was shipped out, but the attempt was finally abandoned when the aircraft refused to take off at the start of the flight. A second attempt by another crew in the same aircraft also failed to break the record, but did manage to cross the Atlantic.

In September 1933, the Dragon Mk II was introduced on the production line, the main external differences being the replacement of the cabin perspex by individually framed windows. With the cancellation of the Stag Lane airfield license on 5 January 1934, all flying ceased and Dragon production was moved to Hatfield.

A Dragon Mk II was sold in Canada in February 1935, and like many aircraft before, was fitted with floats in the summer and skis in the winter. In Australia, a Dragon joined the Royal Flying Doctor Service in 1940, whilst many others were used on ambulance duties in Ethiopia and photographic survey in Australia. In addition to 115 Dragons being built in Britain when the production finished in May 1937, a further 87 were completed by de Havilland Australia as urgently needed radio and navigation trainers, the first flying on 29 September 1942. Now few of these aircraft remain, but one is preserved by the Science Museum at Wroughton.

Data
Variant: D.H.84 Dragon Mk II
Power plant: Two 97 kW (130 hp) D.H. Gipsy Major 1 inline engines
Accommodation: Pilot and six to eight passengers in a cabin

Fuel capacity: 273 ltr (60 Imp gal)
Wing span: 14.43 m (47 ft 4 in)
Wing area: 34.93 sq m (376 sq ft)
Length: 10.52 m (34 ft 6 in)
Height: 3.07 m (10 ft 1 in)
Weight empty: 1,060 kg (2,336 lb)
Max t/o weight: 2,041 kg (4,500 lb)

Max level speed: 216 km/h (134 mph)
Service ceiling: 4,420 m (14,500 ft)
Endurance/range: 877 km (545 miles)
Production Total of 202: prototype G-ACAN; Dragon Mk I: de Havilland/UK (61); Dragon Mk II: de Havilland/UK (53) and de Havilland Australia (73)

DE HAVILLAND D.H.85 LEOPARD MOTH

First flight: 27 May 1933

Type: Cabin touring aircraft
Notes: The Leopard Moth developed the ideas of the Puss Moth by providing more power, improving the passenger accommodation by widening the fuselage so that two persons could sit side-by-side, and saving weight by returning to a plywood-covered wood fuselage. The rearward-folding wings were tapered to reduce drag.

The early flight testing was so promising that three Leopard Moths were entered in the 1933 King's Cup Air Race and de Havilland himself was the winner at an average speed of 224.5 km/h (139.51 mph) over the 1,294 km (804 miles) course, gaining good publicity for the aircraft. A total of 132 Leopard Moths were built during its three years in production, selling in Britain and overseas, with deliveries commencing in 1933. When Stag Lane closed in January 1934, production was moved to Hatfield.

As well as being popular for private flying, other Leopard Moths were used for business flying, charter and air taxi. Like other de Havilland aircraft, Leopard Moths also made a number of epic long distance flights, collecting a few records in the process. One of the most significant of these flights was by Bernard Rubin and Ken Waller in spring 1934 to survey the route to Australia for the Mac-Robertson Air Race. Waller was to gain valuable experience for his attempt in the Comet Racer, and the record for the round trip was broken in an elapsed time of eight days and twelve hours. Redesignated D.H.85A, the Leopard Moth tested the Gipsy Six R engine and propellers for the Comet Racer.

Of the 71 Leopard Moths sold in Britain 44 were impressed at the outbreak of war for communications duties, as were many of the Commonwealth aircraft.

Using a collection of spare parts, a final Leopard Moth was built by Peter Franklin at White Waltham, England, making its first flight on 8 August 1963.

Data
Variant: D.H.85 Leopard Moth
Power plant: One 97 kW (130 hp) D.H. Gipsy Major inline engine
Accommodation: Pilot and two passengers in a cabin
Fuel capacity: 160 ltr (35 Imp gal)
Wing span: 11.43 m (37 ft 6 in)
Wing area: 19.14 sq m (206 sq ft)
Length: 7.47 m (24 ft 6 in)
Height: 2.67 m (8 ft 9 in)
Weight empty: 624 kg (1,375 lb)
Max t/o weight: 1,009 kg (2,225 lb)
Max level speed: 228 km/h (141.5 mph)
Service ceiling: 6,550 m (21,500 ft)
Endurance/range: 1,151 km (715 miles)
Production Prototype G-ACHD plus 131 production aircraft built at Stag Lane and Hatfield to 1937. G-APKH built at White Waltham 1963.

A small number of D.H.85 Leopard Moths remain as privately owned vintage aircraft (*P. J. Birtles*)

DE HAVILLAND D.H.86

D.H.86B SU-ABV was delivered to Misr Airwork in December 1936 (*Hawker Siddeley*)

First flight: 14 January 1934

Type: 10-passenger feeder-liner
Notes: de Havilland's first four-engined airliner, the D.H.86, was built to a Qantas specification issued on 23 September 1933, to cover the Singapore to Brisbane sector of the England to Australia air route. The Gipsy Six engine was specially developed as a six-cylinder version of the Gipsy Major, four of which provided the required safety over the inhospitable terrain. Construction was traditional de Havilland practice of wood with fabric covering. The biplane wings were high aspect ratio with all four engines mounted on the lower mainplanes, and the aircraft featured a fixed undercarriage.

Following the maiden flight from Stag Lane, concentrated flight trials were conducted at Martlesham Heath. The prototype and first two production aircraft were single pilot operation, but the Qantas requirement called for the security of two crew, which resulted in a wider nose being fitted before delivery to Australia on 13 October 1934 of the first of six aircraft. Delays to service entry were caused by two unexplained accidents in October and November 1934, resulting in some precautionary modifications. However, international flights commenced on 25 February 1935 from Brisbane, arriving at Singapore three days later. The Qantas D.H.86s continued to operate successfully until 1941 when they were impressed into RAAF service for ambulance duties.

Due to the simple efficiency of the design, a number of other airlines in Britain, Egypt and New Zealand found the aircraft economical to operate.

The improved D.H.86A was adopted by Imperial Airways with an order for six for their European and Empire routes, services commencing in February 1936.

To improve lateral control, auxiliary fins were fitted to the tailplane changing the designation to D.H.86B. All the surviving D.H.86As were modified to this standard, and a further 10 were built bringing production to 62 aircraft.

A few D.H.86Bs survived war service on communications and aircrew training duties, but the last D.H.86 was destroyed while landing at Madrid on 21 September 1958.

Data
Variant: D.H.86B
Power plant: Four 140 kW (200 hp) D.H. Gipsy Six inline engines
Accommodation: Two crew and 10 passengers in an enclosed cabin
Fuel capacity: 528 ltr (116 Imp gal); oil 55 ltr (12 Imp gal)
Wing span: 19.66 m (64 ft 6 in)
Wing area: 59.55 sq m (641 sq ft)
Length: 14.05 m (46 ft 1 in)
Height: 3.96 m (13 ft)
Weight empty: 2,943 kg (6,489 lb)
Max t/o weight: 4,649 kg (10,250 lb)
Max level speed: 267 km/h (166 mph)
Service ceiling: 5,300 m (17,400 ft)
Endurance/range: 1,287 km (800 miles)
Production Total of 62: 4 single-pilot D.H.86, 28 two-pilot D.H.86, 20 D.H.86As, 10 D.H.86Bs

DE HAVILLAND D.H.87 HORNET MOTH

First flight: 9 May 1934

Type: Two-seat cabin training aircraft
Notes: The Hornet Moth was unusual as a training aircraft, not only because it had the comfort of an enclosed cabin, but also the then unfamiliar side-by-side seating giving improved view and communications. With provision for luggage behind the crew, the aircraft also made a useful tourer. The front section of the aircraft consisted of a welded square section steel tube structure, while the remainder was the traditional wood, with overall fabric covering.

The Hornet Moth was the first new prototype to make its maiden flight from the new airfield at Hatfield, flown by Geoffrey de Havilland himself. The prototype had rounded wing-tips, but two further prototypes and initial production aircraft were built with tapered wings of increased span. In practice, these D.H.87As were found unsuitable for any but the most experienced pilot and were hardly ideal trainers. Rectangular wings were then fitted to most of the early batch and all subsequent production, becoming D.H.87Bs. Production continued at Hatfield until May 1938 when a total of 165 had been completed.

de Havilland Canada adapted one aircraft to operate from water and four were adapted at Felixstowe in Britain as seaplane trainers in 1938 by fitting floats. They later reverted to wheel undercarriages, and two still survive in private ownership.

Many of the Hornets were impressed for wartime communications and calibration of early radar installations. At least 24 survived to return to the postwar flying clubs, half of which are still airworthy in Britain. A surprise winner of the 1968 King's Cup Air Race was Hornet Moth

G-ADKM flown by F. R. E. Hayter at an average speed of 194.7 km/h (121 mph).

Data
Variant: D.H.87B Hornet Moth
Power plant: One 97 kW (130 hp) D.H. Gipsy Major inline engine
Accommodation: Two crew side-by-side in a cabin
Fuel capacity: 160 ltr (35 Imp gal); oil 12 ltr (2.6 Imp gal)
Wing span: 9.73 m (31 ft 11 in)
Wing area: 22.71 sq m (244.5 sq ft)
Length: 7.61 m (24 ft 11½ in)
Height: 2 m (6 ft 7 in)
Weight empty: 563 kg (1,241 lb)
Max t/o weight: 885 kg (1,950 lb)
Max level speed: 200 km/h (124 mph)
Service ceiling: 4,511 m (14,800 ft)
Endurance/range: 998 km (620 miles)
Production Prototype G-ACTA; 2 prototype D.H.87As plus 27 production aircraft (many converted to D.H.87B standard); 135 D.H.87Bs

Four D.H.87B Hornet Moths were fitted with floats for training at Felixstowe (*Hawker Siddeley*)

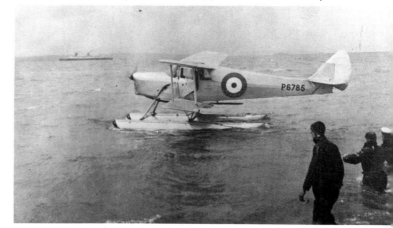

DE HAVILLAND D.H.88 COMET RACER

First flight: 8 September 1934

Type: Long-range racing aircraft
Notes: Worldwide interest was generated in the Melbourne Centenary Air Race in 1934, to be held between London and Melbourne for the

MacRobertson Trophy, with prizes amounting to £15,000 offered by Sir MacPherson Robertson. From the early stages it appeared that the Americans would easily win, while Britain had nothing in existence with the speed and range to have any hope of success. However, not to be beaten, de Havillands decided in January 1934, with only ten months to go, to offer a suitable aircraft if sufficient orders were obtained by the end of February. A nominal price of £5,000 was set for each aircraft and a speed of 322 km/h (200 mph) was guaranteed.

Three orders were received from Jim and Amy Mollison, the racing motorist Bernard Rubin, and A. O. Edwards, Managing Director of the Grosvenor House Hotel, allowing the start of an intense design and construction programme of an all-wood, low wing, twin-engined aircraft of exceptional aerodynamic cleanliness. Among the new features in British aircraft was a retractable undercarriage, variable-pitch propellers and flaps, in addition to the stressed wood skin structure, later to be invaluable in the construction of the Mosquito. Although the Comet was designed for the race, it had also to comply with international standards and therefore hold a current certificate of airworthiness.

The race start was from Mildenhall in Suffolk on 20 October 1934, flown in two sections. One was the fastest time with five compulsory stops, and the other a handicap section based on a combination of speed and payload. There were twenty starters, including the three Comet Racers, flown by Jim and Amy Mollison, Owen Cathcart-Jones and Ken Waller, and C. W. A. Scott and Tom Campbell Black. Other aircraft included a Douglas DC-2 with a full load of passengers entered by KLM, while other de Havilland aircraft entered the handicap section.

Early in the race the Mollisons took the lead, but were forced to retire with engine trouble. They were soon overtaken by Scott and Black in the Comet Racer sponsored by the Grosvenor House Hotel, who gained first place, completing the 18,840 km (11,700 miles) in an elapsed time of 70 hours 54 minutes and 18 seconds at an average speed of 257.5 km/h (160 mph). The Dutch-flown DC-2 came second, gaining the prize in the handicap section. The remaining Comet Racer flown by Cathcart-Jones and Waller gained fourth place in the speed section, made a rapid turn-round and flew back to England with newsreel film of the race finish.

The Mollisons' Comet Racer *Black Magic* was sold to Portugal for experimental high-speed long-range air mail services, and soon after Jones and Waller's aircraft went to France on similar duties. The victorious Comet Racer, G-ACSS, continued to break long-distance records, including round trips from England to Cape Town and New Zealand. It was also used experimentally by the Air Ministry.

Two further Comet Racers were built, one for the French Government joining the earlier aircraft to expand the experimental mail services, but both French aircraft were broken up at Istres during the war under German instructions. The fifth Comet Racer, G-ADEF, was built purely as a record breaker, but its life was short, as it had to be abandoned by the crew over Sudan on 22 September 1935 during an attempt to fly to Cape Town.

Fortunately G-ACSS, the winning aircraft, still survives and is being restored to flying condition by the Shuttleworth Trust assisted by many other organisations.

Data
Variant: D.H.88 Comet Racer
Power plant: Two 172 kW (230 hp) D.H. Gipsy Six R inline engines
Accommodation: Two crew in tandem under a canopy
Fuel capacity: 1,173 ltr (258 Imp gal)
Wing span: 13.4 m (44 ft)
Wing area: 19.74 sq m (212.5 sq ft)
Length: 8.84 m (29 ft)
Height: 2.74 m (9 ft)
Weight empty: 1,329 kg (2,930 lb)
Max t/o weight: 2,517.5 kg (5,550 lb)
Max level speed: 362 km/h (225 mph)
Service ceiling: 6,400 m (21,000 ft)
Endurance/range: 4,747 km (2,950 miles)
Production Total of five aircraft: G-ACSP *Black Magic* (later CS-AAJ *Salazar*); G-ACSR (later F-ANPY); G-ACSS *Grosvenor House* (later briefly *The Burberry*)/K5084/G-ACSS; F-ANPZ; and G-ADEF *Boomerang*

Second D.H.88 Comet Racer on a test flight at Hatfield (*Hawker Siddeley*)

DE HAVILLAND D.H.89 DRAGON RAPIDE

A number of the D.H.89A Dragon Rapides were used on wartime domestic routes (*Hawker Siddeley*)

First flight: 17 April 1934

Type: Five-seat local service airliner

Notes: The Dragon Rapide was a scaled down twin-engined version of the D.H.86 to replace the Dragons. It was powered by two Gipsy Six engines and construction was traditional de Havilland practice. The launch customer, as with the Dragon, was Hillman Airways, followed by a number of other local service airlines, long since merged into larger organisations.

A New Zealand registered example (ZK-ACO) was fitted with extra fuel tanks to extend its range by 1,609 km (1,000 miles) for the MacRobertson Air Race. It gained fifth place in the speed section, and sixth in the handicap, with a flying time of 106 hours 54 minutes and 28 seconds.

Exports commenced to the Middle East at the end of 1934, and an early military sale was to Australia. The military Rapide, known as the D.H.89M, lost out to the Avro Anson for coastal reconnaissance duties, but the work of arming it with defensive guns and bomb racks was not in vain as orders came from Spain, Iran and Lithuania for this version.

Among the earlier overseas civil sales was the aircraft purchased by the New Zealand Melbourne Centenary Air Race Committee, and many more were to be sold worldwide to airlines in developing countries in remote areas. Sales to Canada included the traditional adaption to wheel, ski or float undercarriages, a dorsal fin being fitted to balance the floats.

In 1935 and 1936 a number of improvements were introduced, including a landing light in the nose, cabin heating and flaps, which resulted in some increase in weight. This version became the D.H.89A, and some of these modifications were retrofitted to earlier aircraft.

Two significant sales were made in 1935, one to the King's Flight and the other to the RAF as a VIP transport with No. 24 Squadron at Hendon.

Further significant RAF orders were placed in 1938 for transport, wireless and navigation training, the military version eventually being named the Dominie.

With the outbreak of war, all transport aircraft came under the control of the Government, either on military communications, or operated necessary internal services under the Associated Airways Joint Committee, still carrying their civil registration. Impressment did not provide sufficient aircraft and production continued at Hatfield on the D.H.89B Dominie Mk 1 navigation and W/T trainer, and the Mk 2 communications aircraft. These were ordered by the RAF and Fleet Air Arm, production being moved to Brush Coachworks at Loughborough in 1942, to make space for Mosquitoes.

When the war ended, many of the Dominies were restored to civilian use by the de Havilland Repair Unit at Witney near Oxford. These aircraft were used to re-commence local air services, the tasks eventually being absorbed by British European Airways. The Rapides were particularly useful on the routes around the Channel Islands, Scilly Isles, Isle of Man, and the Scottish Highlands and Islands. In Scotland, they provided a valuable service on medical duties, helping sick and injured people in remote areas.

A small number of Rapides were used for business purposes, an example being Fox's Glacier Mints, and others were operated on air taxi and charter work. In its later life, the Rapides earned their keep on joy-riding and as mounts for parachute jumping.

In early postwar years, an attempt was made to introduce Mark numbers to differentiate between the versions. The surviving prewar examples were Mk 1s, and the civil conversions were Mk 2 and Mk 3 carrying respectively two crew and six passengers, or one pilot and eight passengers. The Mk 4 was powered by Gipsy Queen Mk 2 engines giving an improved all round performance. The sole Mk 5 had variable-pitch propellers, and the Mk 6 had improved airways radio and navigation equipment.

A few Rapides now survive preserved in flying condition by enthusiasts or shut away in museums, and at least one is still being used for joy-riding to give people an experience of the past.

Data
Variant: D.H.89A Dragon Rapide
Power plant: Two 149 kW (200 hp) D.H. Gipsy Queen inline engines
Accommodation: One or two crew and up to eight passengers in an enclosed cabin
Fuel capacity: 364 ltr (80 Imp gal)
Wing span: 14.6 m (48 ft)

Wing area: 31.2 sq m (336 sq ft)
Length: 10.5 m (34 ft 6 in)
Height: 3.12 m (10 ft 3 in)
Weight empty: 1,486 kg (3,276 lb)
Max t/o weight: 2,495 kg (5,500 lb)
Max level speed: 252.7 km/h (157 mph)
Service ceiling: 5,940 m (19,500 ft)
Endurance/range: 925 km (578 miles)
Production Total of 730:
Dragon Rapide: de Havilland/Hatfield (206);
Dominie: de Havilland/Hatfield (186); Brush Coachworks Ltd/Loughborough (336; 10 cancelled);
2 Witney rebuilds from spares (G-AJGS and G-AKJS), and many conversions

DE HAVILLAND D.H.90 DRAGONFLY

First flight: 12 August 1935

Type: Five-seat executive aircraft
Notes: The Dragonfly was probably the first custom-built business aircraft, with accommodation for five including the pilot in an enclosed cabin. It looked generally similar to the Rapide, but the fuselage consisted of a stressed monocoque shell of pre-formed ply stiffened with spruce stringers, as developed with the Comet Racer. The tapered wings were slightly swept back with a deep centre section, eliminating wire bracing in the inner bay.

As well as being ideal as a business communications aircraft, the D.H.90 was also suited to pilot training, photographic survey and casualty evacuation. For the latter duties, a special door could be installed on the starboard side of the nose for stowing a stretcher.

The Gipsy Major II-powered production version was designated the D.H.90A and the high price of the aircraft because of the new method of construction largely restricted sales to business flying, charter or pilot training. A few were sold in 1936–37 to wealthy industrial business owners and a number were purchased by airlines for charter and crew training. In government service they were used for pilot training by the air forces of Denmark and Sweden. Four were acquired by the Mounties for aerial customs surveillance along the coastline of Nova Scotia, all being converted to floatplanes by de Havilland Canada.

After the outbreak of hostilities in 1939 a number of Dragonflies were impressed for military service in Britain, Canada and Australia, but few survived the war due to difficulties with repairing the fuselage structure.

As far as it is known, only two Dragonflies are still extant, one which was sold to the USA in 1964 and appears to have vanished, and the other which was sold to the USA in 1983.

D.H.90 Dragonfly VP-KCA was used on ambulance duties *(Hawker Siddeley)*

Data
Variant: D.H.90A Dragonfly
Power plant: Two 108 kW (145 hp) D.H. Gipsy
Major II inline engines
Accommodation: One pilot and four passengers in
an enclosed cabin
Fuel capacity: 386 ltr (85 Imp gal)
Wing span: 13.1 m (43 ft)
Wing area: 23.78 sq m (256 sq ft)

Length: 9.65 m (31 ft 8 in)
Height: 2.8 m (9 ft 2 in)
Weight empty: 1,128 kg (2,487 lb)
Max t/o weight: 1,814 kg (4,000 lb)
Max level speed: 233 km/h (145 mph)
Service ceiling: 4,880 m (16,000 ft)
Endurance/range: 1,424 km (885 miles)
Production Total of 67: one prototype G-ADNA
plus 66 Hatfield-built production aircraft

DE HAVILLAND D.H.91 ALBATROSS

First flight: 20 May 1937

Type: Long-range airliner
Notes: The significance of the result of the Mac-Robertson Air Race was not lost on Imperial Airways. Although the specially produced Comet Racer was the overall winner, the DC-2 airliner was not far behind, and would therefore be a very competitive transport aircraft in the future. Using much of the Comet Racer experience, de Havillands proposed a four-engined monoplane airliner featuring stressed skin monocoque structure and capable of flying at over 322 km/h (200 mph). It was accepted by the Air Ministry, who placed an order for two experimental transatlantic mail planes to Specification 36/35 in January 1936.

The aircraft was a very graceful design, with great attention to detail, giving a higher speed for less power than had previously been possible with the same payload capability.

The wooden monocoque fuselage structure consisted of inner and outer layers of pre-formed ply, with a stabilising balsawood sandwich in between. The one-piece wooden wing consisted of a central box spar structure with a double layer stressed skin ply covering, giving a very smooth finish. Similar

construction was later to be used on the Mosquito. Power came from four Gipsy 12 engines faired smoothly into the wings giving minimum drag.

During the development flying, it was found necessary to change the original inset fins for more elegant cantilever units. Problems were also experienced with the undercarriage, resulting in a wheels-up landing in March 1938, but thanks to the strength of the wooden structure damage was not serious. During overload tests at Hatfield in autumn 1938, the aircraft was carrying 1,361 kg (3,000 lb) over normal landing weight, and on the third landing the rear door sprung open at low speed and the fuselage broke in half. Little other damage occurred, and repairs and strengthening had been made within two weeks, with an increase in weight of only 5.67 kg (12.5 lb).

Following the two experimental mail carriers, Imperial Airways ordered five Albatross airliners for use on the Empire routes. The cabin was divided into three saloons to accommodate 23 passengers. For long night-time journeys, the cabin could be converted to 12 sleeping berths.

The two Air Ministry aircraft were never to undertake their long-range experimental mail flights, being initially allocated to crew training

D.H.91 Albatross was one of de Havilland's most graceful designs

and later to join the Imperial Airways fleet. Services commenced from London to Paris in November 1938, and extended to Alexandria in time for Christmas. The performance of the aircraft was so good that in the first ten weeks of operation it set the fastest times on the routes from Croydon to Paris, Zürich and Brussels.

The outbreak of the Second World War put an end to further prospects of sales and the two mail carriers were allocated to No. 271 Squadron for courier flights between Britain and Iceland. Both aircraft were destroyed in landing accidents in Iceland within 18 months.

Meanwhile, the five Imperial Airways aircraft were put into service between Britain and Alexandria, and also on the London to Paris routes, with Lisbon added later.

Two of the Albatross courier aircraft were lost in non-fatal accidents, one due to structural failure, and a third was sabotaged and destroyed by fire at Bristol. As a result of the structural failure, the remaining two aircraft were found to be in poor condition and they were scrapped in the autumn of 1943.

Data
Variant: D.H.91 Albatross
Power plant: Four 391 kW (525 hp) D.H. Gipsy Twelve I inline engines
Accommodation: Four crew and up to 23 passengers in an enclosed cabin
Fuel capacity: 6,000 ltr (1,320 Imp gal)
Wing span: 31.9 m (104 ft 8 in)
Wing area: 100 sq m (1,078 sq ft)
Length: 21.3 m (70 ft)
Height: 6.14 m (20 ft 2 in)
Weight empty: 9,207 kg (20,298 lb)
Max t/o weight: 13,381 kg (29,500 lb)
Max level speed: 362 km/h (225 mph)
Service ceiling: 5,460 m (17,900 ft)
Endurance/range: 1,674 km (1,040 miles)
Production Total of seven: two mail carriers (G-AEVV *Faraday* and G-AEVW *Franklin*) and five airliners (G-AFDI *Frobisher*, G-AFDJ *Falcon*, G-AFDK *Fortuna*, G-AFDL *Finegal*, and G-AFDM *Fiona*)

DE HAVILLAND D.H.92 DOLPHIN

First flight: 9 September 1936

Type: Experimental six-seat light passenger transport
Notes: In 1936 de Havillands decided to develop a new local service airliner, using the combined experience of the Rapide, D.H.86 and Dragonfly. A single prototype known as the D.H.92 Dolphin was built in the Experimental Shop at Hatfield, using pre-formed ply monocoque structure. Two crew sat side-by-side as in the D.H.86 and a luggage locker was located behind a hinged nose. The passenger cabin had a toilet compartment and behind this was a further luggage compartment. Wings had a similar sweepback to the Dragonfly, the deep centre-section of the lower wing supporting the engines, and the undercarriage retracting into the engine nacelles. Flaps were fitted under each stub wing. The strength of the centre-section avoided the use of bracing wires, making passenger access easier, and reducing drag.

Before the retractable undercarriage was fitted, trial installations were made with faired and unfaired fixed undercarriage. Despite its similarity

No photographs exist showing a complete view of D.H.92 Dolphin (*de Havilland*)

to earlier aircraft, the majority of the main assemblies were of entirely new design.

The civil registration G-AEMX was allocated but not applied, as its brief flight trials were carried out with undercoat and Class B markings E-3. The aircraft was found to be structurally overweight, and as the factory was fully employed on the Albatross development and large scale production of Tiger Moths, staff were not available for solving the weight problems. The project was therefore abandoned and the prototype scrapped in October 1936.

For many years it was thought that no photographs of this aircraft were taken, but after some investigations in early 1976 some views of the undercarriage installation were located at Hatfield. No overall view of the aircraft appears to exist.

Data
Variant: D.H.92 Dolphin
Power plant: Two 151 kW (204 hp) D.H. Gipsy Six II inline engines
Accommodation: Two crew and six passengers in an enclosed cabin
Wing span: 15.4 m (50 ft 6 in)
Wing area: 36.5 sq m (393 sq ft)
Length: 11 m (36 ft)
Max t/o weight: 2,994 kg (6,600 lb)
Max level speed: 259 km/h (161 mph)
Production One prototype E-3/G-AEMX.

DE HAVILLAND D.H.93 DON

First flight: 18 June 1937

Type: Aircrew trainer and communications aircraft
Notes: The Don was produced to Air Ministry Specification T.6/36 for a combined trainer and communications aircraft. The aircraft was built using the stressed monocoque ply structure but the 391 kW (525 hp) Gipsy King I engine barely possessed sufficient power to lift the overloaded aircraft off the ground. Accommodation was provided for two pilots sitting side-by-side, with adequate cabin space for a radio trainee, and a rear turret for gunnery practice. The specification simply called for too many duties from one small aircraft. When fully loaded, the technique for take-off was to set out across the airfield until a large enough bump was hit, throwing the aircraft into the air. At this instant, the undercarriage was retracted to reduce drag.

A production order for 250 aircraft was commenced at Hatfield in 1937 while the prototype attempted acceptance trials at Martlesham Heath. However, official policy changed and the order was reduced to 50 aircraft, all to be in the communications configuration. Conversion commenced with the fifth aircraft, and following acceptance trials, a small number were issued to No. 24 Squadron at Hendon and to several RAF Station flights.

In the event only 30 aircraft were completed and issued to the RAF. The remaining 20 incomplete Dons were also delivered to the service and used for ground instruction at a number of Technical Training Schools and Air Training Cadet Squadrons.

D.H.93 Don communications version (de Havilland)

The D.H.93 soon faded into the obscurity which it deserved, although through no fault of the manufacturer.

Data
Variant: D.H.93 Don
Power plant: One 391 kW (525 hp) D.H. Gipsy King I inline engine
Accommodation: Two pilots, a radio operator and trainee gunner
Wing span: 14.48 m (47 ft 6 in)
Wing area: 28.24 sq m (304 sq ft)
Length: 11.38 m (37 ft 4 in)
Height: 2.87 m (9 ft 5 in)
Weight empty: 2,291 kg (5,050 lb)
Max t/o weight: 2,962 kg (6,530 lb)
Max level speed: 304 km/h (189 mph)
Service ceiling: 7,100 m (23,300 ft)
Endurance/range: 1,432 km (890 miles)
Armament: (intended) one Armstrong-Whitworth gun turret
Production Total of 50: 30 completed, 3 unassembled, 17 engineless airframes

DE HAVILLAND D.H.94 MOTH MINOR

D.H.94 Moth Minor was a return to the simple basic trainer formula (*Flight*)

First flight: 22 June 1937

Type: Two-seat basic trainer

Notes: The original concept of the Moth was to produce a practical and economic training aircraft. de Havilland felt that the cost of the Moth successors had crept up to an undesirable level for the more popular market, and the decision was made to return to the primary principles, using the task as a training exercise for a young team. This would enable them to gain the experience of leading a relatively simple exercise in order to effectively participate in a more complex aircraft at a later date.

The simple, yet robust new trainer was a low wing two-seat open cockpit aircraft with a fixed undercarriage. In September 1938 production commenced at Hatfield, the aircraft featuring wheel brakes, an airbrake and folding wings for a basic price of £575, and a coupé tourer for £690.

The training version satisfied the requirements of the newly formed Civil Air Guard, aimed at training many more pilots in the event of war. It could be flown solo from either cockpit and was fully aerobatic. A nose wheel undercarriage, and a covered rear cockpit were also tested in late autumn 1939.

In addition to orders from British flying clubs and private owners, export sales were made to South Africa and Australia. When war com-

menced, the jigs and tools, together with stocks of airframe parts were shipped to Australia where 42 Moth Minors were completed at the Bankstown factory.

More than 30 British-owned Moth Minors were impressed for use in training and communications; among others, coupé Moth Minor G-AFOJ was used by de Havillands for wartime communications. Twelve Moth Minors survived to return to civil flying after the war, including G-AFOJ, but now only a handful are still preserved in flying condition.

Data
Variant: D.H.94 Moth Minor
Power plant: One 60 kW (80 hp) D.H. Gipsy Minor inline engine
Accommodation: Two crew in tandem cockpits, either open or coupé top
Fuel capacity: 59 ltr (13 Imp gal)
Wing span: 11.15 m (36 ft 7 in)
Wing area: 15.05 sq m (162 sq ft)
Length: 7.44 m (24 ft 5 in)
Height: 1.93 m (6 ft 4 in)
Weight empty: 435 kg (960 lb)
Max t/o weight: 703 kg (1,550 lb)
Max level speed: 190 km/h (118 mph)
Service ceiling: 5,610 m (18,400 ft)
Endurance/range: 483 km (300 miles)
Production Total of 115: 63 trainer and 10 coupé versions built at Hatfield, and 42 in Australia

DE HAVILLAND D.H.95 FLAMINGO

First flight: 28 December 1938

Type: 12 to 18-passenger medium-range airliner
Notes: The Flamingo was de Havilland's first all-metal airliner, and as no suitable de Havilland

engines were available, two Bristol Perseus radials were selected, giving a high cruising speed. The high wing gave the passengers an excellent view from the spacious cabin. With the 12-passenger layout, stages of over 1,609 km (1,000 miles) were possible, but on the higher density short routes up to 20 passengers could be carried in addition to the crew of three.

The initial customer was Jersey Airways who ordered three Flamingoes in spring 1939, and used the prototype for evaluation during the summer of 1939. The granting of the C of A on 30 June allowed passenger services to commence less than seven months after the maiden flight.

In April 1939 the King's Flight ordered a VIP Flamingo, with two more ordered for the Air Council, to be operated by No. 24 Squadron at Hendon. On 1 May, an order for 40 Flamingoes was announced as a troop transport to Air Ministry Specification 19/39, but these were later cancelled in favour of using American transport aircraft, leaving Britain free to concentrate on combat types. As with the Albatross and the Moth Minor, the start of the Second World War ended a potentially successful project, although by June 1940 eight Flamingoes were on the Hatfield production line, incorporating a number of improvements including more powerful engines and a greater range.

The Jersey Airways aircraft were impressed for military transport use joining the other aircraft with No. 24 Squadron, while the King's Flight aircraft stood by to evacuate the Royal Family, if necessary. Only a prototype of the military transport was flown. Known as Hertfordshire, it joined No. 24 Squadron, but was lost in a fatal accident after take-off from Hendon. The cause was found to be control problems, which were cured at Hendon, but de Havillands were not told the reason for the crash nor the subsequent cure.

BOAC placed an order for eight of the improved Flamingoes in early 1940, but one was impressed by the Royal Navy and a further aircraft was built as a replacement. These aircraft were ferried to Cairo, following crew training at Whitchurch, for use on a number of Middle East routes. Regrettably, the control problems found at Hendon began repeating themselves, and following two more crashes in 1943 the cause was investigated by de Havillands. It was discovered that the elevator shroud distorted, resulting in control jamming.

The BOAC aircraft were withdrawn at the end of 1943 and shipped to Croydon for storage. The surviving RAF Flamingoes were withdrawn in 1944, one going to Donibristle as spares for the RN aircraft, and the other two being scrapped at Hendon. The RN aircraft was used on communications around Scotland and Northern Ireland, until being abandoned by No. 782 Squadron at Gatwick in August 1945 after ground looping. It was later returned to its civil markings of G-AFYH and restored to flying condition using the stock of BOAC spares. Three of the BOAC aircraft were also to have been restored, but all were abandoned and scrapped at Croydon in 1950, leaving G-AFYH as the sole survivor at Redhill. Unfortunately, with the closure of this airfield in May 1954, this Flamingo was also scrapped.

de Havillands had considered a number of Flamingo improvements including increasing the power with a pair of Twin Wasp radials, enlarging the cabin and increasing the all-up weight. In store at Hatfield were up to 50 sets of parts in various stage of manufacture, which could have been used. Towards the end of the war, a jet-powered version was also considered, but none of these materialised.

Data
Variant: D.H.95 Flamingo
Power plant: Two 694 kW (930 hp) Bristol Perseus XVI radial engines
Accommodation: Three crew and 12–20 passengers in an enclosed cabin
Fuel capacity: 1,496 ltr (329 Imp gal)
Wing span: 21.3 m (70 ft)
Wing area: 60.5 sq m (651 sq ft)
Length: 15.7 m (51 ft 7 in)
Height: 4.6 m (15 ft 3 in)
Weight empty: 5,137 kg (11,325 lb)
Max t/o weight: 8,165 kg (18,000 lb)
Max level speed: 391 km/h (243 mph)
Service ceiling: 6,370 m (20,900 ft)
Endurance/range: 2,165 km (1,345 miles)
Production 15 Flamingoes and one Hertfordshire prototype completed

D.H.95 Flamingo was the first de Havilland all-metal airliner (Hawker Siddeley)

DE HAVILLAND D.H.98 MOSQUITO

First flight: 25 November 1940

Type: High speed, twin-engine unarmed bomber, photo-reconnaissance, day and night fighter, fighter-bomber

Notes: The Mosquito was not only a significant aircraft for de Havillands, but also Britain. de Havillands had a great deal of experience in wooden construction, and studied a high-speed unarmed bomber using the methods of construction developed in the Comet Racer and Albatross airliner. The argument used was if the drag of defensive armament was removed, together with the weight and space of the extra crew and equipment, a smaller aircraft would result powered by two, instead of four engines, and capable of higher speeds. The aircraft defensive guns could only be effective against other aircraft, and if the speed was high enough, the Mosquito could outrun the hostile fighters, dodge the flak from the ground, and spend less time at risk over enemy territory. With only two crew, a pilot and navigator, less manpower was required.

The wooden construction used non-strategic material, and was tough and easy to maintain. Despite these compelling arguments, the Air Ministry resisted the introduction of a wooden aircraft. To overcome the resistance to a bomber, an unarmed reconnaissance prototype was ordered to specification B.1/40 in early 1940. As a security measure, design and construction commenced at the isolated Salisbury Hall near St Albans in October 1939, and on 1 March 1940, an initial batch of 50 bomber-reconnaissance Mosquitoes were ordered.

The flight trials were so successful that further production orders rapidly followed, and the initial batch included reconnaissance, fighter and bomber versions. Top speed was found to be 624 km/h (388 mph) at 6,700 m (22,000 ft) and the estimated service ceiling was 10,330 m (33,900 ft).

Early Mosquito night fighters had an arrowhead AI radar aerial on the nose (*Hawker Siddeley*)

Production built up quickly at Hatfield, the first deliveries to the RAF being reconnaissance versions to the No. 1 Photo Reconnaissance Unit (PRU) at Benson ready for the first operational sortie on 20 September 1941, less than two years after the start of design. The Mosquito PR 1 was fitted with three vertical and one oblique camera, and could fly longer ranges than the Spitfires, with the greater precision achieved with a navigator. Both low-level and high-altitude sorties could be flown, to assess bomb damage at close quarters or to plan the next attacks.

The next development was the Night Fighter Mk II to Specification F.18/40 with AI Mk IV radar. This version and its day fighter equivalent were armed with four .303-in (7.7 mm) Browning machine guns in the nose, and four 20 mm Hispano cannon under the cockpit floor. The night fighters were initially painted matt black overall, and the day intruder version had the radar equipment removed, but could carry two 227 kg (500 lb) bombs in a reduced bomb-bay with a 113 kg (250 lb) bomb under each wing.

No. 157 Squadron formed at Debden on 13 December 1941 as the first Mosquito night fighter unit, but it was some time before they received their first fully equipped aircraft. The Mosquito night fighter force then began to build up covering the various approaches to Britain from the Continent.

The dual-control Trainer Mk III, based on the fighter version was followed by the first bomber version, the B.Mk IV, capable of carrying a 907 kg (2,000 lb) bomb load. The first bomber was delivered to No. 105 Squadron on 15 November 1941 for training to commence, and enough aircraft were on hand for the first operation to Cologne at the end of May 1942. It was shown that the Mosquito could outfly the defending fighters, and as well as high and low-level night attacks, the new aircraft were found to be particularly suited to low-level daylight precision raids. With the addi-

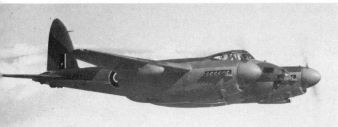

Mosquito B.Mk XVI could carry one 1,814 kg (4,000 lb) bomb (*Hawker Siddeley*)

Coastal strike Mosquito FB.Mk VI carried underwing unguided rockets (*C. E. Brown*)

tion of special radio and navigational aids, the Mosquito was introduced to pathfinder duties, pinpointing targets with flares for the main bomber force.

Using the experience gained with the Intruder Mk II, the Fighter-Bomber Mk VI was produced with the normal fighter armament and room for two 227 kg (500 lb) bombs in the bomb-bay, and two 227 kg (500 lb) bombs or additional fuel tanks under the wings. Early deliveries were to No. 418 (Intruder) Squadron at Ford in May 1943. The 2nd TAF was formed in June 1943 and Mosquito FB.Mk VIs were delivered to No. 464 (RAAF) and No. 487 (RNZAF) Squadrons in August at Sculthorpe. 140 Sculthorpe Wing was completed with No. 21 Squadron converting to Mosquitoes beginning September 1943.

Mosquito fighter-bomber operations were also flown against the Japanese in the Far East, but initially there were problems with glue joints com-

ing apart in the heat and humidity. This was overcome by using formaldehyde glue in manufacture.

The FB.Mk VI was also fitted with underwing racks for the carriage of unguided rocket projectiles and issued to Coastal Command squadrons where they made potent anti-shipping aircraft. Eight Mosquito Mk VIs were used with some bombers by BOAC on unarmed high-speed courier and urgent mail flights from Scotland to Scandinavia. These services began in 1942 using Hudsons and Lodestars. After proving flights with Mosquitoes, the first was delivered to BOAC on 15 December 1942, and commenced operations on 4 February 1943.

The major development of the FB.Mk VI was the FB.Mk XVIII, on which the four cannons were replaced by a modified 57 mm (6 pdr) Molins gun. A total of 30 such conversions were made and shared out among the Coastal Command squadrons, being particularly suitable against U-boats.

Development of the photo-reconnaissance Mosquitoes was generally paired with bomber improvements, since both airframes were similar. Only six PR.Mk VIIIs were built powered by two-stage Merlin engines for high-altitude operations. The Mk IX was produced in both bomber and PR versions, powered by Merlin 72 engines giving a ceiling of over 10,970 m (36,000 ft). The bomber version could carry four 227 kg (500 lb) bombs internally and two more under the wings, while by bulging the bomb doors a 1,814 kg (4,000 lb) bomb could be carried internally. A number of B.Mk IXs were used on pathfinder duties and the PR.IX had a range of over 3,220 km (2,000 miles).

The Mk XVI was a specially developed pressurised pathfinder version of the Mk IX with extra power, increased load capacity and special bombing aids. Only five of the lightened PR.32s were built.

The ultimate PR development was the PR.Mk 34 powered by a pair of Merlin 113/114 engines giving very long range and high altitude

PR Mosquitoes were used for low- and high-level unarmed photo reconnaissance (*C. E. Brown*)

Naval Mosquitoes could carry a torpedo under the fuselage (de Havilland)

performance with a pressurised cockpit. With extra fuel tanks in the bulged bomb-bay the maximum still air range was 5,633 km (3,500 miles) at 9,144 m (30,000 ft); there was also a provision for underwing drop tanks. The equivalent bomber version was the B.Mk 35 which served with the peacetime RAF, ending its career as a high-speed target tug.

The other major line of Mosquito development was the night fighter family. Following the early Mk II was the Mk XII with Mk VIII centimetric AI radar protection by a thimble radome. A total of 97 Mk IIs were converted to this standard retaining the cannon armament, and 270 similar Mk XIIIs were built with increased fuel tankage.

The Mosquito Mk XV was a rapidly produced high-altitude fighter to combat the pressurised Ju 86P reconnaissance bombers which flew over Britain in August and September 1942 at over 12,200 m (40,000 ft). The RAF did not have any fighters capable of catching these raiders and early in September 1942 Mosquito MP469 was rapidly modified as a high-altitude interceptor, but these high-altitude daylight raids were discontinued. Four additional Mosquitoes, designated NF.Mk XV, were fitted with Mk VIII AI radar and delivered to Ford by mid-March 1943 in case these high-altitude raiders changed to night operations, but no contact was made.

The Mk XVII was a night fighter conversion of the Mk II fitted with American SCR 720 centimetric AI radar (designated Mk X in RAF service) but was otherwise similar to the Mk XII. It was first flown in March 1943. The Mk XIX was based on the NF.Mk XIII, but fitted with improved radar under a thimble nose radome. The NF.30 was an unpressurised night fighter fitted with either AI Mk 8 or Mk 10 radar and powered by high altitude Merlin 76 engines.

The ultimate Mosquito night fighters were the similar Mk 36 and Mk 38. The Mk 36 was the last of the type to serve with the RAF, and the Mk 38 with British Mk 9 AI radar in place of the Ameri-

can radar was sold to Yugoslavia. The last Mosquito completed was a Mk 38 which was rolled out at the Chester factory on 15 November 1950.

The mark numbers from XX to XXIX (changed to Arabic figures in 1944) were allocated to Canadian production, the Mk XX being a Packard Merlin-powered bomber, similar to the Mk IV. Early examples were used for training and issued to the USAAF, but later aircraft supplemented British production for RAF service. The Mk XXI was a fighter-bomber and the Mk XXII was a trainer similar to the T.III, but both were only produced in small numbers. The B.Mk 25 was powered by improved Packard Merlin 225 engines, some going to the Royal Navy for special duties. The FB.Mk 26 was the main Canadian fighter-bomber equivalent of the British Mk VI, 200 of which were sold to China after the war. The Mk 27 and Mk 29 were both Canadian trainer versions, the former developed from the T.Mk 22 and the latter from the FB.Mk 26. A total of 1,034 Mosquitoes were built in Canada.

The Fleet Air Arm also made use of the Mosquito, fitting arrester hooks, folding wings and other naval equipment for deck operations. The first deck landing by a two-engined aircraft was made on HMS *Indefatigable* on 25 March 1944 by a Mosquito FB.Mk VI, and as a result of these successful trials the Mosquito TR.Mk 33 was developed to specification N.15/44. It had American ASH radar in the nose, and provision for JATO gear for rapid take-off. The usual four 20 mm cannon were fitted and as alternatives to the internal load of two 227 kg (500 lb) bombs, a 907 kg (2,000 lb) torpedo, bomb or mine could be carried externally under the fuselage. Developed from this version was the TF.Mk 37 torpedo fighter-bomber, of which 14 were built, fitted with British ASV Mk 13 radar in the nose. The final British version of the Mosquito was the TT.Mk 39, a shore-based target tug conversion of the Mk XVI for the Royal Navy to Specification Q.19/45, the work being the responsibility of General Aircraft.

The last versions of Mosquito from Mk 40 onwards were allocated to the de Havilland Australia production. The FB.Mk 40 was a Packard Merlin 31 (later 33)-powered aircraft based on the British FB.Mk VI. Six of the early aircraft were converted to PR.Mk 40s and were so successful that many of the final batch were modified to PR.Mk 41s for the aerial survey of Australia. Only one FB.Mk 42 was completed, powered by Merlin 69 engines. The final version was the T.Mk 43, similar to the T.Mk III, a total of 22 being converted from FB.Mk 40s. The Australian production were used in the Asian theatre, and did not supplement UK production like the Canadian aircraft.

At the end of the war, a number of Allied and friendly countries needed Mosquitoes to build up their defences. Fighter-bombers were supplied to Turkey, Dominica, France, Norway, Czechoslovakia and Burma. Night fighters were sold to Sweden and Belgium, and South Africa used photo reconnaissance Mosquitoes during and after the war. Mosquitoes also continued in service with the RAF at home and overseas in a number of roles, until replaced by the first generation jet fighters and bombers.

Data
Variant: D.H.98 Mosquito B.Mk IV
Power plant: Two 1,089 kW (1,460 hp) R-R Merlin 21 or 23 inline engines in earlier versions; two 1,275 kW (1,710 hp) R-R Merlin 76, 77 or 114A inline engines in later versions
Accommodation Two crew seated side-by-side under canopy

Fuel capacity: 2,450 ltr (539 Imp gal)
Wing span: 16.5 m (54 ft 2 in)
Wing area: 42.18 sq m (454 sq ft)
Length: 12.34 m (40 ft 6 in)
Height: 3.81 m (12 ft 6 in)
Weight empty: 6,078 kg (13,400 lb)
Max t/o weight: 9,735 kg (21,462 lb)
Max level speed: 612 km/h (380 mph)
Service ceiling: 10,360 m (34,000 ft)
Endurance/range: 3,283 km (2,040 miles)
Armament: (Mk IV Srs 2) No guns. 1 × 454 kg (1,000 lb) and 2 × 227 kg (500 lb) bombs, or 4 × 227 kg (500 lb) or 4 × 113 kg (250 lb) bombs internally. Specially modified Srs 2 carried 1 × 1,616 kg (4,000 lb) bomb in internal bomb bay.
Production Total of 7,747 of all versions built: de Havilland/Hatfield (3,324); de Havilland/Leavesden (1,648); de Havilland/Chester (96); The Standard Motor Co Ltd/Coventry (1,066); Percival Aircraft Co Ltd/Luton (245); Airspeed Ltd/Christchurch (122); de Havilland Canada Ltd (1,034); and de Havilland Australia Ltd (212)

DE HAVILLAND D.H.100 VAMPIRE

First flight: 20 September 1943

Type: Single-seat jet day fighter-bomber
Notes: de Havilland's first jet-powered aircraft was the Vampire, produced to an experimental specification E.6/41, but with provision for carrying armament. Built under great secrecy at Hatfield, the Vampire was powered by a 1,225 kg (2,700 lb) thrust Goblin I engine, and featured wooden fuselage structure similar to the Mosquito with tapered unswept metal wings, twin tail booms and tail surfaces. The twin boom layout gave maximum efficiency to the low-powered engine. Despite being a new airframe with a new type of propulsion, it proved successful enough on flight trials to be developed into a fighter.

Three prototypes were built, the third being armed with four under-fuselage-mounted 20 mm cannon, followed by the initial contract for 120 (later 300) Vampire F.Mk I fighters built by the English Electric Company at Preston. The Vampire was the second British jet fighter to fly, and the first British aircraft to exceed 805 km/h (500 mph), but was too late for combat in the Second World War. The second prototype was modified for naval use and became the first

carrier-borne jet aircraft after carrying out deck trials on HMS *Ocean* on 3 December 1945.

The Vampire F.Mk I first entered service with No. 247 Squadron at Odiham in April 1946, and subsequently equipped all three units in the Odiham Wing. These were followed by No. 3 Squadron in the 2 TAF, as well as three Auxiliary Squadrons (Nos. 605, 501 and 608).

The improved Vampire F.Mk 3 was designed to specification F.3/47 with better longitudinal stability and strengthened wings for the carriage of underwing stores. This version went into service with the RAF at Odiham, in Germany, Cyprus and the Middle East. In July 1948, six Vampire F.Mk 3s of No. 54 Squadron became the first jet aircraft to fly across the Atlantic.

Vampire F.Mk 1s entered service with No. 247 Squadron in April 1946 (C. E. Brown)

Over half Vampires were exported, in this case to Venezuela

The major production version was the FB.Mk 5 adapted for low level ground attack with reduced span and provision for the carriage of bombs or rockets under the wings. This version was adopted as the standard jet fighter for the 2 TAF in Germany where it combined ground attack and interception duties. Squadrons were also equipped with Vampire FB.Mk 5 in the Middle East and Asia.

The Vampire FB.Mk 9 was developed for use in the hotter climates featuring a more powerful Goblin 3 engine and a refrigeration unit to keep the cockpit cool. No. 28 Squadron in Hong Kong became the last RAF front-line unit to operate Vampires when they re-equipped with Venoms in February 1956.

The single-seat Vampires, with their docile handling and lack of complication, made good training aircraft to prepare pilots for Vampire, Venom and Hunter operations. They served with a number of Flying Training Schools (FTS) and Operational Conversion Units (OCU).

As a result of the successful deck trials, the Royal Navy ordered six Vampire development aircraft and a further 30 production aircraft, known as the Sea Vampire F.Mk 20. This version was fitted with an arrester hook and stronger undercarriage, and its modest size avoided the need for wing folding. The first production F.Mk 20 was flown in October 1948. A further experimental naval development was the F.Mk 21 adapted for operations from rubber mats without the use of the normal undercarriage to save structural weight. Trials were carried out at Farnborough and on board the carrier HMS *Warrior* early in 1949, but damage to the aircraft and their immobility resulted in the idea being abandoned.

The Vampire was also adopted by many overseas air forces, either directly from Britain, or produced under license. The Swedish Government were the first overseas customer when they placed an order in February 1946, to be followed five months later by the Swiss. Their initial orders were for the F.Mk 1, but later batches were the F.Mk 6, an export version of the RAF FB.Mk 5. The Swiss Air Force continues to operate Vampires in the training role.

The first Commonwealth order came from Canada, some of their surplus aircraft later being acquired by Dominica and Mexico. License production was also undertaken in Australia and India. One of the largest Vampire customers was France, where it was adapted and produced under license as the S.E.535 Mistral powered by a French-built Rolls-Royce Nene engine. Other countries to adopt the Vampire were Norway, South Africa, Italy, Egypt, Venezuela, New Zealand, Finland, Iraq and Southern Rhodesia, production closing at over 3,000 aircraft.

Data
Variant: D.H.100 Vampire FB.Mk 5
Power plant: One 1,406 kg (3,100 lb) thrust D.H. Goblin 2 centrifugal jet engine
Accommodation: Pilot under bubble canopy
Fuel capacity: 2,410 ltr (530 Imp gal), including 2 × 455 ltr (100 Imp gal) wing drop tanks
Wing span: 11.58 m (38 ft)
Wing area: 24.34 sq m (262 sq ft)
Length: 9.37 m (30 ft 9 in)
Height: 2.69 m (8 ft 10 in)
Weight empty: 3,290 kg (7,253 lb)
Max t/o weight: 5,607 kg (12,360 lb)
Max level speed: 861 km/h (535 mph)
Service ceiling: 12,190 m (40,000 ft)
Endurance/range: 1,883 km (1,170 miles)
Armament: Four 20 mm Hispano Mk 5 cannon, plus 2 × 227 kg (500 lb) bombs or 8 × 27 kg (60 lb) rockets.
Production Total of 1,571 (including 3 prototypes) for the RAF and RN: 172 F.Mk 1, 117 F.Mk 3, 30 F.Mk 20/21, 931 FB.Mk 5, and 317 FB.Mk 9
Under License: Switzerland (Federal Aircraft Plant/Emmen & consortium) 103; Italy (SpA Fiat/Turin and Aeronautica Macchi SA/Varese) 80; India (Hindustan Aircraft Ltd/Bangalore) 247; France (SNCASE/Marseilles) 433 (including 250 Mistrals and direct deliveries); de Havilland Australia Ltd 80
Exports: Sweden 183 (70 + 113); Finland 6; Iraq 12; Lebanon 4; SAAF 50; RNZAF 38; RCAF 85; Switzerland 79; Ceylon 2; Norway 29; Southern Rhodesia 24; Venezuela 15; India 39

DE HAVILLAND D.H.103 HORNET AND SEA HORNET

First flight: 28 July 1944

Type: Single-seat long-range twin-engined fighter

Notes: The Hornet was a cantilever mid-wing monoplane of similar wooden construction to the Mosquito, but using for the first time a composite light alloy and wood bonded structure in the wing spars and ribs. The bottom wing skin, wing leading edge and tail unit were also of metal construction. Power came from two especially developed Rolls-Royce Merlin engines with opposite-handed propellers. These engines and the very slim design made it the fastest piston-engined fighter to enter production. Armament consisted of four 20 mm cannon mounted under the nose, and underwing racks could carry either two 454 kg (1,000 lb) bombs or eight 27 kg (60 lb) rockets.

de Havillands started design of the Hornet as a private venture in late 1942 to provide a very-long-range fighter for use in the Pacific war. The aircraft was adopted officially in June 1943 when Specification F.12/43 was written around it. The prototype was flown from Hatfield by Geoffrey de Havilland Jnr only thirteen months later, and soon demonstrated its excellent high speed performance. A second prototype joined the test programme and an initial production batch of 60 Hornet F.Mk 1s was ordered, but there were insufficient available for the Far East Air Force before the war with Japan ended.

Following the F.Mk 1 was the PR.Mk 2, a long-range unarmed photo-reconnaissance aircraft, but only a handful were built and not used in service. The F.Mk 3 was an improvement of the Mk 1 with greater internal fuel capacity, provision for the carriage of two 909 ltr (200 Imp gal) wing drop tanks and improved directional stability with the addition of a dorsal fin. The final RAF version was the F.Mk 4, similar to the F.Mk 3 but with an F.52 vertically-mounted camera and slightly reduced internal fuel tankage.

Four RAF squadrons in Britain were equipped with Hornets commencing with No. 64 in March 1946. The other units were Nos. 19, 41 and 65 Squadrons, but in 1951 the type was withdrawn from Fighter Command to replace Spitfires and Beaufighters in the campaign against Malayan terrorists. Here they equipped Nos. 33, 45 and 80 Squadrons on ground attack duties as the last piston-engined fighter-bombers in RAF service until replaced by Vampires during the first half of 1956.

Near the end of 1944 specification N.5/44 was issued to cover the naval adaptation of the aircraft, to be known as the Sea Hornet. Heston Aircraft Co had the design authority and converted three Mk 1s to have high drag flaps, Lockheed power folding wings, arrester hook, catapult pick-up points and Airdraulic undercarriage legs to cope with the high rates of descent on deck landings. The first partially navalised aircraft flew on 19 April 1945 and the fully navalised version commenced deck trials on 19 August. The Royal Navy then placed a production order for the Sea Hornet F.Mk 20 as their first twin-engined long-range strike fighter, the first production aircraft flying on 13 August 1946. Apart from training units only one front-line Fleet Air Arm unit used the Sea Hornet F.Mk 20, No. 801 Squadron, which reformed at Ford on 1 June 1947. A development

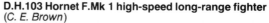

D.H.103 Hornet F.Mk 1 high-speed long-range fighter
(C. E. Brown)

of this version was the unarmed PR.Mk 22 with two F.52 cameras for day photography and a Fairchild K19B for nocturnal photo reconnaissance.

The other major version was the NF.Mk 21 built to an urgent specification N.21/45 for a high performance naval night fighter. Modifications included the installation of ASH radar inside a nose-mounted thimble radome and the addition of a second crew member's cockpit above the wing trailing edge. Following successful trials, No. 809 Squadron was commissioned at Culdrose on 20 January 1949 as the only front-line unit to use the type. It disbanded in 1954, the remaining aircraft continuing on training duties until retirement at the end of 1955, when they were all scrapped.

Data
Variant: D.H.103 Hornet F.Mk 3
Power plant: Two 1,544 kW (2,070 hp) R-R

Merlin 130/131 inline engines
Accommodation: Pilot under bubble canopy
Fuel capacity: 2,518.5 ltr (554 Imp gal)
Wing span: 13.72 m (45 ft)
Wing area: 33.54 sq m (361 sq ft)
Length: 11.18 m (36 ft 8 in)
Height: 4.32 m (14 ft 2 in)
Weight empty: 5,842 kg (12,880 lb)
Max t/o weight: 9,480 kg (20,900 lb)
Max level speed: 760 km/h (472 mph)
Service ceiling: 10,670 m (35,000 ft)
Endurance/range: 4,828 km (3,000 miles)
Armament: Four 20 mm Hispano cannon, plus 2 × 454 kg (1,000 lb) bombs or 8 × 27 kg (60 lb) rockets
Production Total of 391: two prototypes, 60 F.Mk 1, 5 PR.Mk 2, 132 F.Mk 3, 12 F.Mk 4, 79 F.Mk 20, 78 NF.Mk 21 and 23 PR.Mk 22

DE HAVILLAND D.H.104 DOVE

First flight: 25 September 1945

Type: Twin-engined feeder liner
Notes: The Dove was designed to the Brabazon Type 5B Specification to replace the Rapide and to Air Ministry Specification 26/43 as a local service all-metal airliner using for the first time metal to metal bonding. Power came from two Gipsy Queen 70 engines driving three-blade D.H. reverse pitch/feathering propellers. The Dove was designed to carry up to 11 passengers in a high density layout and provision was made for two crew. The Dove was ideal for local service scheduled airlines, charter and business use, with modern travelling standards at economic levels of operation and maintenance.

It was initially designed to fulfil the five different tasks of aircrew training, communications, survey, ambulance and pest control, and at a later date, for airways calibration. The military variant was known as the Devon, and all versions operated in a wide range of climatic conditions from the Arctic Circle to the Equator. One Dove was fitted with floats by de Havilland Canada in 1947.

The Dove Mk 1 was the initial airline version and the Mk 2 was the executive equivalent, the first of which was delivered to Vickers in 1948. The Mk 3 was a proposed high-altitude survey version, which was not built, and the Mk 4 became the military Devon to specification C.13/46 which was

ordered by the RAF and RN, still continuing in service for communications. Other Devon orders came from India, South Africa and New Zealand.

Among the early airline customers were BOAC, Airwork, Central African Airways and the Airlines of Western Australia. Demand for the Dove grew rapidly, the largest single customer being the Argentine government who ordered a total of 70 aircraft for transport, ambulance duties, and locust control. Doves were used widely throughout Africa, Asia and Europe, followed by North America where they were delivered unpainted and unequipped. They were then completed in various finishing centres for business travel and commuter operations.

In 1953, more powerful Gipsy Queen 70 Mk 2 engines were installed resulting in the Dove Mk 5 for airline use and the executive Mk 6. The aircraft for the American market carried the suffix A after each number, and suffix B covered the rest of the world. The airframe itself changed little, but with these versions role change was made easier. Dove production had started at the Hatfield factory, but was moved to Chester in 1951 to make room for Comet construction.

In the summer of 1960, the six-seat Dove Mk 8 was announced, which featured uprated Gipsy Queen 70 Mk 3 engines, an enlarged Heron type canopy and improved equipment. Not only was the performance improved, but so also was the payload-range capability. The executive Mk 8 first flew in February 1960, and the high density airline

D.H.104 Doves were sold widely to airlines, business users and governments (*Hawker Siddeley*)

version was the Mk 7. This version was only sold in its VIP business aircraft configuration outside North America, where there was a preference in replacing the Gipsy Queen engines with lighter, cheaper and more effective Continental engines. In the mid-1960s, the RAF commenced the conversion of most of their Devons to the Mk 8 standard, with the more powerful engines and new canopy.

The last of the 544 Doves to be built was delivered in early 1970 to Dowty Ltd, having been in store at Chester for some years, but it was destroyed in April of the same year in a fatal crash at Wolverhampton. Despite their increasing age many Doves and Devons are still flying throughout the world, and will no doubt continue for many years to come.

Data
Variant: D.H.104 Dove Mk 8
Power plant: Two 298 kW (400 hp) D.H. Gipsy Queen 70 Mk 3 inline engines
Accommodation: Two crew in cockpit compartment, plus six to eleven passengers in the cabin
Fuel capacity: 1,000 ltr (220 Imp gal)
Wing span: 17.37 m (57 ft)
Wing area: 31.21 sq m (335 sq ft)
Length: 11.96 m (39 ft 3 in)
Height: 4.06 m (13 ft 4 in)
Weight empty: 2,985 kg (6,580 lb)
Max t/o weight: 4,060 kg (8,950 lb)
Max level speed: 378 km/h (235 mph)
Service ceiling: 6,610 m (21,700 ft)
Endurance/range: 1,891 km (1,175 miles)
Production Total of 544 Doves and Devons (including 2 prototypes) built at de Havilland/Hatfield and de Havilland/Chester. The last Dove completed was c/n 04542 G-AVHV

DE HAVILLAND D.H.106 COMET

First flight: 27 July 1949

Type: Medium-range four-engined jet airliner
Notes: Designed to Brabazon Type IV specification of 1943, the Comet was the world's first pure jet airliner, to compete with the American postwar lead in commercial transports. Serious design work commenced in September 1946 allowing construction of two prototypes and initial production for BOAC and British South American Airways, who were later to merge. During design considerable research was undertaken on pressurisation, insulation, structures and engines.

Power for the Comet was from four D.H. Ghost 50 jet engines, initial testing being in a pair of converted Lancastrians for endurance and a Vampire for high altitude performance.

During its development flying programme, the aircraft was found to achieve all its specification requirements allowing 36 passengers to be carried over 4,185 km (2,600 miles), or up to 48 passengers on shorter ranges. The first public appearance of the Comet was at Farnborough in September 1949 and it gained the first commercial jet Certificate of Airworthiness on 22 January 1952. The first passenger service was from London to Johannesburg with 36 passengers on 2 May that year, giving Britain a lead in passenger jet operations of four to five years.

The first export order came from the Canadian Pacific Airlines for two improved Comet 1A jet airliners on 15 December 1949, but they were never to enter service due to an accident to their first aircraft on its delivery flight. It suffered a ground stall at Karachi on 3 May 1953, killing all aboard. A similar accident befell BOAC Comet 1 G-ALYZ at Rome on 26 October 1952 and another BOAC Comet 1 G-ALYV broke up in a violent storm at Calcutta on 2 May 1953 with the loss of 43 lives. Export orders were received from the UAT and Air France for three each and the RCAF for two of the improved Series 1A standard with increased fuel capacity and all-up weight.

As the axial-flow jet engines offered better economics than the centrifugal Ghost type, the 6th Comet airframe was fitted with Rolls-Royce Avon 503 units to become the prototype Series 2. Shortly after the maiden flight from Hatfield on 16 February 1952, BOAC ordered 11 of this version in May 1953, followed by Panair do Brasil. The Brazilian airline also took options on the stretched Comet 3, first announced at Farnborough in September 1952. The Comet 3 could carry up to 70 passengers 60 per cent further than the Comet 2 and was fitted with more powerful Avon 523 engines. With the growth of orders additional production capacity was obtained at the Short Brothers factory at Belfast.

Canadian Pacific and British Commonwealth Pacific Airlines both ordered Comet 2s and BOAC placed an order for five Comet 3s for the North Atlantic route, with options on additional aircraft. Further Comet 2 orders came from Air France, Japan Airlines, Linea Aeropostas Venezolana, followed by a major breakthrough into the American market with an order for three Comet 3s from Pan Am, plus options for seven more in October 1953. Air India joined the queue for Comet 3s, and with orders for over 100 more Comets under active negotiation, supplementary production capacity was allocated at the Chester factory.

D.H.106 Comet prototype was the world's first commercial jet airliner (*Hawker Siddeley*)

A number of Comet Srs 2s were delivered to the RAF to serve with No. 216 Squadron (*de Havilland*)

Then came the major blow to the Comet programme with the initially unexplained loss of BOAC Comet 1 G-ALYP off Elba on 10 January 1954 and G-ALYY off Stromboli on 8 April 1954. Following an exhaustive investigation metal fatigue was found to be the cause. The existing aircraft were capable of modification, but in most cases it was uneconomic. The RCAF Comets were strengthened and two of the ex-Air France aircraft were used for testing. Most of the Comet 2s under construction were modified and entered service with the RAF as jet transports or on signals duties. Two others were used by BOAC to route-prove the more powerful Avon RA.29 jet engines.

The Comet 3 was developed into the similar, but stronger and more powerful Comet 4 powered by four of the RA.29 Avon engines. Confidence was restored in the Comet by an order for 19 from BOAC, the maiden flight of this new version being from Hatfield on 27 April 1958. Production of the Series 4s was shared between Hatfield and Chester, the C of A being issued on 29 September 1958. Deliveries started in time for the first commercial transatlantic scheduled jet service to commence on 4 October that year.

The first export order was by Capitol Airlines of USA who required four Comet 4s and 10 of a developed Comet 4A, which was a short to medium range version with a 1.01 m (40 inch)

Only one Comet 3 was built, leading to the development of Comet 4 (*Hawker Siddeley*)

fuselage extension and reduced wing span, similar to the later Comet 4B. Due to financial difficulties, the Capitol order was later cancelled. Comet 4s were ordered by Aerolineas Argentinas and East African Airways. The high capacity, shorter range Comet 4B was ordered by BEA, now part of British Airways, as their initial jet equipment, and by Olympic Airways.

The final civil version of the Comet was the Mk.4C combining the high density fuselage of the Comet 4B with the long range wing of the Comet 4. This became the most successful export version with an initial order for three from Mexicana. This was followed by Misrair, later renamed United Arab Airlines, who eventually had a fleet of nine Comet 4Cs; Middle East Airlines; one for Aerolineas Argentinas; Sudan Airways and Kuwait Airways. A VIP version was sold to King Ibn Saud of Saudi Arabia, but this aircraft was lost in the Alps in March 1963 near Cuneo a year after its maiden flight.

The RAF placed an order for five Comet C Mk 4s, the RAF equivalent of the Comet 4C, to replace the Comet C Mk 2s with No. 216 Squadron which were retired in March 1967. The final Comet 4C sale was to the Ministry of Defence, to operate as a flying laboratory for the testing of radio and navigation equipment, which still operates from the A and AEE at Boscombe Down.

Two uncompleted Comet 4C airframes left at the Chester factory were shortened to the Comet 4 fuselage length and converted as development aircraft for the Nimrod maritime reconnaissance aircraft. One retained the Avon engines, but the other had more extensive modifications to incorporate the Rolls-Royce Spey engines, which powered the production Nimrod. The first Nimrod prototype was flown on 23 May 1967, the first production Nimrod MR.Mk 1 on 28 June 1968.

When the original airlines began to dispose of their Comets commencing with BOAC in November 1965, five were purchased by Malaysian Airways. Most of the remainder were bought by Dan-Air, who eventually were to purchase at one time or other just about every surviving Comet, either for inclusive tour operations or spare parts. Meanwhile, the BEA Comet 4Bs were operated by British Airtours starting in March 1970, and the ex-Olympic aircraft were taken over by Channel Airways.

On 30 June 1975, No. 216 Squadron disbanded and their Comets were purchased by Dan-Air and delivered to their Lasham base by early September. With the so-called fuel crisis, the Comet's Avon engines were becoming uneconomic but the passenger appeal, reliability and ease of maintenance of the Comets, particularly the relatively underutilised ex-RAF aircraft made them sufficiently attractive for a few more years until the last Comet commercial flight on 9 November 1980.

Comet 4B was the high-density short range version (*P. J. Birtles*)

Data
Variant: D.H.106 Comet 4C
Power plant: Four 4,763 kg (10,500 lb) thrust
R-R Avon 525B jet engines
Accommodation: Three flight crew and up to 101
passengers in a pressurised cabin
Fuel capacity: 40,668 ltr (8,946 Imp gal)
Wing span: 35 m (114 ft 10 in)
Wing area: 197 sq m (2,121 sq ft)
Length: 35.97 m (118 ft)
Height: 8.69 m (28 ft 6 in)
Weight empty: 36,106 kg (79,600 lb)

Max t/o weight: 73,483 kg (162,000 lb)
Max level speed: 809.48 km/h (503 mph)
Service ceiling: 11,890 m (39,000 ft)
Endurance/range: 4,265 km (2,650 miles)
Production Total of 112, including four
prototypes (two Comet 1, one Comet 2 and one
Comet 3). Series: 9 Comet 1, 10 Comet 1A, 15
Comet 2, 28 Comet 4 (plus one test airframe), 18
Comet 4B, 28 Comet 4C. Two airframes
converted to Nimrod prototypes by Hawker
Siddeley Aviation.

DE HAVILLAND D.H.108

First flight: 15 May 1946

Type: Single-seat, single-engine tailless jet
research aircraft
Notes: The D.H.108, unofficially named Swallow,
was designed to Specification E.18/45 to gain
experience with swept-wing aircraft. To speed the
design of this revolutionary aircraft, captured
German information, particularly Messerschmitt
calculations and research data for design and construction of swept wings was used. It was a tailless
aircraft with a 40-degree swept-back metal wing
attached to a wooden Vampire fuselage. A swept
fin and rudder were fitted to the rear of the nacelle.

Two prototypes were ordered, one for low speed
and the other for high speed research. Construction of the first low speed aircraft was completed in
the Experimental Department in seven months,
but as the runway at Hatfield had yet to be built,
the prototype was taken to RAF Woodbridge for
its maiden flight. Power came from a Goblin 2
engine.

The high-speed prototype joined the programme on 1 August, powered by a slightly
uprated Goblin 3 engine. Despite low power, the
efficiency of the airframe gave a potentially
record-breaking performance. It was decided to
attempt to beat the absolute world speed record of
991 km/h (616 mph) achieved by a Meteor. During an early practice the D.H.108 reached
1,025 km/h (637 mph) at 2,743 m (9,000 ft), but
on the final low level practice on 26 September
1946, the aircraft broke up killing Geoffrey de
Havilland Jnr.

A third prototype, incorporating a number of
improvements, was ordered to continue the high-
speed research programme. A Vampire fuselage
was again used, but had a more pointed nose, new

canopy and strengthened structure. It first flew on
24 July 1947, and successfully broke the 100 km
closed circuit record on 12 April 1948 flown by
John Derry, a de Havilland test pilot, who
achieved 973.997 km/h (605.230 mph) at low
level. On 6 September 1948 the third D.H.108,
again flown by John Derry, became the first British
aircraft to exceed the speed of sound, in a dive.

The surviving aircraft were delivered to Farnborough for further development, but both
crashed fatally. The high-speed prototype,
VW120, was lost at Birkhill, Bucks on 15 February
1950 in an unexplained accident, but most probably due to lack of oxygen for the pilot. The original low-speed prototype crashed near Hartley
Wintney the following 1 May while in a spin.

Data
Variant: D.H.108 2nd prototype
Power plant: One 1,701 kg (3,750 lb) thrust D.H.
Goblin 4 jet engine
Accommodation: Pilot under bubble canopy
Wing span: 11.89 m (39 ft)
Wing area: 30.47 sq m (328 sq ft)
Length: 7.47 m (24 ft 6 in)
Max t/o weight: 4,064 kg (8,960 lb)
Max level speed: 1,030 km/h (640 mph)
Production Three prototypes: TG283, TG306
and VW120

Third D.H.108 prototype used for high speed research
(*Hawker Siddeley*)

Sea Vixen FAW.2 had leading edge pinion fuel tanks
added ahead of the tail-booms (*P. J. Birtles*)

DE HAVILLAND D.H.110 SEA VIXEN

First flight: 26 September 1951

Type: Two-seat, twin-engine, all-weather naval jet fighter

Notes: Designed to a joint Naval Specification N.40/46 and RAF Specification F.44/46 issued in January 1947, the D.H.110 had 40-degree swept-back wings and the familiar twin-boom layout. It was powered by a pair of Rolls-Royce Avon engines.

Initial service interest was high, with orders for development prototypes coming from the RAF and RN; however the RAF order was later reduced to two prototypes, and the RN selected the cheaper interim Sea Venom to replace the Sea Hornets.

John Cunningham, the new Chief Test Pilot, took off the first aircraft on its maiden flight from Hatfield in September 1951, and it became the first operational aircraft to exceed the speed of sound, in a shallow dive, on 9 April 1952. Tragically, the first prototype broke up in low-level flight during the Farnborough Air Show in September 1952, killing John Derry, his observer Tony Richards and 29 spectators.

The competing Gloster Javelin was selected by the RAF in 1953 as the standard all-weather fighter despite problems in its development programme, leaving the future of the D.H.110 in some doubt. However, there was still a naval requirement for a more advanced all-weather fighter to specification N.14/49, to which de Havillands submitted a much modified D.H.110 powered by more powerful Avon engines.

The surviving prototype was strengthened and modified, and was joined by a Christchurch-built semi-navalised prototype, the aircraft by now having been named Sea Vixen. This aircraft made its maiden flight on 20 June 1955, and had all the basic naval features apart from folding wings and radar equipment. The long-awaited production order for 78 Sea Vixens was placed in January 1955, and included an initial batch of 21 pre-production aircraft to speed the development and trials programme of this complicated weapons system.

The airframe had been about 80 per cent redesigned compared to the original D.H.110 and featured power-operated folding wings for carrier stowage, catapult gear, arrester hook, a new cockpit canopy, long stroke undercarriage, steerable nosewheel, an all-flying tailplane, and the latest AI radar housed under a pointed nose radome. Armament consisted of four D.H. Firestreak infra-red homing missiles, supplemented by 28 2-in (50 mm) RPs in a retractable ventral pack. Additional rockets, stores and fuel tanks could be mounted on underwing pylons, giving this potent night fighter a very effective strike capability.

The first production Sea Vixen FAW.Mk 1 flew on 20 March 1957, and deliveries commenced to RNAS Yeovilton in November 1958 to No. 700Y Service Trials Unit, later commissioned as No. 892 Squadron.

A second substantial order was announced in June 1959 and No. 766 Squadron became the training unit at Yeovilton, supplying crews to Nos. 890, 893 and 899 Squadrons.

In early 1960, modest improvements were made to the aircraft by increasing the fuel capacity in leading edge extensions to the tail booms, and making room for the equipment to replace Firestreaks with the later Red Top homing missiles. This modification became the FAW.Mk 2, and in addition to a new production order for this version, built at the Chester factory, many of the FAW.Mk 1s were modified during overhaul to the new standard. Electronic equipment consisted of an AI Mk 18 radar with its scanner enclosed in a nose radome.

With the rundown of naval fixed wing operations and withdrawal of the aircraft carriers, the Sea Vixen units began to decommission, No. 899 Squadron being the last naval squadron to cease Sea Vixen operations in January 1972.

Subsequently, the Sea Vixens served for a short while with the Air Directors School at Yeovilton until replaced by Canberras in January 1974. Apart from the non-flying examples preserved in museums, a small number of Sea Vixens were retained for conversion into pilotless target drones by Flight Refuelling but due to a shortage of finance this programme continues at a very slow pace, without any apparent plans to undertake any series conversions of the aircraft stored at Farnborough.

Data
Variant: D.H.110 Sea Vixen FAW.Mk 2
Power plant: Two 5,094 kg (11,230 lb) thrust R-R Avon 208 jet engines
Accommodation: Two crew, pilot on port side under canopy, and observer on starboard side in fuselage

Fuel capacity: 4,700 ltr (1,034 Imp gal) plus 2 × 910 ltr (200 Imp gal) drop tanks
Wing span: 15.24 m (50 ft)
Wing area: 60.2 sq m (648 sq ft)
Length: 16.94 m (55 ft 7 in)
Height: 3.28 m (10 ft 9 in)
Max t/o weight: 16,783 kg (37,000 lb)
Max level speed: 1,030 km/h (640 mph)
Service ceiling: 14,630 m (48,000 ft)
Endurance/range: 3 hr 6 min; max 2,260 km (1,404 miles) with 2 × 910 ltr (200 Imp gal) drop tanks
Armament: Four D.H. Red Top air-to-air homing missiles and 28 2-in (50 mm) RPs
Production Total of 151: two D.H.110 prototypes, one Sea Vixen prototype, and 148 series production Sea Vixens

DE HAVILLAND D.H.112 VENOM AND SEA VENOM

First flight: 2 September 1949

Type: Single-seat single-engined fighter-bomber, two-seat night fighter and all-weather naval fighter
Notes: The Venom was designed to specification F.15/49 as an interim replacement for the Vampire fighters to exploit the more powerful D.H. Ghost jet engine. The layout and structure were generally similar to the Vampire, but the major changes included sweep-back on the wing leading edge and provision for the carriage of 341 ltr (75 Imp gal) wing-tip fuel tanks.

The first 17 aircraft were completed at Hatfield before the main production was moved to Chester, and small batches were built by Faireys at Ringway and Marshalls at Cambridge. The first RAF delivery was to the Central Fighter Establishment at West Raynham in April 1952, followed by the equipping of three fighter-bomber wings with Venoms in West Germany at Wunstorf, Fassberg and Celle. As well as being particularly suited to ground attack, its better manoeuvrability over the faster interceptors made it useful in air to air combat.

In addition to service in Germany, the Venom fighter-bombers also provided colonial protection in the high ambient temperatures of Cyprus, the Middle East, Africa, and Asia. In the Middle East, Venoms were operated in Jordan, Iraq and Aden, later moving to Cyprus, while in Asia the aircraft were based in Malaya and Hong Kong.

When it was realised that the Venom was more than an interim design, particularly because the early Hunters were not suited to ground attack and the Swifts were a failure, the improved FB.Mk 4 was developed, the prototype flying on 29 December 1953 for the first time. One of the RAF Germany Wings had its FB.Mk 1s replaced by the new version, but most of the Mk 4s were used to re-equip the Cyprus squadrons in time to participate in the Suez crisis in November 1956. No. 8 Squadron in Aden and No. 60 Squadron in Malaya also re-equipped, the latter passing their aircraft on to No. 28 Squadron in Hong Kong. No. 208 Squadron were equipped with Venoms for operation in East Africa and Aden. No. 28 Squadron

Among overseas customers for the early Venoms was Iraq (Hawker Siddeley)

Venom night fighters joined RAF service in the mid-1950s
(Hawker Siddeley)

flew the last RAF Venom sortie on 27 June 1962, when they were replaced by Hawker Hunters.

There was a need to bridge the gap between the Vampire Night Fighter and the late arrival of the more complex Gloster Javelin. The Venom was therefore adapted as an interim measure by lengthening the wooden fuselage nacelle to accommodate two crew side by side and AI radar in the nose. First flight of the private venture prototype was from Hatfield on 22 August 1950, and it was adopted by the RAF as the Venom NF.Mk 2. Only No. 23 Squadron at Coltishall was equipped with this aircraft, as it suffered a high accident rate and without ejector seats the crew had difficulty in escaping, particularly at low level. The improved NF.Mk 3 was then developed, featuring power-operated ailerons, a clear-view canopy and improved radar, but still no ejector seats for the crew. A number of the Mk 2s were modified to a similar standard, becoming the NF.Mk 2A.

Deliveries of these improved aircraft commenced in mid-1955, equipping eight of the UK-based night fighter squadrons at Waterbeach, Coltishall, Driffield, Stradishall and Leuchars. The last Venom night fighters were withdrawn in September 1961.

Both RAF versions of the Venom gained valuable export sales as it was an economic and effective aircraft for ground attack and night fighting. Italy were to undertake license production of the fighter-bomber, and ordered two aircraft, but did not proceed. Venom fighter-bombers were ordered by Iraq and Venezuela, but the largest overseas user was the Swiss Air Force who license-built 250, of which 150 were the improved FB.Mk 4 equipped with ejector seats. The rest were retired in November 1983.

Sweden was the only overseas buyer of the night fighter version when 62 were ordered in September 1952. Designated J33 in the Swedish Air Force, they equipped three squadrons, and after retirement four were retained as target tugs until 1967.

Following evaluation of the Venom Mk 2, the Royal Navy selected an adaptation to specification N.107, naming it the Sea Venom. The first two semi-navalised prototypes were built at Hatfield, but the main production and development was at Christchurch. The first fully navalised Sea Venom, with folding wings, arrester hook and other modifications flew in July 1952, followed by an initial production batch known as the FAW.Mk 20. The first unit to be equipped was No. 890 Squadron in March 1954, but during the initial period afloat arrester hooks broke under landing loads, and the aircraft were relegated to shore-based all-weather training.

The FAW.Mk 21 was developed as the Fleet Air Arm equivalent of the NF.Mk 3, but with additional improvements including long-stroke undercarriage, and provision for rocket-assisted take-off. Later in the production run Martin Baker Mk 4 ejector seats were fitted, and earlier aircraft

Switzerland built the Venom FB.4 under licence
(Swiss Air Force)

Fleet Air Arm used Sea Venoms as all-weather ship-borne fighters (*Royal Navy*)

were retrofitted. Power was from an uprated Ghost 104 engine, which was replaced by the Ghost 105 in the final FAW.Mk 22 series.

Four Fleet Air Arm squadrons received Sea Venom FAW.Mk 21s commencing in May 1955, and after training they were ready for action. This came at short notice on 31 October 1956 with the Suez crisis. Following this, two more FAA front-line units equipped with Sea Venoms, one using the aircraft in the electronic warfare role. Three training squadrons were formed, two for pilot training and one for observers.

The Sea Venom was also used for development work on the Firestreak IR homing missile, including service trials with No. 893 Squadron, preparing the way for a smooth introduction of the Firestreak-armed Sea Vixen.

Retirement of the Sea Venom from front-line service commenced with the introduction of the Sea Vixen in July 1959, and was completed when No. 891 Squadron decommissioned in July 1961. Sea Venoms continued in service with Airwork at Yeovilton on Fleet requirement duties until October 1970 when the last was flown to Culdrose for fire fighting practice.

The Sea Venom also had export success in Australia and France. The Royal Australian Navy ordered 39 FAW.Mk 53s, an export version of the FAW.Mk 21. The first squadron formed at Culdrose in August 1955 using borrowed aircraft, and departed for Australia in March 1956 with the new aircraft. They were withdrawn from front-line service in Australia in August 1967 but a small number continued on training duties until 1970.

In France, the Sea Venom was adapted for the French Navy and license-built in modified form as the Aquilon by Sud Aviation, the first French-built aircraft flying in October 1952. Four versions were built, the Aquilon 201 advanced prototype, similar to the FAA Mk 20, the Aquilon 202 with ejector

seats under a rearward-sliding canopy and a stronger undercarriage (first flown on 24 March 1954), the Aquilon 203 single-seater fitted with American radar and clear-view canopy, and the Aquilon 204 two-seat unarmed trainer conversion of the 203. A total of three *Flotillas* of the French naval aviation were equipped with the Aquilon until the type was withdrawn in 1963. All Aquilon versions were powered by Ghost 48 Mk 1 jet engines.

Data
Variant: D.H.112 Sea Venom FAW.Mk 22
Power plant: One 2,404 kg (5,300 lb) thrust D.H. Ghost 105 jet engine
Accommodation: Two crew side-by-side under a clear-view canopy
Fuel capacity: 2,073 ltr (456 Imp gal) including 685 ltr (150 Imp gal) in wing-tip tanks
Wing span: 13.08 m (42 ft 11 in)
Wing area: 25.99 sq m (279.75 sq ft)
Length: 11.15 m (36 ft 7 in)
Height: 2.6 m (8 ft 6¼ in)
Weight empty: 5,126 kg (11,300 lb)
Max t/o weight: 7,167 kg (15,800 lb)
Max level speed: 925 km/h (575 mph)
Service ceiling: 12,190 m (40,000 ft)
Endurance/range: 1,135 km (705 miles)
Armament: Four 20 mm Hispano Mk 5 cannon
Production Venom: Total of 749 for the RAF: five prototypes, 379 FB.Mk 1, 90 NF.Mk 2, 129 NF.Mk 3, 150 FB.Mk 4.
Export: Total of 349: Sweden 60, Italy 2, Iraq 15, Venezuela 22, and Switzerland (license-built) 250.
Sea Venom: Total of 299 for the FAA: four prototypes, 50 FAW.Mk 20, 167 FAW.Mk 21, 39 FAW.Mk 22, and 39 for the RAN.
French license production: Total of 94: four Aquilon prototypes, 25 Aquilon 201, 25 Aquilon 202 and 40 Aquilon 203.
Overall total: 1,491 aircraft

D.H.113 VAMPIRE NIGHT FIGHTER

First flight: 28 August 1949

Type: Two-seat, single-engine jet night fighter

Notes: Developed from the Vampire Mk 5, the D.H.113 was a private venture low cost night fighter for the export market. It featured a lengthened side-by-side two-seat fuselage nacelle, and AI Mk. 10 radar in the nose. A more powerful Goblin 3 engine was fitted, otherwise the remainder of the aircraft was similar to the fighter version.

The initial production order was for 12 aircraft for Egypt, but before they could be delivered an arms embargo was imposed by the British Government and the aircraft were adopted by the RAF, with further production as the NF.Mk 10. It became the first jet night fighter with the RAF when it replaced Mosquito NF.36s at West Malling with No. 25 Squadron in July 1951. The aircraft made a useful stop-gap night fighter, but was criticised for its lack of ejector seats for the crew.

A total of three home defence units operated the Vampire Night Fighter, the others being at Coltishall and Leuchars, but in November 1953 the short operational life of the aircraft began to come to an end when No. 23 Squadron started to receive Venom NF.2s.

Exports included one to Switzerland for evaluation in January 1951, and 14 to Italy. Unused and surplus aircraft available after withdrawal from RAF service were released for export, and 30 were purchased by India in 1954.

Many of the remaining aircraft had the radar removed and were modified for advanced navigation training with a new clear-view canopy, but still without ejector seats. These aircraft were used by 1 Air Navigation School (ANS) at Topcliffe and 2 ANS at Thorney Island until retirement in mid-1959. The biggest user of the Vampire Mk 10s was the Central Navigation and Control School (CNCS) at Shawbury between May 1954 and September 1959.

Data

Variant: D.H.113 Vampire NF.Mk 10

Power plant: One 1,520 kg (3,350 lb) thrust D.H. Goblin 3 jet engine

Accommodation: Two crew side-by-side under upward opening canopy

Fuel capacity: 2,410 ltr (530 Imp gal) including 2 × 455 ltr (100 Imp gal) wing drop tanks

Wing span: 11.58 m (38 ft)

Wing area: 24.25 sq m (261 sq ft)

Length: 10.54 m (34 ft 7 in)

Height: 2 m (6 ft 7 in)

Weight empty: 3,168 kg (6,984 lb)

Max t/o weight: 5,942 kg (13,100 lb)

Max level speed: 866 km/h (538 mph)

Service ceiling: 12,190 m (40,000 ft)

Endurance/range: 1,963 km (1,220 miles)

Armament: Four 20 mm Hispano Mk 5 cannon

Production Total of 124: one prototype, 78 to RAF, one to Switzerland, 14 to Italy, 30 to India

D.H.113 Vampire was an interim and export low-cost night fighter *(Hawker Siddeley)*

DE HAVILLAND D.H.114 HERON

D.H.114 Heron was developed from the Dove as a four-engined feederliner (*de Havilland*)

First flight: 10 May 1950

Type: 14 to 17-seat four-engine feeder airliner
Notes: First announced in April 1950, the Heron was designed to carry a 1,524 kg (1½ ton) payload over stages of up to 644 km (400 miles). It featured simplicity of design, which included a fixed undercarriage, four ungeared Gipsy Queen engines driving two-blade propellers, and no hydraulics. For ease of production and spare parts, the Heron utilised a number of Dove main components including outer wings, nose, rear fuselage and tail unit. During flight trials however, the tailplane had to be given some dihedral to improve control.

Less than a year after its first flight an unrestricted C of A was achieved, and early orders came from Norway, Brazil and Indonesia. Following the prototype only seven Herons were built at Hatfield before production was moved to Chester; the last Hatfield Heron was the prototype Srs 2 with a retractable undercarriage and increased range, first flown on 14 December 1952.

The Heron entered airline service with Braathens SAFE in Norway on 8 August 1952, achieving a load factor of 69 per cent. It worked well in all climates including airline services in Australia, Brazil, what was then French Equatorial Africa, New Zealand, Uruguay, Japan and the Channel Islands.

The Heron Srs 2 prototype completed a demonstration tour of Africa, the Middle East and India resulting in sales to airlines and business users in India, Turkey, South Africa, Saudi Arabia and the Belgian Congo. In North America an executive model was sold in Canada and one was allocated to the British Embassy in Washington DC. In September 1954, the royal approval was given to the Heron when the first of four was ordered for the Queen's Flight, remaining in service until replaced by Andovers in 1964.

Further Heron 2s were sold in West Africa and the Bahamas, and in late 1954 BEA ordered two Herons to replace the Rapides on the Scottish Ambulance services, which continued to use them until 1972.

Shell, Vickers and Rolls-Royce were amongst British business users, and another joined a pair of Doves with the Moroccan royal family in 1957. The East African DCA used a Heron for the calibration of radio aids. Military users of the Heron included the Royal Navy who operated five acquired from civil sources, two each to the SAAF, R. Iraqi AF, the Luftwaffe, R. Jordanian AF and the RMAF. The Ceylon Air Force operated four Herons and five Devons.

Aviaco of Spain operated a fleet of eight 14-seat Herons on their local services, while in the UK Cambrian and Morton used Herons on domestic and continental routes. It was a Morton Heron 1 G-AOXL which operated the last scheduled service from Croydon Airport on 30 September 1959 before the airport ceased operations after 43 years.

Apart from detailed modifications, the Heron changed little once the Series 2 had been produced. The final version was the Series 2D with an increased all-up weight, and the last production aircraft was used on company communications by Hawker Siddeley Aviation from January 1968 until offered for sale in 1972.

The basic Heron was not a great success in North America until the engines were replaced by four 253.5 kW (340 hp) Lycoming GSO-480s. A large fleet was modified and operated by the Carribean commuter airline, Prinair. Saunders Aircraft of Montreal developed a comprehensive modification programme which became the ST-27. Under this, two United PT6A engines replaced the four Gipsy Queens, and the fuselage was extended by 2.59 m (8 ft 6 in) to accommodate 24 passengers and three crew. When good second-hand

Herons were not available, the plan was to produce aircraft from scratch, but due to financial difficulties the company collapsed and the project was cancelled after only a small number had been delivered.

Data
Variant: D.H.114 Heron Srs 2D
Power plant: Four 186 kW (250 hp) D.H. Gipsy Queen 30 Mk 2 inline engines
Accommodation: Two crew and up to 14 passengers
Fuel capacity: 1,900 ltr (418 Imp gal)

Wing span: 21.79 m (71 ft 6 in)
Wing area: 46.36 sq m (499 sq ft)
Length: 14.78 m (48 ft 6 in)
Height: 4.75 m (15 ft 7 in)
Weight empty: 4,177 kg (9,209 lb)
Max t/o weight: 6,124 kg (13,500 lb)
Max level speed: 295 km/h (183 mph)
Service ceiling: 5,240 m (17,200 ft)
Endurance/range: 2,502 km (1,555 miles)
Production Total of 149: one prototype Srs 1 and one prototype Srs 2 both Hatfield-built. Six Hatfield-built Srs 1s plus 44 Chester-built Srs 1s, 97 Chester-built Srs 2s

DE HAVILLAND D.H.115 VAMPIRE TRAINER

First flight: 15 November 1950

Type: Two-seat, single-engined advanced jet trainer
Notes: The Vampire Trainer was the last aircraft type wholly produced by de Havilland before the mergers. It was an all-purpose advanced trainer for pilot, gunnery, rocketry, bombing and radar instruction, seating the crew side-by-side in a pressurised cockpit. As with earlier Vampires, it had a wooden fuselage nacelle and the remainder was metal construction. With its armament of two or four 20 mm cannon under the fuselage and provision for the carriage of two 454 kg (1,000 lb) bombs or eight RPs under the wings, the aircraft could be used operationally if required.

Following successful completion of service trials with the private venture prototype in 1951, it was ordered into production for the RAF as the Vampire T.Mk 11, and later for the FAA as the T.Mk 22. Production was shared between Christchurch, Chester and Hatfield, with a few assembled by Fairey. The early aircraft were fitted with the old Night Fighter type canopy with a hinged upward opening lid and no ejector seats. However, the 144th and subsequent production aircraft were fitted with a rear-hinged upward opening clearview canopy, ejector seats and dorsal fillets to the fins, the earlier aircraft being retrofitted.

The first training unit to receive the T.11s was 5 Flying Training School (FTS) at Oakington, the initial course commencing in June 1954, to complete the first advanced jet training. Other units to follow included 7 FTS at Valley, the RAF College at Cranwell, 229 Operational Conversion Unit (OCU) at Chivenor and the Fighter Weapons School at Leconfield, as well as most fighter squadrons for continuation training. Other users were the Central Navigation and Control School

D.H.115 Vampire Trainer was designed as an advanced jet trainer

(CNCS) at Shawbury and No. 3 Civil Anti-Aircraft Co-operative Unit (CAACU) at Exeter as tactical targets for the Army. The Fleet Air Arm used their T.22s with three or four training squadrons and station flights.

As with the Vampire and other de Havilland aircraft, the Vampire Trainer was a great success in the export market, many going to air forces already equipped with the single-seaters, as well as new customers.

The first overseas sale was to Australia in 1951 who bought an initial batch of 35 T.Mk 33s for the RAAF and five similar T.Mk 34s for the RAN, with deliveries commencing on 26 May 1952. A total of 69 improved T.Mk 35 trainers with modified fins, clear-view canopy, ejector seats and increased fuel tankage were license-built locally. New Zealand placed an order later the same year, followed by South Africa who ordered the export version known as the T.Mk 55. The first European customer was Norway. This was followed by an order from Venezuela (first delivered in September 1952) and Portugal (end of 1952). One of the largest export orders came from Sweden in 1952. Switzerland license-built the metal parts and fitted them to the de Havilland supplied fuselages.

The largest order for Vampire Trainers came from India who followed the 53 from de Havillands (delivered from mid-1953 to the end of 1957) with 60 more built under license. Smaller orders came from the Lebanon, Iraq, Chile, Finland, Burma, Southern Rhodesia, Egypt, Indonesia, Jordan and Ireland. One was supplied to Japan for evaluation but the type was not adopted and two frustrated orders were from Ceylon and Syria, the latter due to an arms embargo. The last overseas order came from Austria in January 1957 who ordered five new aircraft, and added three ex-RAF T.11s in January 1964.

The Vampire T.11s were finally retired from training duties with the RAF on 29 November 1966 when the last were withdrawn from 3 FTS at Leeming. Some continued in service at Shawbury until November 1970 and at No. 3 CAACU at Exeter until December 1971.

Two Vampire T.11s still fly in Britain, one with the RAF as part of the Vintage Pair with a Meteor, and the other is privately owned. Overseas, the type is still in service in Switzerland. Many were disposed of to museums and cadet units to ensure examples will be preserved for many years.

Data
Variant: D.H.115 Vampire T.Mk 11
Power plant: One 1,588 kg (3,500 lb) thrust D.H. Goblin 35 jet engine
Accommodation: Two crew side-by-side under clear-view canopy
Fuel capacity: 2,410 ltr (530 Imp gal) including 2 × 455 ltr (100 Imp gal) wing drop tanks
Wing span: 11.58 m (38 ft)
Wing area: 24.25 sq m (261 sq ft)
Length: 10.49 m (34 ft 5 in)
Height: 2 m (6 ft 7 in)
Weight empty: 3,348 kg (7,380 lb)
Max t/o weight: 5,806 kg (12,800 lb)
Max level speed: 866 km/h (538 mph)
Service ceiling: 11,580 m (38,000 ft)
Endurance/range: 1,352 km (840 miles)
Armament: Two 20 mm Hispano Mk 5 cannon, plus up to two 454 kg (1,000 lb) bombs
Production Total of 610 for the RAF and RN: one prototype and two pre-production aircraft, 534 T.Mk 11 for the RAF, 73 T.Mk 22 for the RN.
Exports: Australia 109 (including license-built), RNZAF 6, SAAF 27, Norway 6, Venezuela 6, Portugal 2, Sweden 45, Switzerland 30, India 53 (plus 60 under license), Lebanon 4, Iraq 7, Chile 6, Finland 4, Burma 8, Egypt 12, Indonesia 8, Japan 1, Ireland 6, Ceylon 5, Syria 2, Austria 5.
Total exports: 412.
Overall Vampire Trainer production: 1,022 aircraft

DE HAVILLAND D.H.121 TRIDENT

First flight: 9 January 1962

Type: Medium-range three-engine jet airliner
Notes: It was announced in Parliament on 12 February 1958 that BEA would follow the Comet jet operations with the second generation D.H.121 airliner. To comply with government wishes, the new airliner was to be produced by a consortium of companies led by de Havilland and consisting of Hunting and Fairey. This company revived the name Airco and was incorporated in February 1958.

The original D.H.121 was to be powered by three Rolls-Royce Medway by-pass engines, being specially developed for this airliner. The aircraft was to be capable of carrying up to 111 passengers on stage lengths up to 2,897 km (1,800 miles) at over 966 km/h (600 mph), but still be capable of operating from 610 m (2,000 yd) runways. It was ordered by BEA on 12 August 1959, the contract covering 24 aircraft, with options for a further twelve.

However, following a 10 per cent drop in passenger growth for BEA in 1958, the airline considered the existing aircraft too large. The length of the fuselage was therefore reduced, the less powerful Rolls-Royce Spey engines were substituted for the Medways, and at the same time the range was reduced to 1,287 km (800 miles). With the aircraft tailored so closely to the transient needs of one airline it was unsaleable to any others, and had severely restricted development potential. This reduction in size was even more regrettable because the BEA passenger figures increased again, more than justifying the original aircraft.

The D.H.121 had a number of unique features, including the grouping of the three engines around the tail to give a quieter cabin and more efficient wing; triplication of all major systems giving added safety; and full provision for automatic landings, a feature still not common to all of today's modern airliners.

On 17 December 1959, de Havillands merged with the Hawker Siddeley Group to become part of Hawker Siddeley Aviation, thereafter becoming fully responsible for the Trident, as the aircraft became known.

The first Trident was rolled out at Hatfield on 4 August 1961, but the first flight was delayed until the following January due to non-availability of the Spey engines, caused by the short development time with the demise of the Medway. The first six aircraft were used in the development programme, including one aircraft which pioneered automatic landing, first accomplished on 5 March 1964. The first fare-paying passengers landed automatically on 10 June 1965, and the first automatic landing in fog by a civil airliner was made at London Airport on 4 November 1966. All other movements had been brought to a halt, and the major problem was to find the terminal buildings from the runway.

The C of A was awarded to the Trident on 18 February 1964, ready for *ad hoc* services to commence on 11 March, and regular schedules on 1 April, just over two years from the maiden flight of this advanced airliner.

The first development of the Trident was the Mk 1E with an increased all-up weight, more powerful Spey 511-5 engines and improvements to the flaps and wing leading edge devices. This version was more attractive in the export market and gained its first order for two from Kuwait Airways in 1962.

Further Trident 1Es were sold to Iraqi Airways, Pakistan International Airlines, and another one to Kuwait Airways. The remaining five of this version on the production line at Hatfield were converted to the Mk 1E-140 with an increased all-up weight for greater payload or range, for Channel Airways. This airline only took delivery of two, another two going to the Newcastle-based BKS, later Northeast Airlines, and one to Air Ceylon.

On 28 August 1965, BEA placed an order for 15 Trident 2Es powered by uprated Spey engines, carrying more fuel to extend the range to 4,023 km (2,500 miles), and increasing the all-up weight. First flight was on 27 July 1967, followed by C of A, and delivery to BEA on 17 April 1968. With two and a half times the range and 20 per cent more power than the Trident 1, the new aircraft

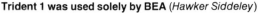

Trident 1 was used solely by BEA (*Hawker Siddeley*)

141

The ultimate Super Trident 3, two of which were ordered by China (*Hawker Siddeley*)

fitted in well on the longer European routes. Two were ordered by Cyprus Airways, who previously had operated in a pool with BEA.

BEA still had a need for a high-capacity, short-range aircraft, the Trident 3 being offered for this requirement. The fuselage was stretched by 5.03 m (16 ft 5 in) giving room for up to 180 passengers, and more powerful Spey engines fitted. BEA made it known that they preferred the Boeing 727-200 and demanded a government subsidy to compensate them for operating British aircraft; in fact, an aircraft which had suffered from the airline's own miscalculations. To cope with hot and high airfields on some of the BEA network, a Rolls-Royce RB.162 boost engine was installed at the base of the rudder. Subsequently BEA placed an order for 26 of this version known as the Trident 3B in August 1968, and the maiden flight was the following 11 December, with services commencing on 1 April 1971.

A significant second-hand sale was the Pakistan International Airlines aircraft to China in 1970. As a result, CAAC of China required more Tridents for their domestic routes, eventually ordering 33 Trident 2s and two modified Super Trident 3Bs with increased range and all-up weight.

British Airways have now retired all their Trident 1s and many of the Trident 2s, but the remainder will remain in operation until their use-

ful life is finished. The Trident was developed effectively from the modest Trident 1, and had it had a better start, it would no doubt have sold more widely.

Data
Variant: D.H.121 Trident 3B
Power plant: Three 5,411 kg (11,930 lb) thrust R-R Spey, plus one 2,381 kg (5,250 lb) thrust RB.162
Accommodation: Three flight crew and up to 180 passengers
Fuel capacity: 25,548 ltr (5,620 Imp gal)
Wing span: 29.87 m (98 ft)
Wing area: 138.7 sq m (1,493 sq ft)
Length: 40.03 m (131 ft 2 in)
Height: 8.61 m (28 ft 3 in)
Weight empty: 36,855 kg (81,250 lb)
Max t/o weight: 68,040 kg (150,000 lb)
Max level speed: 885 km/h (550 mph)
Service ceiling: 9,140 m (30,000 ft)
Endurance/range: 3,597 km (2,235 miles)
Production Total of 117, all from Hatfield: 24 Trident 1 for BEA, 15 Trident 1E, 50 Trident 2 and 28 Trident 3

DE HAVILLAND D.H.125

First flight: 13 August 1962

Type: Six to eight-passenger, twin-engine business jet
Notes: Although strictly speaking the D.H.125 was produced over two years after the merger with Hawker Siddeley, it was the last aircraft to carry the 'D.H.' initials and was produced by essentially

the same team who had conceived the earlier D.H. aircraft. The D.H.125 was a private venture business jet, using the Comet and Trident experience scaled down to a Dove-sized aircraft. Power came from two rear fuselage mounted Bristol Siddeley Viper engines giving jet comfort and speed over ranges of 1,609 km (1,000 miles) and beyond. A unique feature of the aircraft was the bolting of the unobstructed fuselage directly on top of the slightly swept-back wing.

The two prototypes were built at Chester, but assembled at Hatfield for their maiden flights. Production was then set up at the Chester factory, which is still making developed versions of the 125. All development flying, crew training, design, sales and product support remains at Hatfield.

The company authorised an initial production batch of 30 aircraft, the first example going to Bristol Siddeley Engines for Viper development flying, with others being used for demonstration or sold to individual companies. An early significant order was for 20 navigation trainers for the RAF, known as the Dominie T.Mk 1, which now serve with 6 FTS at Finningley.

Following the first batch was another batch of 30 with the rear cabin window deleted and an improved all-up weight, known as the Srs 1A for North America, and Srs 1B for the rest of the world. America was to be a major market for the 125, the aircraft being completed structurally and flown across the Atlantic for equipping, furnishing and painting to the individual customer's requirements. The Srs 2 was the RAF Dominie, and the Srs 3 featured a further increase in all-up weight and revised electrical and air conditioning systems. The first of these was Number 111 off the line, apart from two earlier crew training aircraft for Qantas. A later improvement to this model was the addition of a ventral long-range fuel tank which became the Srs 3AR or 3BR.

The first major change was the Srs 400 with

D.H.125 prototype had a shorter fuselage and reduced wing span than later versions (de Havilland)

uprated Viper 522 engines, cleaning up of the external shape, increased all-up weight and a narrower outward opening door which featured integral air stairs. By this time known as the HS 125 it was a highly successful aircraft capable of operating unsupported at unsophisticated airfields.

In August 1972, the stretched Srs 600 was announced with a 0.61 m (2 ft) extension to the cabin, adding back the sixth window. The airframe was further cleaned up and the more powerful Viper 601 engines installed. Handling in the air was improved and the interior was transformed with a new flight deck and comfortable cabin. All the civil versions of the 125 have been offered with their own private toilet, and the galley and baggage compartments accessible in flight. Its walk-round cabin has always been an advantage on longer flights over the smaller and cheaper business jets. Not only has the 125 been sold to business organisations all over the world providing secure, rapid transport, but also for aircrew training, the checking of ground navigation aids, ambulance flights and charter.

A recent and most successful version to date is the Srs 700 which is basically the Srs 600 airframe fitted with Garrett Airesearch quiet fuel-efficient fan engines. A prototype conversion of a Srs 600 first flew from Chester on 28 June 1976 and production deliveries commenced in mid-1977. The new Srs 800 with an improved wing and many aerodynamic improvements was unveiled in June 1983. To date, over 550 of the 125s have been sold with prospects for many more in the future. Development is expected to continue.

Data
Variant: HS.125-400
Power plant: Two 1,633 kg (3,600 lb) thrust BS (later R-R) Viper 522 jet engines
Accommodation: Two crew and six to eight passengers
Fuel capacity: 5,170 ltr (1,137 Imp gal)
Wing span: 14.33 m (47 ft)
Wing area: 32.79 sq m (353 sq ft)
Length: 14.45 m (47 ft 5 in)
Height: 5.03 m (16 ft 6 in)
Weight empty: 5,114 kg (11,275 lb)
Max t/o weight: 10,569 kg (23,300 lb)
Max level speed: 821 km/h (510 mph)
Service ceiling: 12,500 m (41,000 ft)
Endurance/range: 3,122 km (1,940 miles)
Production Two prototypes, eight Srs 1, 78 Srs 1A/1B, 62 Srs 3 of all types, 118 Srs 400, 71 Srs 600.
Over 200 Srs 700 and continuing in production, while Srs 800 becomes established.

Appendix 1
The Overseas Companies and Their Aircraft

DE HAVILLAND AUSTRALIA

The Australian company was the first overseas company to be formed by the parent organisation, on 7 March 1927 in Victoria, to support the aircraft in service within the Dominion. Major Hereward de Havilland headed the company, established in a semi-derelict warehouse at Melbourne for the assembly of crated Moths which had arrived by sea. They were towed by road to the aerodrome at Essendon, some 11.25 km (7 miles) away.

The demand for Moth variants began to grow for private owners, club and military use. In 1930, a move was made to better premises at Mascot Aerodrome, near Sydney, where aviation prospects were improved. From February 1931, the company handled sales, service and maintenance, including manufacture of components for spares, and later wing production, the more complicated fuselages being shipped from Britain. In 1932, the company practically closed due to the effects of the world depression and a particularly bad drought in Australia, but with the arrival of the Fox Moths, Dragons and D.H.86s their fortunes began to improve.

Efforts were made to develop the productive capacity, but there was a lack of encouragement from the Australian Government. However, three Moths and two Fox Moths were built locally and Australian personnel had visited the British company to gain experience in the manufacturing techniques.

With the British re-armament programme gaining momentum in 1937, Australia agreed for their branch of the company to commence the manufacture of propellers. Eventually over 2,000 propellers were produced for Australian use during the war at a new factory in New South Wales.

The first 20 Tiger Moths were ordered in 1938, Australia building the wooden parts and Britain supplying the engines and metal fuselages. These were followed by 41 Moth Minors which were replaced on the production line by more Tiger Moths, produced entirely in Australia. Total production amounted to 1,085 by the end of the war. Many were supplied to the Empire Training Scheme in South Africa and Rhodesia, as well as to India and the Dutch East Indies.

In October 1941, the Australian government ordered 87 Dragons for navigation training and communications with the RAAF, which required a considerable expansion of production space.

Useful design experience was gained when in March 1942 a troop-carrying glider for the RAAF to Specification 5/42 was ordered. Design of this all-wood aircraft known as the DHG.1 was completed in three months, and to simplify manufacture it used the nose and cockpit section of the Dragon. The specification was altered somewhat, requiring a 75 per cent re-design as the DHG.2, for which a production order was placed. However, it was abandoned after only six were built due to production difficulties, the changing military situation, and ready availability of other Allied gliders.

DHG.2 Glider was DH Australia's first original design to be built (*RAAF*)

Total of 212 Mosquitoes were built in Australia for the RAAF (de Havilland)

The major D.H. Australia wartime effort was the production of RAAF Mosquitoes. A new factory was built at Bankstown near Sydney for the production of a fighter-bomber version known as the FB.Mk 40, with an initial order for 150 aircraft. The first drawings from Britain arrived in June 1942 and a Mosquito Mk II was shipped out the same month. This sample aircraft was flown on 17 December 1942, but the first locally-produced Mosquito did not make its maiden flight until 23 July 1943, having been delayed for about four months due to problems with the supply of special parts from Britain. First deliveries to the RAAF were also about eight months late due to glueing problems which were thought to be the cause of the fatal accident to A52-12 on its pre-acceptance flight. However, wing flutter at high speed and high 'G' forces were found to be the actual cause of this crash. Once these problems had been cured production continued at Bankstown until 1948, the total output amounting to 212 Mosquitoes. By the end of the war, over 5,300 people were employed in 21 factories covering 65,030 sq m (700,000 sq ft).

To maintain work for as many employees as possible, the design team commenced their only powered project to reach production, the DHA.3 Drover. The Drover was a light, economical, simple and robust transport powered by three Gipsy Major engines. The first of 20 production aircraft flew on 23 January 1948, with a capability of carrying six to nine passengers. Construction was all-metal using Dove experience, and a fixed tailwheel undercarriage was used.

An order was placed in August 1948 for a total of 12 aircraft by the Australian Government to be used by the Department of Civil Aviation and the airlines. The first production aircraft was handed over to Qantas on 13 September 1950 for use as a convertible freighter in New Guinea capable of carrying 12 passengers. The most well-known use of the Drover was with the Royal Flying Doctor Service (RFDS) with a capability of carrying two stretcher patients. This service extended to cover twelve bases over the continent, replacing veteran Dragons.

Improvements made to the aircraft included changing the variable-pitch propellers to Fairey Reed fixed-pitch type as the Drover Mk 1F. The Mk 2 had its plain flaps changed to double slotted type and the Mk 3 had its Gipsy Majors replaced by three Lycoming O-360-A1A engines with Hartzel propellers. The tailplane was given dihedral and the all-up weight was increased. Drovers were finally phased out of RFDS service by 1970.

In August 1945, proposals were made for local manufacture of Vampire jet fighters for the RAAF, which were accepted in September 1946.

DHA.3 Drover, a rugged three-engined transport (de Havilland)

The initial production version, powered by a Rolls-Royce Nene engine, was the F.Mk 30 of which 57 were ordered powered by CAC-built Nene 2-VH jet engines. The first flew on 29 June 1949 and was delivered three months later. The FB.Mk 31 was then developed, an order for 23 being placed, and the last 28 F.30s were modified to the same standard. These Vampires remained in service until retirement in June 1960.

Early deliveries of the Vampire Trainers were made to the RAAF from Britain, but an order was placed for 36 T.Mk 33s, followed by five T.Mk 34s for the RAN. The last T.33 was modified to the later British standard with clear-view canopy and ejection seats to become the T.Mk 35, of which 68 were ordered in 1955 for the RAAF and one, a T.34A, for the RAN. The earlier production versions were later modified to the same standard.

In 1960, D.H. Australia was merged with the parent company into Hawker Siddeley Group, and became Hawker de Havilland Australia Pty Ltd.

Australian-built Vampires were powered by RR Nene engines (*RAAF*)

SPECIFICATIONS FOR D.H. AUSTRALIA AIRCRAFT

Variant: DHG.2
Accommodation: Seven-seat troop-carrying glider
Wing span: 15.39 m (50 ft 6 in)
Wing area: 30.89 sq m (332.5 sq ft)
Length: 10.06 m (33 ft)
Weight empty: 658 kg (1,450 lb)
Max t/o weight: 1,474 kg (3,250 lb)
Towing speed: 209 km/h (130 mph)
Production One prototype DHG.1 and six production DHG.2s

Variant: DHA.3 Drover Mk 1
Accommodation: Two crew and eight passengers
Power plant: Three 108 kW (145 hp) D.H. Gipsy Major 10 Mk 2 inline engines
Wing span: 17.37 m (57 ft)
Wing area: 30.19 sq m (325 sq ft)
Length: 11.12 m (36 ft 6 in)
Height: 3.05 m (10 ft)

Weight empty: 1,900 kg (4,190 lb)
Max t/o weight: 2,948 kg (6,500 lb)
Max level speed: 225 km/h (140 mph)
Ceiling: 4,880 m (16,000 ft)
Range: 901 km (560 miles)
Production 20 aircraft

Australian unbuilt projects:

DHA.1: Single-seat fighter powered by one Pratt & Whitney 1830 radial engine
DHA.2: Two-seat basic trainer powered by a D.H. Gipsy Major inline engine
DHA.4: All-metal 18-seat airliner powered by four D.H. Gipsy Queen 70 inline engines
DHA.5: Lightweight two-seat jet trainer powered by a single R-R Viper engine

DE HAVILLAND AIRCRAFT OF CANADA

Officially announced in March 1928, de Havilland Aircraft of Canada was formed in a wooden railside shed at Mount Dennis, Ontario, the initial task being the assembly of Moth aircraft. To cope with the increasing popularity of the Moth, a new factory was built at Downsview, Ontario and officially opened in September 1929. A batch of 25 Puss Moths followed the D.H.60s, but a major portion of the early business was to adapt the parent company's aircraft to operate in the uncharted parts of Northern Canada by fitting float, wheel or ski undercarriages and other modifications.

In 1937, with war approaching, Tiger Moths were modified to meet local requirements, and an order was placed for an initial batch of 25 for the RCAF to be produced in Canada. The tide was turned when the British organisation ordered 200 Tiger Moth fuselages and other components from Canada, but work in the factory stagnated until a further order was placed for Tiger Moths in February 1940 for the Empire Air Training Scheme. A total of 1,553 D.H.82Cs were produced by D.H. Canada in addition to the fuselages. In 1940, 375 Avro Ansons were built under license as trainers for the RCAF, the factory covering 12 acres and employing over 7,000 people.

In 1941, organisation of Mosquito manufacture commenced in Canada and by September 1942 the first of 1,135 rolled off the production line, supplying Europe with much needed aircraft. Production rate eventually increased to 120 aircraft per month.

The end of the war brought the expected readjustment, and the first postwar activity for the factory was the production of over 50 modernised D.H.83C Fox Moths, using many Tiger Moth components.

In October 1945, design work led by the expatriate Polish engineer W. Jakimiuk commenced on

The original D.H. Canada premises were used for Moth assembly (*de Havilland*)

the first aircraft to be totally conceived by de Havilland Canada. His last design in Poland had been the advanced all-metal P.50a fighter, the sole prototype of which was shot down in error by a Polish AA battery in September 1939. The aim of the company was to produce an all-metal low-wing monoplane trainer to succeed the Tiger Moth. Named DHC-1 Chipmunk, this versatile training aircraft was designed to cover the range from primary instruction to advanced aerobatics and instrument training.

DHC-1 Chipmunk was used by a number of air forces including the RAF (*de Havilland*)

D.H. Canada adapted the Tiger Moth for local conditions by fitting a canopy (*Canadian Forces*)

An initial batch of 157 Chipmunks were produced between 1946 and 1952, delivered to the RCAF and a number of overseas air forces and flying schools. In 1955, the production line was reopened for 60 Chipmunks to an improved T.Mk 30 standard with a larger one-piece clear-view canopy.

In April 1948, the Chipmunk was chosen as the standard elementary trainer for the RAF Reserve flying schools, the first deliveries being to Oxford University Air Squadron in February 1950. Production lines were set up initially at Hatfield, and later at Chester, where a total of 1,000 were produced for the RAF, the British Army, the Royal Navy, civil flying schools and export, the last being delivered to Saudi Arabia in February 1956.

One of the major Chipmunk modifications, handled by de Havillands, was the Agricultural Mk 23. This version had a hopper in place of the front seat and the pilot was located in a raised cockpit in the rear seat. For top dressing with liquids, spray bars were fitted under the wings. de Havillands only completed one conversion before abandoning the scheme, but three more were converted by Farm Aviation.

In 1946, the Ontario Provincial Government was looking for a new bush aircraft. As a result of a questionnaire circulated to many Canadian bush pilots, de Havilland Canada commenced work on the DHC-2 Beaver, a light STOL (Short Take Off and Landing) transport capable of operating from restricting areas of land, water and snow. Normal load was up to six passengers or 508 kg (half a ton) of freight, and it could be used for feeder operations from more remote strips, casualty evacuation, supply dropping, crop protection, border and coastal patrols, aerial survey, mining and oil exploration and supply, paratroop operations and forest fire protection.

Two Beavers were evaluated by the USAF in 1950, resulting in substantial orders, and in the following year some 800 were also ordered by the

DHC-2 Beavers were fitted with ski undercarriages for operations off ice and snow (de Havilland)

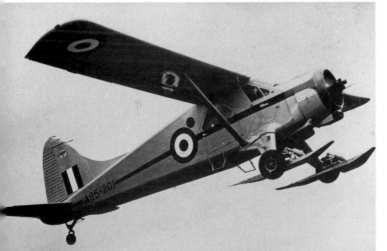

Like many D.H. Canada aircraft, DHC-3 Otter could be fitted with floats (de Havilland)

US Army. A number of overseas air forces ordered Beavers, some examples being used in the extreme conditions of the Antarctic. A total of 46 Beavers were ordered by the British Army in 1959 and assembled at Chester.

The only major development was the Turbo Beaver which had its original Wasp Junior radial engine replaced by a United PT6-A6 propeller turbine giving 30 per cent more power. The cabin was also extended by 0.76 m (30 in) making room for two more passengers. The prototype made its maiden flight on 30 December 1963, and the overall performance improvement was more than 30 per cent. A total of 60 of this version were produced, in addition to over 1,600 of the earlier version.

With the enormous success of the Beaver a need was seen for a similar aircraft, with the same performance, but double the payload. This aircraft was the DHC-3 Otter, powered by a single Pratt & Whitney Wasp radial engine. A total of 466 were built alongside the Beavers, and they could carry up to 14 passengers from land, water or snow. Initial orders were from the RCAF and the Ontario Department of Lands and Forests, with many going to Beaver operators including 84 to the US Army. As with the Beaver, the Otter was a very rugged aircraft flown in all climates for a wide variety of duties and making good use of its STOL capabilities.

In 1954 work commenced on the license production of 100 Grumman Trackers for carrier based anti-submarine duties with the Royal Canadian Navy (RCN).

A year later, DH Canada commenced work on the first multi-engine design, a STOL utility transport, which became the DHC-4 Caribou. Powered by two Pratt & Whitney R-2000 radial engines, the aircraft had an upswept rear fuselage with high tail to allow loading of vehicles and freight through a rear ramp. This door could be opened in flight for parachute dropping of men and equipment. Up to

DHC-4 Caribou has a large door in the rear fuselage (*DHC*)

27 passengers could be carried on feeder operations, or 22 stretchers for casualty evacuation.

The prototype Caribou made its first flight from Downsview on 30 July 1958, and a stretched version was ordered by the US Army who took delivery of 78, later passing them on to the USAF. A number of other air forces ordered the Caribou, as it was ideally suited to tactical transport duties from a variety of surfaces in all climates. The Caribou was not fitted with floats as it would probably have been too large, but a wheel/ski undercarriage was developed for operations from snow. The production line closed in 1972 after 307 were produced, to be followed by the prop-jet Buffalo.

The DHC-5 Buffalo was generally similar in concept to the Caribou, but was powered by two General Electric turbo-prop engines, and took advantage of the later techniques in design and construction. The prototype made its first flight from Downsview on 9 April 1964 in US Army markings, but they did not place the expected orders due to political moves which transferred the medium-lift tactical transport duties to the USAF. A launch order was however placed by the RCAF for 15 aircraft. Once again it bore the DH Canada trade mark of a dramatic STOL performance, carrying up to 44 passengers with twin engine security. Other major customers were the Brazilian Air Force who ordered 24, and Peru who had 16 Buffaloes.

Two Buffaloes were used for development work, the most extensively modified being one for Augmentor Wing Research for NASA, converted by Boeing and powered by two Rolls-Royce Spey jet engines. The other development programme was the fitting of an inflatable air cushion landing system to allow operations from any reasonably level unprepared surface such as swamps, snow or gravel.

In 1974, a civil DHC-5E was offered, changes including the fitting of more powerful General Electric T64 turbo-props. This new version was renamed Transporter, and both versions remain in production as highly effective tactical transport aircraft, with over 100 operating in extreme environments.

When investigating the original Caribou specification, a twin-engined Otter had been considered, but offered little advantage at that time. However, with the availability of the United PT-6 turbo-prop engine, the design was revised as the highly successful DHC-6 Twin Otter. The new design proved to be ideally suited to third level and commuter routes in the USA and the rest of the world. It provided a relatively unsophisticated, but efficient aircraft, and once again the full range of undercarriage options were available. Up to 15 passengers could be carried economically on stages of between 161 and 966 km (100 and 600 miles). Like its predecessors, it could be used for a wide range of duties including executive transport, air ambulance, forestry patrol, water bomber, geophysical survey as well as passenger and cargo transport. First flight was from Downsview on 20 May 1965, taking-off in just three times its own length.

In April 1968 the improved Twin Otter Series 200 was announced with a longer nose giving more baggage space, a larger passenger entry door and an increase in landing weight. In August 1969 the Series 300 was announced with more powerful PT6A engines, giving a capability of carrying up to

DHC-5 Buffalo carries freight or passengers from short rough strips

DHC-6 Twin Otter commuter airliner has a sprightly take-off performance (*P. J. Birtles*)

20 passengers. The engine overhaul life had reached 3,000 hours, with 4,500 hours in some special cases.

A recent addition to the range has been a specially-equipped military Series 300M for maritime reconnaissance and light strike, but by far the greatest demand has been for the commuter routes, mostly with North American operators. With over 800 sold by the end of 1982, the type remains in production for the foreseeable future.

In 1972, the go ahead was given for the 50 passenger DHC-7, known as the Dash 7. It is a STOL commuter airliner powered by four quiet PT6A-50 turbo-prop engines, capable of operating from down-town airports. This was the first aircraft produced by D.H. Canada for regular commercial operations with major airlines, as well as commuter operators. Originally the aircraft had been designed with rugged, bush features, but

these were deleted during the initial lull in sales interest. Canadian Government backing was awarded in October 1972. Early customers were Wideroe of Norway and Rocky Mountain Airways of Denver, and over 80 have been sold, mainly for airline operations, but also for the Canadian Armed Forces and the Venezuelan Navy.

When de Havilland merged with Hawker Siddeley, the Canadian company was included in the deal. In so doing, they inherited the large ex Avro factory at Malton which they used for the sub-contract production of DC-9 wings and rear fuselages. Due to the high costs of tooling, this operation later had to be taken over by McDonnell Douglas. In 1974, the Canadian Government exercised their option to purchase the company from Hawker Siddeley to ensure a national interest in the organisation, and much to the relief of the British owners.

The name lives on as de Havilland Aircraft of Canada, the eventual aim being for the Canadian Government to sell their interests nationally, but this is yet to happen.

The most recent product from this company, which never fails to produce a winner, is the DHC-8 or Dash 8, powered by two Pratt & Whitney PW 120 turbo-props. It is a 36-seat commuter airliner/corporate aircraft. The first prototype made its maiden flight on 20 June 1983, and over 115 options have already been received.

De Havilland Canada are now the only part of the Enterprise surviving and keeping the pioneer name alive.

STOL DASH-7 commuter airliner can carry over 50 passengers (*DHC*)

DASH-8 is the latest STOL development by D.H. Canada

SPECIFICATION FOR D.H. CANADA AIRCRAFT

Variant: DHC-1 Chipmunk T.Mk 10
First flown: 22 May 1946
Type: Basic trainer
Accommodation: Two crew in tandem under a rearward sliding canopy
Power plant: One 108 kW (145 hp) D.H. Gipsy Major 1C inline engine
Wing span: 10.45 m (34 ft 4 in)
Wing area: 16.03 sq m (172.5 sq ft)

Length: 7.75 m (25 ft 5 in)
Height: 2.13 m (7 ft)
Weight empty: 646 kg (1,425 lb)
Max t/o weight: 953 kg (2,100 lb)
Max level speed: 233 km/h (145 mph)
Ceiling: 4,880 m (16,000 ft)
Range: 781 km (485 miles)
Production 217 from DH Canada, 1,000 from DH in Britain, 60 from OGMA Portugal.

Variant: DHC-2 Beaver
First flown: 16 August 1947
Type: STOL bush transport
Accommodation: One pilot plus six passengers
Power plant: One 336 kW (450 hp) Pratt & Whitney Wasp Junior radial engine
Wing span: 14.63 m (48 ft)
Wing area: 23.23 sq m (250 sq ft)
Length: 9.24 m (30 ft 4 in)
Height: 2.74 m (9 ft)
Weight empty: 1,275 kg (2,810 lb)
Max t/o weight: 2,313 kg (5,100 lb)
Max level speed: 237 km/h (147 mph)
Ceiling: 4,800 m (15,750 ft)
Range: 1,333 km (828 miles)
Production 1,632 standard Beavers, plus 60 Turbo Beavers

Variant: DHC-3 Otter
First flown: 12 December 1951
Type: STOL bush transport
Accommodation: One pilot plus 14 passengers
Power plant: One 447 kW (600 hp) Pratt & Whitney R-1340 Twin Wasp radial engine
Wing span: 17.68 m (58 ft)
Wing area: 34.84 sq m (375 sq ft)
Length: 12.75 m (41 ft 10 in)
Height: 3.83 m (12 ft 7 in)
Weight empty: 2,010 kg (4,431 lb)
Max t/o weight: 3,629 kg (8,000 lb)
Max level speed: 257 km/h (160 mph)
Ceiling: 5,730 m (18,800 ft)
Range: 1,408 km (875 miles)
Production 466 aircraft

Variant: DHC-4 Caribou
First flown: 30 July 1958
Type: STOL military transport aircraft
Accommodation: Two crew and up to 32 troops or 3,048 kg (3 tons) freight
Power plant: Two 1,081 kW (1,450 hp) Pratt & Whitney R-2000 radial engines
Wing span: 29.15 m (95 ft 7½ in)
Wing area: 84.72 sq m (912 sq ft)
Length: 22.12 m (72 ft 7 in)
Height: 9.68 m (31 ft 9 in)
Weight empty: 7,997 kg (17,630 lb)
Max t/o weight: 8,677 kg (19,130 lb)

Max level speed: 291 km/h (181 mph)
Ceiling: 8,110 m (26,600 ft)
Range: 2,060 km (1,280 miles)
Production 307 aircraft

Variant: DHC-5 Buffalo
First flown: 9 April 1964
Type: STOL military tactical transport
Accommodation: Two crew and up to 44 passengers
Power plant: Two 2,215 kW (2,970 shp) General Electric CT64-820-1 turbo-prop engines
Wing span: 29.26 m (96 ft)
Wing area: 87.79 sq m (945 sq ft)
Length: 24.08 m (79 ft)
Height: 8.74 m (28 ft 8 in)
Weight empty: 16,783 kg (37,000 lb)
Max t/o weight: 22,317 kg (49,200 lb)
Max level speed: 438 km/h (272 mph)
Ceiling: 9,390 m (30,800 ft)
Range: 3,384 km (2,103 miles)
Production 100 plus, and continuing

Variant: DHC-6 Twin Otter Srs 300
First flown: 20 May 1965
Type: STOL commuter airliner
Accommodation: Two crew and 20 passengers or 2,404 kg (5,300 lb) of freight
Power plant: Two 486 kW (652 shp) United PT6A-27 turbo-prop engines
Wing span: 19.81 m (65 ft)
Wing area: 39.02 sq m (420 sq ft)
Length: 15.77 m (51 ft 9 in)
Height: 5.94 m (19 ft 6 in)
Weight empty: 3,062 kg (6,750 lb)
Max t/o weight: 5,670 kg (12,500 lb)
Max level speed: 338 km/h (210 mph)
Ceiling: 8,140 m (26,700 ft)
Range: 1,704 km (1,059 miles)
Production Over 800, and continuing

Variant: DHC-7 (Dash 7)
First flown: 27 March 1975
Type: STOL regional airliner
Accommodation: Two crew plus up to 54 passengers
Power plant: Four 835 kW (1,120 shp) Pratt & Whitney (Canada) PT6A-50 turbo-prop engines
Wing span: 28.35 m (93 ft)
Wing area: 79.90 sq m (860 sq ft)
Length: 24.58 m (80 ft 7¾ in)
Height: 7.98 m (26 ft 2 in)
Weight empty: 10,079 kg (22,220 lb)
Max t/o weight: 19,958 kg (44,000 lb)
Max level speed: 420 km/h (261 mph)
Ceiling: 6,400 m (21,000 ft)
Range: 2,148 km (1,335 miles)
Production Continuing, with over 125 sold

Appendix 2
De Havilland Projects

D.H.7   Single-seat fighter biplane powered by one R-R Falcon engine. Design not completed due to non-availability of engine.

D.H.8   Two-seat biplane fighter with pusher engine, armed with one 37 mm (1½ pdr) COW gun in front cockpit. Design not completed due to delays in gun development and non-availability of specified engine.

D.H.12   Improved D.H.11 with mid-upper gunner moved to new position between the spars of the upper wing. Design only.

D.H.13   Not used, probably due to superstition.

D.H.17   Advanced 16-seat passenger airliner biplane powered by two R-R Condor engines. Enclosed cabin, semi-retractable undercarriage. Design work completed but despite intensive sales campaign aircraft not built for lack of orders due to postwar slump.

D.H.19   Two-seat cabin biplane powered by one 205 kW (275 hp) R-R Falcon engine. Design not completed.

D.H.20   Single-seat sports biplane powered by one ABC Wasp radial engine. Span 10.06 m (33 ft); length 7.92 m (26 ft); wing area 30.657 sq m (330 sq ft).

D.H.21   Design study for a large civil transport prepared for the Aircraft Manufacturing Co Ltd. Two engines driving a single geared propeller.

D.H.22   Pusher-engined biplane with normal rear fuselage instead of outriggers. Engine mounted on the upper mainplane.

D.H.23   Four-seat biplane flying boat powered by one 336 kW (450 hp) Napier Lion engine. Detail design almost completed and allocated official Air Ministry registration G-EARN on 9 March 1920, but aircraft not built.

D.H.24   Enlarged development of the D.H.18 powered by one Napier Lion engine. Not proceeded with.

D.H.25   Large 10-seat (plus two crew) civil transport biplane powered by three 298 kW (400 hp) Liberty engines driving a single propeller. Span 26.21 m (86 ft); length 19.20 m (63 ft); estimated all-up weight 7,004 kg (15,440 lb).

D.H.26   Commercial transport powered by one 172 kW (230 hp) Puma engine featuring a thick-section internally-braced monoplane wing, designed in 1920 despite official disapproval of the monoplane. Design estimates showed such promise that the Air Council ordered two prototypes of a larger version as the D.H.29, and D.H.26 not proceeded with.

D.H.28   Troop carrier biplane to Air Ministry Type 12 Specification. One 746 kW (1,000 hp) Napier Cub engine, two crew in open cockpits. Similar layout used on later D.H.54. Span 26.52 m (87 ft); length 19.81 m (65 ft).

D.H.30   Reconnaissance fighter to Air Ministry D. of R. Type 3 requirement of 1922. Possibly named Denbigh. Three unbuilt prototypes allocated serials J6915-J6917.

D.H.31   Design layout to an unspecified Air Ministry requirement.

D.H.32   Commercial transport to Air Ministry Specification 18/21 as an improvement of the successful D.H.18. Two crew on upper wing plus 18 passengers in cabin with air conditioning. Aerodynamically cleaner design, hence one 269 kW

(360 hp) R-R Eagle engine. Detail design completed, but shortly before start of construction work on the prototype interested operators specified the well-tried Lion engine. As a result the D.H.32 shelved for the larger D.H.34. Span 15.24 m (50 ft); all-up weight 2,603 kg (5,738 lb); estimated maximum speed 177 km/h (110 mph).

D.H.33   Single-seat shipborne fighter biplane. Design layout only.

D.H.35   Two-seat reconnaissance biplane to Air Ministry Specification D. of R. Type 3A. One A.S. Jaguar engine. Span 14.02 m (46 ft); length 8.38 m (27 ft 6 in).

D.H.36   Single-engined coastal defence torpedo-bomber biplane to Air Ministry Specification D. of R. Type I. Three crew. Layout only, similar to D.H.27. Span 26.2 m (86 ft); length 18.6 m (61 ft).

D.H.38   Two-seat general purpose biplane powered by one 336 kW (450 hp) Napier Lion engine. Layout similar to D.H.14. Detailed design prepared for the Greek Government, but no orders resulted. Span 15.62 m (51 ft 3 in); estimated maximum speed 201 km/h (125 mph).

D.H.39   Proposed alternative version to the D.H.38 powered by 269 kW (360 hp) R-R Eagle VIII engine.

D.H.40   Proposed two-seat forestry patrol variant of the D.H.39 for the Canadian Air Board.

D.H.41   Proposed two-seat reconnaissance variant of the D.H.38 to Air Ministry Specification D. of R. Type 3. One Napier Lion engine. Layout only.

D.H.43   Large freight-carrying biplane powered by one 298 kW (400 hp) Liberty 12 engine. Large cargo door on the port side of fuselage. No detail design completed.

D.H.44   Passenger transport biplane powered by one Siddeley Puma engine, 1923. Preliminary design study only.

D.H.45   Three-seat torpedo-bomber/coastal defence biplane. Two 336 kW (450 hp) Napier Lion engines. Layout based on the D.H.11. Span 26.2 m (86 ft); length 18.3 m (60 ft).

D.H.46   Single-seat lightweight sports monoplane. Span 11.43 m (37 ft 6 in); length 7.57 m (24 ft 2 in). Design layout only; later D.H.53 Humming Bird similar.

D.H.47   Single-seat glider; no detail design completed. Span 11.58 m (38 ft); length 8.25 m (27 ft 1 in); wheel track 0.76 m (2 ft 6 in). Later D.H.52 similar.

D.H.48   Single-seat forestry patrol and survey aircraft for the RCAF. Based on, and similar to D.H.9A, but powered by 149 kW (200 hp) Wolseley Viper engine and equipped with W/T. No detail design completed. Span 11.28 m (37 ft); length 8.68 m (25 ft 6 in).

D.H.49   Modernised version of the D.H.9A powered by 276 kW (370 hp) R-R Eagle IX engine. Incorporated similar improvements to the D.H.9J Stag; estimated all-up weight 2,495 kg (5,500 lb). Offered for reconnaissance, light bombing and general purpose duties, but not accepted by the Air Ministry.

D.H.55   Airliner biplane for seven passengers powered by three 89 kW (120 hp) Airdisco engines. Based on the D.H.54 Highclere. Design layout only.

D.H.57   Airliner biplane for 12 passengers powered by three 172 kW (230 hp) Puma engines. Also based on the D.H.54 Highclere. Span 24.08 m (79 ft); length 16.3 m (53 ft 6 in); wing area 118.9 sq m (1,280 sq ft); estimated all-up weight 5,216 kg (11,500 lb). Prepared in 1926.

D.H.58   Scaled-up version of the D.H.57 for two crew plus 20 passengers powered by three 336 kW (450 hp) Napier Lion engines. Span 31.4 m (103 ft); length 20.98 m (68 ft 8 in); wing area 199.7 sq m (2,150 sq ft); estimated all-up weight 9,752 kg (21,500 lb).

D.H.59   Proposed unspecified airliner scheme.

D.H.62   Commercial transport for eight passengers powered by two Siddeley Puma engines. Crew of two in open cockpit in the nose. Span 20.73 m (68 ft); length 15.4 m (50 ft 6 in). No detailed design drawings completed.

D.H.63   Scaled-down version of the D.H.61 for pilot and four passengers, powered by 179 kW (240 hp) Siddeley Puma engine. Span 13.72 m (45 ft); length 9.5 m (31 ft 2 in). No detail drawings completed.

D.H.64 Enlarged version of the D.H.62 for 14 passengers powered by two A.S. Jaguar radial engines. Span 23.47 m (77 ft); length 16.69 m (54 ft 9 in); wing area 111.48 sq m (1,200 sq ft); estimated all-up weight 5,216 kg (11,500 lb). Investigated in September 1926.

D.H.68 Executive version of the D.H.67 for two crew and six passengers powered by two A.S. Jaguar engines. Cabin with toilet facilities. Span 17.83 m (58 ft 6 in); length 12.04 m (39 ft 6 in); wing area 78.5 sq m (845 sq ft); estimated all-up weight 3,402 kg (7,500 lb). Preliminary investigation in 1927.

D.H.69 High-performance two-seat day bomber to an Air Ministry Specification. Similar to the D.H.65A Hound but powered by an R-R Type F engine. Pilot in open cockpit, observer had prone bombing position on the fuselage floor. Span 10.97 m (36 ft); length 8.07 m (26 ft 6 in). Design study only, 1927.

D.H.70 Army Co-operation biplane for the Australian Government. Layout only, not proceeded with.

D.H.73 High-altitude survey development of the D.H.67, proposed in March 1927. Two 224 kW (300 hp) ADC Nimbus engines. Several optional cockpit layouts as tandem or side-by-side; aircraft could be adapted as a seaplane. Span 15.54 m (51 ft); length (landplane) 10.11 m (33 ft 2 in); (seaplane) 11.87 m (38 ft 9 in); wing area 57.6 sq m (620 sq ft); estimated all-up weight (landplane) 2,481 kg (5,470 lb).

D.H.74 Light commercial transport for pilot and four passengers, based on the D.H.65 Hound and intended as D.H.50 replacement. No engine type specified; design study only.

D.H.76 Airliner for 20 passengers, powered by three Bristol Jupiter radial engines. Intended as D.H.66 replacement, but no detailed drawings prepared.

D.H.78 Two alternative schemes for multi-engined commercial transports, not proceeded with.

D.H.96 Primary trainer to Air Ministry Specification T.1/37 of May 1937 powered by Gipsy Queen I engine. Low-wing monoplane, two crew in open tandem cockpits. Front windscreen frame strong enough to protect the crew in case of a nose-over on landing. Fixed main undercarriage with streamlined fairings. Span 11.28 m (37 ft).

D.H.97 Commercial transport powered by three engines. Low-wing monoplane seating eight passengers; airframe of similar construction to the D.H.91 Albatross. Detail design not proceeded with due to the outbreak of war.

D.H.99 Light single-engined biplane, intended as D.H.87 Hornet Moth replacement. Design work abandoned due to the war.

D.H.101 High-speed high-altitude unarmed night intruder to Air Ministry Specification B.11/41 powered by two Napier Sabre engines. Design based on the Mosquito. Despite initial priority over the Vampire jet fighter the shortage of Sabre engines resulted in its abandonment in April 1942 in favour of the lower-powered D.H.102.

D.H.102 Night bomber to Air Ministry Specification B.4/42. Similar to the D.H.101 but with two R-R Griffon or Merlin engines. Designed to carry a bomb load of 2,268 kg (5,000 lb) at lower speed than the Mosquito. Officially approved in April 1942 as the Mosquito Series II, but all work ceased late in 1942.

D.H.105 Three-seat primary trainer with fixed undercarriage to Air Ministry Specification T.23/43, designed in 1946. Production contract won by the competing Percival Prentice.

D.H.107 Proposed development of the D.H.100 Vampire which, like the Vampire FB.Mk 8, eventually became the Venom.

D.H.109 Four-engined airliner. Design study only.

D.H.111 Jet bomber. Comet 1 adaptation to Air Ministry Specification B.35/46 proposed in May 1948. Although it did not meet the Specification in all respects it represented the most advanced aircraft that could be produced with a certainty of success within a reasonable time scale. The Comet wing with its four Ghost jet engines and the tailplane were to be fitted to a thinner fuselage which could carry either one 4,536 kg (10,000 lb) or 18 × 454 kg (1,000 lb) bombs and a crew of four. Pilot/captain located under a bubble canopy offset to port, with co-pilot on the starboard side and two radar navigators/bomb aimers behind the pilot facing aft. Span 35.06 m (115 ft); estimated all-up weight 47,628 kg (105,000 lb).

D.H.116 Naval jet fighter to Specification N.114 powered by one R-R RA.14 Avon jet engine giving an estimated maximum speed of just over Mach 1.0 in level flight. The cockpit and forward fuselage based on that of the Sea Venom, married to a new thin-section swept-back wing of an overall span of 10.36 m (34 ft) (3.66 m/12 ft folded). Project dropped in favour of the D.H.110 which became the Sea Vixen.

D.H.117 Supersonic high-altitude interceptor to RAF Requirement 115 powered by one D.H. Gyron Junior jet engine and a Spectre rocket motor.

D.H.118 Long-range airliner powered by four R-R Conway jet engines. Designed as a successor to the Comet to carry 120 passengers on Transatlantic and similar long-distance routes. Larger than the Comet, the D.H.118 was smaller than the Boeing 707, and promised improved speed and range performance. Announced in the House of Commons on 24 October 1956, the D.H.118 was planned to commence operations in February 1962, but the project was abandoned in February 1957 in favour of the Vickers VC 10.

D.H.119 High-speed short to medium-range high-capacity airliner. Projected in 1956/57, the D.H.119 was based on Comet experience and intended to fulfil a BEA requirement. Standard seating for 95 passengers over stage lengths of 2,012 km (1,250 st miles). Wings and tail surfaces swept back approximately 35 degrees, with the four R-R Avon jet engines in pairs under the wing trailing edge. Span 35.83 m (117 ft 6 in); estimated all-up weight 72,576 kg (160,000 lb); estimated cruising speed 966+ km/h (600+ mph).

D.H.120 Jet airliner development, similar to the D.H.119 but intended to meet the requirements of both BEA and BOAC.

D.H.122 Proposed Trident development to compete with the VC 10. Designation also used for a twin Gnome-powered executive project at Christchurch, which was complimentary to the D.H.123 project as a low-wing Dove replacement.

D.H.123 Feeder liner project intended as Dakota replacement. Two D.H. Gnome turbo-props, high-wing layout, maximum capacity 40 passengers or a payload of 3,538 kg (7,800 lb). Designed for economic operations over very short stages, eg 322 km (200 miles), but with full fuel load the range could be extended to 2,591 km (1,610 miles) with the payload reduced to 1,088 kg (2,400 lb). Span 24.77 m (81 ft 3 in); estimated all-up weight 10,025 kg (22,100 lb). This Christchurch project was abandoned when de Havilland joined HSA and the 748 was also in the group.

At the same time at Hatfield the type number was allocated to a six-seat Vampire Trainer development, similar to more recent plans from other companies, and a mock-up of the fuselage nacelle was built in the late 1950s.

D.H.124 A series of design studies for a twin-jet airliner with BS.75 engines mounted on the rear fuselage and a high-swept tail. Accommodation for 48 passengers with room forward for freight. Similar in size to the Hunting H.107 project.

D.H.126 Twin-jet feeder liner of similar layout to the D.H.125 but designed to carry 26–32 passengers. The design was originally put forward in May 1960, powered by two rear-mounted engines in the 1,588–1,905 kg (3,500–4,200 lb) thrust range. Jet units under consideration were the R-R RB. 173, D.H. BS. 92 and GE CF-700. Span 20.42 m (67 ft); estimated all-up weight 10,886–12,700 kg (24,000–28,000 lb).

D.H.127 Naval strike fighter/reconnaissance aircraft powered by two jet engines with lift jet deflection and braking thrust on either side of the rear fuselage, balanced by two lift engines in the nose. Two crew in tandem, shoulder-mounted thin delta wing, detachable weapons bay. Overall wing span 10.06 m (33 ft)

(6.40 m/21 ft folded). To avoid confusion with the Hawker P.1127 subsequently redesignated D.H.128.

D.H.128 Became a joint exercise with Kingston and Brough and covered a family of aircraft with both fixed and variable geometry wings to meet a joint RAF/RN requirement.

D.H.129 V/STOL military transport to NATO Specification NBMR 4; design studies in 1961–62. Shoulder-mounted swept-back wings, main undercarriage stowed in fuselage blisters, freight door in the rear fuselage under the high-swept tailplane. Propulsion consisted of 16 lift engines in transverse underwing pods at half span to allow full thrust deflection for V/STOL operations. Span 23.77 m (78 ft). Although adjudged the winning design, the requirement was eventually dropped by NATO, as was the NBMR 3 strike fighter which the D.H.129 was intended to support. As a result of this study HSA were selected to co-operate with Dornier in 1963–65 and further developments of the Do 31 for research. This later led to joint projects, the Do/HS 1 and Do/HS 2 military V/STOL transport based on the D.H.129 and Do 31 designs.

Cierva C.24 Autogiro

This two-seat cabin autogiro was produced by de Havilland for the Cierva Autogiro Company. The cabin was based on that used on the D.H.80A Puss Moth. The C.24 had a short-span wing, a tricycle undercarriage and a triple fin tailplane, with a large rudder on the centre fin. Powered by a 89 kW (120 hp) Gipsy III engine, the sole example built was registered G-ABLM. The main contribution from the Cierva Company was the three-blade rotor assembly mounted on cabin roof.

Index

157